"This book is simply the best, most sane, useful extant book on the topic of sustaining desire in long term love relationships."

—**Sue Johnson**, Developer of Emotionally Focused
Couple Therapy; Author of *Hold Me Tight:
Seven Conversations for a Lifetime of Love*

"The McCarthys have, yet again, produced an excellent resource for couples struggling with issues related to sexual desire. Barry McCarthy is a master clinician and educator. Along with his wife, Emily, they have developed a unique ability to present complex therapeutic suggestions in a way that is easily accessible to the mainstream reader. The combination of their warmth, skill, and clinical acumen combine to make this one of the few books on sexual desire that will actually provide useful, accurate, and clinically sound advice and counsel. I know I will recommend it often to my patients."

—**Daniel N. Watter**, EdD, President-Elect,
The Society for Sex Therapy and Research (SSTAR)

"The McCarthys have put a career's worth of wisdom, inspiration, and practical suggestions into this remarkable book. If your sexual desire and couple teamwork are in good shape, this book will help you make things even better. If you are struggling, it will help you relax (you are not alone) and show you a way forward towards more emotional and sexual intimacy."

—**William Doherty**, PhD, Professor, University of Minnesota;
Author of *Take Back Your Marriage*

"Emily and Barry McCarthy do it again—in a clear and lucid style, they teach readers how to be an intimate sexual team, creating a solid basis for rekindling a couple's sexuality. A superb self-help book!"

—**Michael A. Perelman**, PhD, Past-President, The Society for
Sex Therapy and Research (SSTAR); Clinical Professor, Weill
Medical College, Cornell University; Co-Director, Human
Sexuality Program, The New York Presbyterian Hospital

"*Rekindling Desire, 2nd Edition* should be on the bookshelf of every sex/relationship therapist's office, and on the nightstand of every person who is facing questions or concerns about his/her sexual desire. From sexual myths to playful exercises, this book also holds the promise of teaching couples to sustain the flame of desire in long-term partnerships."

—**Lori Brotto**, PhD, Associate Professor,
University of British Columbia, Canada

Rekindling Desire

For more than a decade, *Rekindling Desire* has helped to restore and restructure sexuality in thousands of lives. This expanded edition continues the exploration of inhibited sexual desire and no-sex relationships by respected therapist Barry McCarthy, who brings decades of knowledge and the expertise that comes from having treated almost 3,000 couples for sexual problems. Contained within are suggested strategies and exercises that help develop communication and sexual skills as well as interesting case studies that open the doors to couples' sexual frustrations. The shame, embarrassment, and hesitancy that individuals feel with themselves, and the resentment and blame they can feel toward their sexual partners, are explored and put into context. Whether you are married, cohabitating, or dating, or if you are 25, 45, or 75, reading this book will help renew your sexual desire and put you on the path toward healthy, pleasure-oriented sexuality.

Barry McCarthy, PhD, is a clinical psychologist, professor of psychology, and certified sex and marital therapist. He has published extensively on couples and sexuality and has done more than 350 professional workshops nationally and internationally. He is also the recipient of numerous awards, including the 2009 Smart Marriages® Impact Award.

Emily McCarthy has been working with her husband, Barry, for years, and together they have authored 11 books. She has a degree in speech communication, and her writing provides a balanced, humanistic perspective.

Rekindling Desire

SECOND EDITION

Barry McCarthy and Emily McCarthy

Routledge
Taylor & Francis Group

NEW YORK AND LONDON

Second edition published 2014
by Routledge
711 Third Avenue, New York, NY 10017

and by Routledge
27 Church Road, Hove, East Sussex BN3 2FA

Routledge is an imprint of the Taylor & Francis Group, an informa business

© 2014 Taylor & Francis

First edition published by Routledge 2003

Library of Congress Cataloging-in-Publication Data

McCarthy, Barry W., 1943–
  Rekindling desire / Barry McCarthy and Emily McCarthy. — Second edition.
     pages cm
  Includes bibliographical references.
  1. Sex instruction. 2. Sex in marriage. 3. Women—Sexual behavior.
4. Men—Sexual behavior. 5. Sexual excitement. 6. Sexual abstinence.
7. Sexual desire disorders. I. McCarthy, Emily J. II. Title.
  HQ31.M38 2014
  613.9'6—dc23
  2013026876

ISBN: 978-0-415-82352-4 (pbk)
ISBN: 978-0-203-55012-0 (ebk)

Typeset in New Caledonia
by Apex CoVantage, LLC

CONTENTS

Part 2
Change

Part 3
Relapse Prevention

INTRODUCTION

T HIS EXPANDED EDITION of *Rekindling Desire* focuses on the importance of understanding and changing the hidden, stigmatized problem of the no-sex marriage or relationship. It explores the complex phenomenon of inhibited sexual desire (ISD), the technical term for which is *hypoactive sexual desire disorder*.

The cultural sexual revolution of the 1960s and the scientific sexual revolution of the 1970s, inaugurated by the work of Masters and Johnson (1970), were expected to dramatically enhance sexual function. Why did that not happen? What went wrong? Most important, what does this mean for your marriage or relationship? An astounding increase in knowledge has occurred during the past 40 plus years. Unfortunately, and surprisingly, this has not resulted in improved sexual function or satisfaction. There are as many sexual problems today as there were in the 1970s, although the types of problems have changed.

using this book to revitalize couple sexuality

Rekindling Desire is a resource for both therapists and couples in the healing journey to renewed sexual desire, vitality, and satisfaction. It is not meant to be read like a textbook. Each chapter is self-contained. We encourage you to identify and focus on issues that are personally relevant. The material can be read for information and ideas, but it is best used as an interactive learning medium. We suggest that you first read the material individually, highlighting sections that you find most relevant, and then as a couple discuss the topics that are particularly significant in your situation. Another technique is to take turns reading aloud, stopping at important points to discuss the issues.

Do not just read passively. Try the suggested strategies, involve yourselves in relevant exercises, and develop communication and sexual skills. Most chapters contain a psychosexual skill exercise to make the process of assessment and change personal and concrete. We encourage you to engage in the exercises that you find helpful. Feel free to skip those that you do not find pertinent. These exercises are not rigid or set in concrete. You can redo or individualize them to promote awareness and comfort. This will allow you to get the most from these experiences. Discuss the guidelines and case studies and implement what is meaningful and helpful to you both individually and as a couple. Use the suggested strategies and techniques to empower change. Confront feelings of guilt and shame, which further inhibit desire. Do not beat yourself up or feel stigmatized because of ISD. You deserve to feel good about yourself as a sexual person and to allow sexuality to enhance and energize your intimate bond.

self-help and therapy

This is a book of ideas, guidelines, and exercises, not a "do-it-yourself" therapy manual. The more information and understanding you have, the better decisions you will make. Knowledge is power. However, it is not a substitute for individual, couple, or sex therapy. The most efficacious use of *Rekindling Desire* is as an adjunctive resource while in therapy. Increasing awareness and reducing myths and stigma are crucial. Information, understanding, and a change in attitude challenge ISD, but they are not enough. Understanding and acceptance are only the first steps in the process to break the cycle of the no-sex marriage.

Thus, although this book can help you understand and resolve the complex, draining problem of ISD and the no-sex marriage, we encourage you to seek sex or couple therapy rather than try to change the situation completely on your own. Overcoming desire problems requires awareness, understanding, working as an intimate sexual team, actively confronting avoidance and inhibitions, maintaining motivation, reacting appropriately to difficulties and failures, and using all available resources and support.

who we are and the motivation for this book

We have been married for 47 years and see sexuality as a vital, integral part of our marital bond. Since 1980, we have been a writing team; this is our 12th coauthored book. We have complementary skills: Barry is a PhD clinical psychologist and a certified sex and marital therapist; Emily has a degree in speech communication.

A significant part of Barry's clinical practice has been with couples suffering from ISD or stuck in no-sex or low-sex relationships. He has treated almost 3,000 couples (both married and unmarried, straight and gay) for sexual problems and dysfunction. This volume draws on case studies of some of Barry's clients, with names and details altered to preserve confidentiality. Typically, the problems have gone on for years, and the partners feel ashamed. They mistakenly believe that they are the only couple with this problem and approach therapy with a great deal of embarrassment and hesitancy. The layers of frustration, resentment, and blame that have built up can present a greater threat to the relationship than the sexual problem itself.

Our motivation for writing this book is to provide knowledge, support, and hope for couples facing ISD and a no-sex relationship. Sexual problems need not control a relationship or dominate the partners' feelings. We believe that the partners, working as an intimate sexual team, can make use of a range of affectionate, sensual, playful, and erotic bridges to rekindle desire.

All couples, regardless of sexual orientation or lifestyle, can find the information and guidelines in *Rekindling Desire* useful. We want this material to be as inclusive as possible, so we intermix terms such as *relationship*, *marital bond*, *partner*, and *spouse* throughout the book. Whether partners are straight, gay, married, cohabiting, dating—or are 25, 45, or 75 years old—they deserve sexuality to be a positive, integral part of their lives and relationship. Our hope is that this book will help revitalize your relationship—or at least revive hopefulness and motivate you to seek couple sex therapy that can speed you on the road to a healthy sexual partnership.

PART 1

Awareness

CHAPTER 1

When and Why Couples Lose Sexual Desire

THE NUMBER ONE sexual problem facing American couples is inhibited sexual desire (ISD). The second most common problem is discrepancies in sexual desire. Pundits laugh and ask, "What do you expect from people married 20 years?" In truth, these are not the couples who are in the greatest trouble. Desire problems plague newly married couples as well as unmarried couples who have been together 2 years or longer. Desire problems occur among all types of couples and all age groups but are most destructive in the early years of marriage.

How can you understand and confront ISD? Do many couples experience a no-sex relationship, or is lack of sexual desire a freak occurrence? Before we explore these topics, let's see what you know about sex and marriage, especially the state of sex in your relationship. We urge you to be honest as you take the following true–false test. Do not give politically correct or socially desirable answers.

1. Sex is more work than play.
2. Touching always leads to intercourse.
3. Touching takes place only in the bedroom.

4. You no longer look forward to making love.
5. Sex does not give you feelings of attachment or sharing.
6. You never have sexual thoughts or fantasies about your spouse.
7. Sex is limited to a fixed time, such as Saturday night or Sunday morning.
8. One of you is always the initiator and the other feels pressured.
9. You look back on premarital sex as the best sex in your relationship.
10. Sex has become mechanical and routine.
11. You have sex once or twice a month at most.

If you answered true to five or more statements, true to item 11, or both, you are among the more than 40 million Americans trapped in a low-sex or no-sex or relationship.

The adage in sex therapy is that when sexuality goes well, it is a positive, integral part of your relationship but not a major component— adding 15 percent to 20 percent to couple vitality and satisfaction (McCarthy, 2003). However, when sexuality is dysfunctional or nonexistent, it assumes an inordinately powerful role, robbing your relationship of 50 percent to 70 percent of its intimacy and vitality (Metz & McCarthy, 2010).

The most disruptive sexual problem is ISD. If this inhibited desire degenerates into a no-sex marriage, it puts tremendous pressure on the couple, especially if affection also ceases. Desire is the core dimension of sexuality. No-sex relationships become devitalized, especially when this occurs in the first 5 years of a relationship. Unless something is done to reverse this process, divorce or a breakup is a likely outcome.

The functional benefits of couple sexuality are to create shared pleasure, reinforce and deepen intimacy, and serve as a tension reducer to deal with the stresses of life and marriage. An optional function is to conceive a planned, wanted baby. No-sex marriages negate these benefits. In addition, lack of sexuality robs the couple of special feelings and intimate attachment.

the stigma of desire problems

The initial focus of sex therapy was orgasm dysfunction—premature ejaculation in men and nonorgasmic response (especially during intercourse) in women. The naive assumption was that if both partners had orgasms, everything would be fine. The simplistic concepts were "sex = intercourse" and "orgasm = satisfaction."

Sexuality is complex. It is multicausal and multidimensional, with significant individual, couple, cultural, and value differences (McCarthy & Bodnar, 2005). The new mantra for healthy couple sexuality is desire, pleasure, eroticism, and satisfaction (Foley, Kope, & Sugrue, 2012). When therapists refer to a *primary sexual dysfunction*, it means the problem has always plagued the couple. *Secondary dysfunction* means sexuality was once functional and later became problematic. Secondary ISD is the most common sexual problem facing couples—married and unmarried, straight or gay.

Desire and satisfaction form the core of healthy couple sexuality. It is more socially acceptable to say you have a specific dysfunction—nonorgasmic response, painful intercourse, erectile dysfunction, premature ejaculation, or ejaculatory inhibition—than it is to admit "I am not interested in sex," "I do not like sex," or "I do not find sex enjoyable." In our sex-satiated culture, everyone is supposed to desire sex.

Research studies have found that 1 in 3 women and 1 in 7 men report ISD (Laumann, Gagnon, Michael, & Michaels, 1994). Women are often unfairly blamed for sexual difficulties. In reality, when couples stop being sexual, it is primarily because the man has lost confidence in predictable erections, intercourse, and orgasm. In truth, the majority of couples experience problems involving sexual desire at some time in a relationship. If you are having such problems, you are not alone. Feeling stigmatized and deficient is of no value. Desire problems are the most frequent complaints of couples seeking sex therapy. ISD stresses a relationship more than any other sexual dysfunction.

The extreme of desire problems is the no-sex marriage. The couple falls into the cycle of anticipatory anxiety, performance-oriented sex with intercourse as a pass–fail test, and eventually sexual avoidance. Sex becomes more of a problem than a pleasure. Couples do not plan to have a no-sex marriage; it is a pattern they fall into. A no-sex marriage does not mean total abstinence but that sex occurs less than 10 times a year. A low-sex marriage means being sexual less than every other week (i.e., less than 25 times a year). Approximately 20 percent (1 in 5) of married couples have a no-sex marriage. An additional 15 percent of couples have a low-sex marriage. If you study unmarried couples who have been together 2 or more years, approximately 1 in 3 have a no-sex relationship. Married couples have the most sex while couples who have cohabitated for 2 years or longer have the least sex.

The longer the couple avoids sexual contact, the harder it is to break the cycle. Avoidance becomes a self-fulfilling trap. The longer the partners are in a no-sex relationship, the more they blame each other. And the more shameful they feel, the harder it is to break the cycle. The couple that has not resumed sexual contact 6 months after a baby has been born faces one set of problems, but the couple that has not been sexual for 6 years faces a more daunting task. Yet the strategy for change is the same—renew intimacy, engage in nondemand pleasuring, and add erotic scenarios and techniques. The more chronic the problem, the more difficult the change process. Maintaining motivation is a major challenge. Confronting avoidance and inhibitions is more difficult for the couple that has stopped being affectionate. The good news is that motivated couples are able to reestablish desire, pleasure, eroticism, and satisfaction.

the nonconsummated marriage

The number of couples who do not consummate their marriages is difficult to estimate because it is a shameful secret. One in 4 couples has an unsuccessful or painful first intercourse. As many as 1.5 percent of marriages are not consummated during the 1st year, and about half of these remain unconsummated. Most of these couples were sexually active premaritally but ceased intercourse before marriage and were unsuccessful at resuming. Another pattern is that a specific dysfunction, such as painful intercourse or erectile dysfunction, makes sex very difficult or impossible. Some couples maintain desire and enjoy erotic nonintercourse sexuality. Sadly, most people in nonconsummated marriages avoid any sensual or sexual activity.

Embarrassment over a nonconsummated marriage dominates their lives. If the woman is embarrassed to answer questions about sexual activity, or if she has never had intercourse or suffers from *vaginismus* (spasming of the vaginal opening that make insertion very painful or impossible), she avoids having a gynecological exam or a pap smear. The stigma for the man is just as severe. He views the nonconsummated marriage as an attack on his masculinity. The couple treats the sexual problem as a "shameful secret," not talking to friends, family, doctors, or a minister, which furthers alienation and stigma. The partners do not even talk to each other. It is important to realize that nonconsummated marriages, no-sex marriages, low-sex marriages, and relationships controlled by ISD are more common than thought. Sexual problems can be addressed and resolved. You can revitalize your sexual bond and rebuild desire and function. It requires motivation, focus, and working as an intimate sexual team, most often with the help of a couple's sex therapist.

what is normal sexuality?

Before 1970, there was a lack of scientific information about sexual function and dysfunction; educational materials were of poor quality; and many people suffered from inhibition, guilt, and limited communication. Sexual myths and misinformation were rampant. We now have better scientific information about sexual function and dysfunction than at any time in human history. There is a plethora of educational materials and self-help books. Sexuality is discussed in arenas ranging from pulpits to talk shows. Sexual themes dominate our culture—especially TV, movies, and music. There is an enormous amount of sexual discussion, although the quality is low, with a confusing medley of fact and fiction. Naive, repressive myths have been replaced by unrealistic sex-performance myths. Guilt has been replaced by performance anxiety. There has been no net gain for sexual pleasure. Sexual anxieties, inhibitions, and problems are still the norm today.

Sexuality is a complex, crucial aspect of life and a relationship. We are respectful of individual, couple, value, and cultural differences in the roles and meanings of sexuality. There is no "one right way" to be sexual. Sexually, one size does *not* fit all.

Concepts That Promote Healthy Sexuality

1. Sex is more than genitals, intercourse, and orgasm. Sexuality involves attitudes, feelings, experiences, perceptions, and values. Sexuality is a natural, healthy element in life. It need not be a source of guilt or negative feelings.
2. Sexuality is an integral dimension of your personality. You deserve to feel good about your body and yourself as a sexual person.
3. The essence of sexuality is giving and receiving pleasure-oriented touching.
4. Express sexuality so that it enhances your life and intimate relationship.

The Four Components of Sexual Functioning

Desire—Positive anticipation and the feeling that you deserve healthy sexuality in your life and relationship

Pleasure—Receptivity and responsivity to sensual and sexual touching

Eroticism—Subjective and objective arousal that naturally culminates in orgasm

Satisfaction—Good feelings about yourself as a sexual person and emotionally and physically bonding with your partner after a sexual experience

Healthy sexual functioning allows both partners to enjoy pleasure. A key element in establishing realistic expectations is to accept the inherent variability and flexibility of sexual experiences. Novels and movies emphasize free-flowing, nonverbal, powerful sexuality where desire is intense, arousal is quick, orgasm always occurs for both (simultaneously), and the sexual encounter is marvelous every time. This sells movies and novels but makes real people feel intimidated and deficient. If partners experience powerful desire, arousal, orgasm, and satisfaction twice a month, they can count themselves lucky and celebrate those special times. It is important to be aware that less than half the sexual experiences of well-functioning couples involve equal desire, arousal, and orgasm. Typically, one partner is more into sex, although the other enjoys the experience or at least appreciates going along for the ride. Of total sexual experiences, 5 percent to 15 percent are mediocre, unsatisfying, or dysfunctional. This, too, is normal. You are not a perfectly functioning sexual machine. You are two individuals sharing sexuality. There is a built-in variability in couple sexuality and, occasionally, dissatisfaction or dysfunction (Frank, Anderson, & Rubinstein, 1978).

Sexual dysfunction or dissatisfaction have been experienced by 50 percent of married couples and more than 60 percent of unmarried couples for 6 months or longer, so if you have had these issues you have plenty of company. ISD and discrepancies in desire are the most common complaints. One partner (usually the man) initiates and encourages sexual contact, so even if dysfunctional or unsatisfying, couple sex continues. Some people with desire problems do not have difficulty with arousal and orgasm once the sexual encounter begins. As one client said, "Once stimulation starts, I get turned on and come; it's the wanting to be sexual that stymies me." Pundits call it "lack of wanta."

Occasional lack of desire is normal. At times, it can even be healthy. You wonder about people who have high sexual desire in times of couple conflict, when dealing with an ill child, after a funeral, facing a financial crunch, or during a work crisis. It is unhealthy to use sex to deny or avoid reality. But it is normal to have differences in desire. Sometimes one partner wants a hug and the other wants an orgasm. What is not normal is chronic ISD, a no-sex relationship, or power struggles over sex.

romantic love and sexual chemistry

We have been socialized by movies, songs, and novels to believe that romantic love and sexual chemistry are the powerful, driving forces that carry couples to the heights of ecstasy. Sex is always smooth, passionate, spontaneous, and uninhibited. Movie sex is spectacular sex; the fact that it has nothing to do with real couples' sex lives is ignored in the magical media hype.

Romantic love, with its idealization of the partner and the relationship, plays a powerful role in initial attraction. However, romantic love is inherently unstable, usually ending before marriage; seldom does passionate sex last past the 1st year. Sexual chemistry is very explosive and equally short-lived. Couples report "hot" sex at the beginning of their relationships when they see each other on a more infrequent basis but experience sexual disappointment when living together or married. Where did the passion go? The hot-sex phase based on romantic love and passion (also labeled the *limerance* phase) disappears after 6 months to 2 years, as it should. Romantic love and hot sex cannot maintain desire. Sexual desire is based on emotional and sexual intimacy, not on romance, passion, and drama. Comfort, attraction, and trust nurture desire after the heat of sexual chemistry is long gone. The prescription for maintaining sexual desire is integrating intimacy; nondemand pleasuring; erotic scenarios and techniques; and positive, realistic sexual expectations.

Couples who believe that the way to rebuild desire is to rekindle romantic love and reignite sexual passion are heading into a dead end. The keys to revitalizing couple sexuality are building bridges to desire, increasing intimacy, enjoying nondemand pleasuring, and creating erotic scenarios. Broad-based, flexible sexuality provides a solid foundation for marriage. At its core, sexual desire is interpersonal, not individual. The partners learn to think, talk, act, and feel like an intimate sexual team. Each partner facilitates and reinforces the other's sexual feelings and desires rather than colluding in sexual avoidance.

Maintaining comfort, attraction, and trust is a dynamic process. Each person takes the initiative and designs a pleasurable or erotic scenario. The partner is open and receptive. Inhibitions and avoidance are confronted. This requires commitment and working together as an intimate sexual team. Change is usually gradual rather than dramatic. There will be difficulties, setbacks, disappointments, and lapses, but if you stay with the process, you will succeed. Once sexuality is reestablished, you need to maintain and reinforce gains. Benign neglect subverts sexual desire. Relapse prevention requires active participation. Good intentions and loving feelings are necessary, but not sufficient, to maintain a vital sexual bond.

Sexuality has a major cognitive component: The most important element for desire is positive anticipation. Affirmative attitudes about deserving sexual pleasure and your rights as a sexual person promote healthy sexuality. Yet sexuality is not a cognitive activity. Sexuality involves emotions and behavior—sharing intimacy, pleasure, and eroticism. The more severe and chronic the ISD, the harder it is for a couple to develop the courage to take risks and reinstitute touching and sexual play.

secrets and hidden agendas

ISD and no-sex relationships have a multitude of possible causes. Often these are sexual secrets, some of which can be dealt with and others symbolizing a fatally flawed marriage. Examples of secrets that need to be addressed include shame over childhood sexual abuse, guilt about an idiosyncratic masturbation pattern, and sexual avoidance due to a fear of failure. Examples of secrets that potentially reflect a fatally flawed marriage are a homosexual orientation and hidden sexual life, marrying for convenience or security with no genuine feeling for the spouse, and a comparison affair (an affair that meets emotional and sexual needs at the expense of the marital bond) that subverts the marital bond because emotional and sexual needs are being met through the affair.

Ideally, the trust bond between partners is enhanced by openness. Disclosing sensitive or secret material facilitates trust. Sharing secrets, such as embarrassing or traumatic childhood incidents, helps the individual and increases closeness with her or his partner. Other secrets, such as a wife telling her spouse that one of his children was conceived through an affair, can destroy the marital bond. Secrets inhibit sexual desire and need to be shared with someone—if not your spouse, then a therapist, minister, sibling, or best friend.

Hidden agendas are even more sensitive and explosive. As with secrets, some hidden agendas can be dealt with, whereas others indicate a fatally flawed marriage. Couples can deal with fear of pregnancy, fear of being abandoned, shame about a fetish arousal pattern, lack of desire caused by a side effect of medication, being afraid to raise sexual issues because the spouse might leave, or pretending a lack of desire to protect a partner who is obsessed with sexual performance. Such hidden agendas need to be disclosed and confronted because they destroy sexual anticipation.

No-sex marriages happen; they are not the couple's intention. The exception is when the hidden agenda is sexual avoidance. Examples of such relationship agendas include a spouse who is gay and has married for a convenient cover or a spouse who has a variant arousal pattern (a fetish, cross-dressing, dominance–submission scenarios), with little desire for couple sex. The extreme problem is a deviant arousal pattern such as voyeurism or exhibitionism. Seeking out Internet pornography and chat rooms can become a compulsive pattern, subverting desire for couple sex. These are almost exclusively male patterns. Female hidden agendas include fear of pregnancy or pain during intercourse, resulting in sexual avoidance. In addition, nonsexual hidden agendas include marrying for security, money, social approval, or religious pressure but with lack of attraction or desire for intimacy. In such cases, hidden agendas control the relationship, resulting in a sham marriage There is little hope for these marriages unless both individuals are willing to confront the hidden agenda that blocks becoming a genuine couple and work to rebuild the relationship. Most often, these marriages cannot and should not be saved. The healthy alternative is divorce.

The traditional view was that all marriages could and should be saved. Divorce was viewed as a failure. This is untrue and self-defeating. Marriages that are fatally flawed, abusive, or destructive or that subvert well-being are not worth preserving. We are definitely pro-marriage, but divorce is the healthy alternative when the marriage is fatally flawed or destructive. A marriage that meets needs for intimacy and security is of great value. The marital bond of respect and trust motivates the couple to revitalize sexual intimacy. When respect and trust are lacking, trying to restore intimacy is a useless strategy.

Dealing with secrets or hidden agendas by yourself is extremely difficult. Individual or couple therapy can help the partners understand the dilemma and reach a resolution. Hidden agendas are very hard to address even with objective professional help because of their unpredictable nature and potential explosiveness. Sometimes both people have a hidden agenda, but usually it is one partner. People with hidden agendas fear, often rightly, that these will be used to blame them for all the problems in the relationship or that they will be targeted by lawyers in a divorce proceeding. If the goal is to revitalize the sexual bond, the hidden agenda must be addressed and dealt with to rebuild respect, trust, and intimacy.

is the sexual problem a symptom or a cause?

The question of whether a relationship problem causes a sexual problem or the sexual problem causes relationship dissatisfaction is more than a chicken-and-egg argument. Human behavior is complex, with many causes and many dimensions. Any simple answer is likely to be wrong or at least incomplete.

Sexuality is a positive, integral component of couple intimacy. Although no-sex marriages can function satisfactorily, these are the minority. Some couples maintain a respectful, trusting bond and are good parents even though sexuality is dysfunctional or absent. Other couples have an angry, alienated, nonsupportive marriage, and the only thing that works is sex.

The most common pattern is a couple that has a good relationship but struggles with ISD, which increasingly defines the relationship. The healthy role of sexuality is to energize the couple and reinforce feelings of desire and desirability. Sexual problems undermine marriage by robbing it of intimate attachment and vitality. Over time, the sexual problem becomes severe and chronic, allowing sexuality to play an inordinately powerful role in the relationship, draining positive feelings and tearing at the couple bond.

Another frequent pattern is that relationship conflicts, especially those involving anger, are played out through sexual avoidance. Anger is the main cause of secondary ISD. Withholding or avoiding sex makes a statement; it is a way to fight back. Although this is usually a female reaction, men also can shut down sexually as a way to express anger. Sometimes this is a conscious choice; more often it is not. Anger can involve a sexual issue (demand for oral sex, a discovered extramarital affair, conflict over birth control), but more often anger involves a relationship problem. Common causes of anger are drinking and driving, not feeling supported in a family conflict, out-of-control arguments that include slapping and pushing, conflicts over money, and feeling that your partner is taking advantage of you. As alienation increases, heated, angry thoughts build on themselves. Attempts to bridge the emotional gap with affectionate touch or sexual activity are met with angry rebuffs, increasing frustration and isolation. Emotional and sexual distance feeds the angry cycle. The partners find themselves trapped in an alienated, no-sex relationship.

Infertility problems are also a common cause of ISD. Sex with the intention of becoming pregnant is an aphrodisiac. For 85 percent of couples under 30 and 70 percent of couples over 30, becoming pregnant is easy (often, too easy). Couples in the unlucky minority find that as time goes on, frustration builds. The process of undergoing fertility treatment—with increasingly intrusive, painful, and expensive tests and interventions—weakens the desire of the most ardent couple. Fertility problems are very stressful. Self-blame and blaming the spouse are painful traps. Fertility problems can bring out the worst in people. Infertility dominates self-esteem, the marriage, and sexuality. The couple stops being sexual except during the high-probability week. Sex becomes a pressure and a performance to achieve pregnancy—with little pleasure, warmth, or feelings of connection involved. Partners dealing with a fertility issue need a great deal of support from each other; this includes touching, sensuality, and eroticism to energize their bond during the non-high-probability times of the month.

Another problematic pattern is conflict about intercourse frequency. Instead of broad-based pleasuring and a variety of bridges to desire, sexuality becomes a "yes–no" question: "Are we going to have inter-course? If not, there is no touching." If every touch is regarded as a demand for intercourse, the pressure goes up and the pleasure goes down. Emotional intimacy and nondemand pleasuring are sacrificed to intercourse pressure. The result is ISD. Intimacy, choice, freedom, and pleasure lead to sexual anticipation. Conflict, pressure, and demands lead to ISD. Quality is more important than frequency. Sexuality is more than genitals, intercourse, and orgasm. Guidelines that promote desire include the belief that touching in itself is valued, that touching occurs both inside and outside the bedroom, and that not all touching must result in intercourse.

When sexual dysfunction increasingly dominates the relationship, another common pattern is that one or both partners seek to avoid sexual encounters rather than try to be sexual. The dysfunction—whether an erectile problem, premature ejaculation, nonorgasmic response, or painful intercourse—controls the intimacy. The couple shuns sex to avoid bad feelings on the part of the dysfunctional partner, who feels embarrassed or humiliated. This is an especially destructive trap for men with erectile dysfunction. If a man with this problem cannot be guaranteed an erection sufficient for intercourse, he does not want to be sexually involved. Premature ejaculation or ejaculatory inhibition is frustrating but usually does not cause the couple to stop being sexual. Female dysfunction subverts desire, but the couple is unlikely to stop sexual activity, especially when the man continues to initiate. With painful intercourse, couples can instead engage in erotic scenarios.

If sexual dysfunction does not reverse within 6 months, it is unlikely to spontaneously clear up. The typical outcome is that the problem becomes severe and chronic, negating anticipation and desire. Functional sex alone does not build anticipation, but dysfunctional sex does drain desire.

A myriad of factors inhibit desire and lead to a no-sex relationship. Understanding the pattern is helpful in resolving the problem. Even more important is the commitment to change and restore intimacy and sexuality. No matter what originally started the sexual slide, once the pattern is established, chronicity, blaming, and avoidance solidify ISD.

The individual cannot resolve sexual problems alone or by sheer willpower. The cornerstone of this approach to rekindling desire is that the partners have to work together. The way to build desire is a one–two combination of taking personal responsibility for sexuality and being an intimate sexual team. Trust that the partner will make a good-faith effort to deal with inhibitions, anxieties, and traps. Be open to renewed ways to connect physically and emotionally and build bridges to sexual desire.

maintaining a vital marital and sexual bond

The change process is complex and often difficult, but it is doable. Couples break the sexual hiatus, enjoy pleasuring, build eroticism, and resume intercourse. Once the cycle of the no-sex marriage is broken, you cannot rest on your laurels. To maintain a vital sexual bond, you have to commit time and energy. The most important components in maintaining desire are to be an intimate sexual team; anticipate sexual encounters; realize that sex is more than intercourse and orgasm; focus on sharing pleasure; build bridges to desire; be open to flexible, variable sexual scenarios; and maintain a regular rhythm of affectionate, sensual, playful, erotic, and intercourse touch.

It is normal for 5 percent to 15 percent of sexual experiences to be mediocre, unsatisfying, or dysfunctional. Do not overreact to a negative experience; especially, do not avoid touching. Keeping intimate contact is the best way to ensure that a sexual lapse does not turn into a relapse. Value emotional and sexual intimacy. Both partners can enjoy affection, sensuality, playfulness, eroticism, and intercourse. Not all touching can or should lead to intercourse. Both planned intimacy dates and spontaneous sexual encounters promote a vital sexuality. The greater the number of bridges to desire and openness to variable, flexible sexual scenarios, the more likely that you will maintain your gains. Sexuality energizes your marital bond and reinforces feelings of desire and desirability.

getting all the help you can

Couple sex therapy has a number of advantages over a self-help book. Therapy promotes hope and maintains motivation in the face of frustration and disappointment. The change process is never as easy or straightforward as portrayed in books. The typical process is "two steps forward, one step back." The therapist helps the couple stay focused and reinforces motivation for change. Having a regular therapy appointment and feeling accountable are valuable in breaking the impasse of a no-sex marriage. The therapist's empathy and insights are vital, as are the therapist's respect and concern for each person, which help promote respect and mutual caring between the partners. In addition, the therapist can guide the couple toward other valuable helping resources, including medical interventions. Guidelines for choosing a sex, couple, or individual therapist are presented in Appendix A.

summary

The healthy role of couple sexuality is to energize your bond and reinforce feelings of desire and desirability. Sadly, the negative effects of a low-sex or no-sex relationship have an inordinately powerful negative impact on men, women, and couples. ISD drains intimacy and vitality and can result in separation and divorce.

The good news is that no-sex relationships can be changed. The new mantra for healthy couple sexuality is desire, pleasure, eroticism, and satisfaction. Sexual desire can be rekindled, allowing couple sexuality to again be a shared pleasure, a means to reinforce intimacy, and a tension reducer to help in dealing with the stresses of life and your relationship. The essence of sexuality is giving and receiving pleasure-oriented touching. You can turn to each other as intimate and erotic friends—an intimate sexual team.

Key Points

- One in 5 married couples and 1 in 3 nonmarried couples who have been together 2 years or longer are stuck in the trap of a no-sex relationship.
- Each person is responsible for his or her own sexuality, and together they are an intimate sexual team.
- Rather than remain stuck in a no-sex relationship, you can rebuild intimacy, pleasuring, and eroticism.

CHAPTER 2

Whose Problem Is It?
His, Hers, or Ours?

INHIBITED SEXUAL DESIRE (ISD) and no-sex marriages are not caused by one factor or one person. Sexuality is complex, with many causes and dimensions. In addition, there are individual, couple, and cultural differences in sexual attitudes, experiences, feelings, and values.

Sexual desire and desire problems are best understood as a couple issue. This facilitates emotional problem solving—a way to think about, discuss, address, and enhance sexual desire. The couple approach is especially valuable when considering what maintains, as opposed to what caused, ISD. Regardless of what originally caused the problem, the couple becomes stuck in a self-defeating cycle. It is considerably easier to break this cycle if you approach and talk about sexual desire as a couple issue. The traps of guilt and blame maintain ISD as a chronic drain on your relationship. Viewing ISD as a couple problem reduces guilt, defensiveness, and blaming.

Regarding sexuality as a couple issue is one of the most helpful, yet hardest to accept, guidelines (Meana, 2010). When initially presented to the partners, the couple approach is received enthusiastically as a way to break the sexual deadlock and promote change. The concept of being an intimate sexual team is particularly inviting. However, when they encounter inevitable setbacks, frustrations, and disappointments, it is easy to revert to blaming. It is less taxing to blame your partner than to be responsible for your own sexual attitudes, feelings, and behavior.

A core concept in couple therapy is to take responsibility for yourself. You are not responsible for your partner. Focus on making personal changes in attitudes, behaviors, and feelings, which takes thought, work, and discipline. It is neither your responsibility nor your role to change your partner. Communicate with your partner, share feelings, and make requests for change. You can only influence your partner; you cannot make that person change. Coercion is not effective.

The therapy model we use in assessing, treating, and preventing relapse into sexual dysfunction is the *psychobiosocial* approach (McCarthy & Wald, in press). A core component of this model is a comprehensive couple perspective. Ideally, marriage operates through a positive influence process. Each person is responsible for herself or himself, and the partners are respectful and trusting toward each other. You discuss feelings, make requests, commit to a change process, and support and reinforce individual and couple growth.

In a no-sex marriage, the positive influence process has broken down (at least with regard to intimacy and sexuality). You are caught in a vicious cycle. The more sex is avoided, the lower your sexual desire. You become trapped in a pattern of guilt–blame–alienation–avoidance. The self-defeating cycle culminates in anticipatory anxiety, tension-filled sex, and sexual avoidance. You are not an intimate team working together to understand and resolve the sexual problem. Instead, the sexual problem dominates and drains your relationship. You alternate between self-blame and blaming your partner. You are stuck in a "Whose fault is it?" struggle. When intimacy breaks down into "good partner–bad partner" roles, the possibility of resolution is significantly reduced.

when one partner always pushes sex

Many couples stay stuck in the power struggle in which one spouse reports high desire, always pushes sex, and bitterly complains about being rejected. The other partner, in turn, feels pressured and besieged; it is upsetting to be forced to say no. Consciously or unconsciously, the person with lower desire avoids intimacy. This pursuer–distancer pattern is the opposite of the positive influence inherent in the intimate sexual team approach (Stanley, Markman, & Whitton, 2002).

The partner pushing sex rejects approaching reduced intimacy as a couple problem, preferring to blame her or his spouse and clinging to the belief that ISD is totally the other partner's fault. Typically, it is the husband who pushes sex, but the same pursuer–distancer dynamic occurs when it is the woman who pushes sex. Whether the scenario involves the traditional pattern or a role reversal, the couple dynamic is amazingly similar. The higher desire partner claims there is no reason for him or her to change and blames the lower desire partner. The person with lower desire is mired in guilt and self-blame, which alternates with blaming the partner for being insensitive and coercive. It is hard for either person to stay with the concept of sexual desire as a couple issue. Even when the therapist presents ISD as a couple problem and the couple initially agree, it is easy to slip back into old attitudes and habits at the first disappointment. The partner with higher desire claims it does not help to stop pushing intercourse, and in any case, she or he is not the one with the sexual problem. Even if one person does not overtly make sexual demands, his or her partner still feels the sexual intensity, blaming, and pressure. The ensuing frustration and anger do not invite emotional sharing, touching, or sexual play.

No matter how the ISD pattern started, the higher desire person's attitudes, feelings, and behaviors exacerbate or, at least maintain, the pattern. Blaming and guilt-inducing putdowns are alienating and reduce sexual desire. Seeing the partner as hostile and your worst critic does not facilitate trust or desire. Sex in this case involves conflict and coercion, not pleasure and mutuality. This is not to blame the higher desire spouse or make him or her the "bad guy" but to highlight this partner's role in maintaining the problem. ISD is best dealt with by thinking, talking, and acting as an intimate sexual team. The higher desire spouse who acts unilaterally does not make sex inviting. Sex is a pressured performance to placate the partner and avoid her or his anger.

The valid points the higher desire person makes are that avoidance worsens the problem, that sex is a bonding experience, and that rejection is emotionally alienating. The invalid points are that it is all the partner's fault and that increasing the frequency of intercourse is the key to change.

A prime guideline to successfully address ISD is acknowledging that quality of sexual intimacy and sharing pleasure are more important than intercourse frequency. To break the cycle of a no-sex relationship, sexuality needs to be comfortable, inviting, and pleasurable for both partners. Intimacy, affection, sensuality, playfulness, and eroticism, as well as intercourse, should be valued by both people. The higher desire spouse can change by adopting a nondemand approach to touching and by valuing broad-based sexuality. Not all touching can or should lead to intercourse. The single most important guideline for the higher desire spouse is to respect and honor his or her partner's emotional and sexual feelings and needs, which are as important as those of the higher desire spouse. Intimate coercion has no place in marriage. Coercion poisons sexual desire.

the person with lower sexual desire

In our sex-saturated society, it is hard not to feel deficient or guilty about ISD. Yet it is a problem for 1 in 3 adult women and 1 in 7 adult men—with the male ratio increasing dramatically with age. The more guilty, angry, depressed, and self-blaming the person is, the worse the problem becomes. You pile one negative emotion on top of another, which subverts self-esteem and sexual desire.

What can the lower desire spouse do? The first step is to increase awareness; do not avoid thinking and talking about intimacy, touch, and sexuality. Second, take an emotional problem-solving approach; do not feel ashamed or self-punitive. Third, approach your spouse as your intimate and sexual friend, not as your worst critic. Fourth, carefully assess what you value about intimacy, affection, sensuality, playfulness, eroticism, and intercourse. Take responsibility for your sexuality. Identify aspects of intimacy, touching, and sexuality that you value for yourself and the relationship. Sex to placate your partner reduces your sexual desire.

Persons experiencing ISD feel defensive, guilty, or angry and have lost track of the positive functions of touching, intimacy, and sexuality. Changing ISD is a one–two combination: first, increasing awareness and taking personal responsibility, and second, viewing desire as a couple issue and being an intimate team in revitalizing sexuality.

Are there special issues when the man has ISD? It is more acceptable for him to admit to erection or orgasm problems than admit to not being sexually interested. Traditionally, masculinity and sexuality are closely linked. Too much of the man's self-esteem is tied to his penis.

Male desire problems have a multitude of causes. Among these are

- pressure for perfect performance;
- fear of the female partner becoming pregnant;
- embarrassment because of sexual dysfunction;
- greater confidence with masturbation than with partner sex;
- alcohol or drug abuse;
- a way to maintain emotional distance or punish the spouse;
- a secret, such as a fetish arousal pattern or sexual orientation issue;
- work or money concerns;
- involvement with children or extended family to the detriment of couple time;
- not valuing marital sex;
- a side effect of medication;
- few spontaneous erections, resulting in hesitancy to initiate sex;
- feeling intimidated by his wife's sexual desire;
- a belief that it is unmanly to ask for stimulation to facilitate arousal;
- low self-esteem; and
- depression or anger.

The man has to take responsibility for his ISD and overcome feelings of embarrassment or shame. He needs to ask his partner to be his intimate sexual friend in rebuilding sexual desire and erotic function.

The spouse with ISD wishes her or his partner would "back off" and "reduce the sexual pressure." Although this is necessary to help overcome ISD, it is not sufficient. Building bridges to sexual desire involves interactive intervention. Enlist your partner as a facilitator of desire and pleasure rather than stereotyping him or her as the one who pushes for sex performance. We urge you to confront and change your attitudes toward intimacy, touching, and sexuality. Learn to trust your partner as your intimate sexual friend.

desire discrepancy: an alternative way of thinking and communicating about sexual desire

When you married, you did not decide to enmesh your lives and become one person. A viable marriage involves a balance between individual autonomy and sharing your lives as an intimate sexual couple. If you needed to feel equally desirous to engage in an activity, the relationship would be stagnant and blocked. One spouse may love to dance while the other is enthusiastic about board games. One person prefers the mountains to the ocean; another prefers bed-and-breakfast inns to resort hotels. One spouse enjoys creating elaborate salads; the other's favorite meal is meatloaf with macaroni and cheese. Yet even with these individual differences, couples are able to participate in and share a range of activities. Each partner enjoys certain experiences more, and that is okay. Together they reach a balance that recognizes individuality as well as coupleness. There is no need for a power struggle. Discrepancies in hobbies, vacations, and foods are accepted and enjoyed.

To give a personal example, Emily is a quilter and an antiquer who loves craft shows, especially in small historic towns. Barry appreciates and enjoys these activities, but not as much as Emily does. Barry loves cities, ethnic foods, and plays, which Emily appreciates but finds overwhelming as a steady diet. We accept these differences and cope with them. Each person offers experiences that expand and enrich both partners' lives. Each of us is able to say no to an activity that is aversive or excessive. For example, 2 hours is Barry's maximum at a quilt show; he does his thing (reading, biking, or writing) and meets Emily later for dinner. Emily finds more than 3 days in New York intolerable, so we do not plan more than a weekend trip there. These discrepancies are successfully accommodated. We communicate feelings and requests, use emotional problem-solving techniques, and reach agreements rather than settle for lukewarm compromises.

Can couples use this model in dealing with discrepancies in sexual desire? We believe that they not only can but that this is the preferred approach. It ends power struggles and breaks the guilt–blame cycle. Discrepancies in sexual desire are a couple issue. Each person states feelings, makes requests, and emotionally problem solves. As a couple, develop agreements that nurture desire and sexuality. Accept the desire discrepancy; do not fall into the guilt–blame trap or be coercive. Commit to couple sexuality; enjoy sharing pleasure; and adopt a broad perspective on intimacy, touching, and sexuality. This provides a solid foundation from which to revitalize sexual desire so that it plays a healthy 15 percent to 20 percent role in your life and relationship.

broad-based intimacy and sexuality

There is more to intimacy than sexuality, and more to sexuality than intercourse. A key to change is awareness of the many roles and dimensions of intimacy and sexuality. The prescription for satisfying sexuality is integrating an intimate relationship, nondemand pleasuring, and erotic scenarios and techniques. Even in the best marriages, mutually satisfying sexual encounters do not occur all the time. In fact, the couple is lucky if they occur the majority of the time. Contrary to movies, love songs, and magazines, not all sex is romantic, mutual, or satisfying. There is normal variability and flexibility in couple sexuality.

ISD often reflects an intimacy issue. How emotionally close does each spouse want to be? Is more intimacy better? Some couples prefer the soul mate couple sexual style, with a great deal of closeness; others prefer the complementary couple sexual style of retaining autonomy with moderate closeness; some prefer the traditional couple sexual style, where personal boundaries are strong and life is organized by traditional gender roles; still others adopt the emotionally expressive couple sexual style, where periods of great closeness are mixed with periods of anger and distance. You need to develop a mutually acceptable level of intimacy that fits your emotional needs and life situation while facilitating sexual desire.

The couple relational style is different than the couple sexual style. The *couple relational style* refers to how the couple organizes their lives and marriage, especially how they deal with differences and conflicts. The *couple sexual style* focuses specifically on how the couple integrates intimacy and eroticism into their relationship and how each spouse balances personal autonomy (a distinctive sexual voice) with being an intimate sexual couple. We devote an entire chapter in this book (Chapter 6) to helping you discover the right couple sexual style for you.

Sexuality is one way to express intimacy, but it is not the sole means or even the primary means. Sharing feelings; being affectionate; cuddling on the couch; lying together in bed; disclosing hopes and fears; and sharing your lives as trusting, respectful friends form the core of emotional intimacy.

Sensuality and nondemand pleasuring are the foundation for broad-based sexual intimacy. *Sensuality* involves pleasure-oriented touching—body massage, cuddling, kissing, touching while clothed or semiclothed, back or foot rubs. Touching is valued for itself, occurring both inside and outside the bedroom. Sensual touch is more likely to involve a hug than intercourse. Although a hug could evolve into arousal and orgasm, it normally does not. Cuddling before going to sleep and on awakening provides a solid basis for loving feelings. *Playful touch* integrates genital and nongenital touching. It can include taking a shower or bath together, dancing in the living room to your favorite music while engaging in playful touching, kissing, and whole body massage. Playful touch is inviting and at times serves as a bridge to sexual desire. Giving a neck or back massage while watching TV is a way to maintain connection. Showering together in the morning or before bed can be playful and pleasurable. Nondemand pleasuring and playful touch are the bedrock of a healthy sexual relationship.

Eroticism includes a range of manual, oral, rubbing, and intercourse scenarios and techniques. Eroticism serves as a turn-on for you and your partner. Eroticism includes but is not limited to intercourse. Many couples enjoy erotic scenarios that can be mutual or asynchronous. To increase eroticism, you can engage in multiple stimulation before and during intercourse. Multiple stimulation involves kissing, caressing, breast stimulation, testicle stimulation, anal stimulation, and the use of erotic fantasy.

The broader the intimate, sensual, playful, and erotic repertoire, the easier it is to maintain sexual desire. Both partners are open to a variety of ways to express intimacy, affection, sensuality, playfulness, and eroticism. Sometimes touching is for emotional intimacy and sometimes to enhance affectionate feelings. Sometimes touching is playful; at other times it can be sensual, erotic, or lustful. Communicating feelings and sharing touch help maintain sexual desire.

JILL AND STEFAN

When they finally arrived in the therapist's office, Jill and Stefan were a demoralized couple trapped in the power struggle of whose fault it was that they had a low-sex marriage. They had been married 6 years and had a 3-year-old daughter. Jill very much wanted a second child. Stefan was angry at the lack of sex and feared that Jill only wanted him for "stud" services; he felt he would be trapped in a child-centered, no-sex marriage. Jill thought that Stefan was being irrational and with-holding; before marriage they had agreed to have two children. Stefan counterattacked, saying that Jill had tricked him into believing that she valued sex. Both agreed that their best sex had been premarital. Stefan claimed that Jill had pulled a "bait and switch." When dating, they had sex every night they were together. When they began living together, sex occurred three to five times a week. This decreased to once or twice a week 4 months before marriage. During that time, Jill began experiencing ISD.

Their 2-week honeymoon to Hawaii was the beginning of an intense struggle over sexual initiation and intercourse frequency. Stefan expected daily sex, while Jill's expectation was for a fun, scenic, romantic time. Jill felt coerced by Stefan's sexual pressure. Stefan felt betrayed and played by Jill's sexual avoidance. Jill was not orgasmic during either of the two times they had sex. When the newlyweds returned from Hawaii, friends teased them about what a wonderful, sexy honeymoon it must have been, which further upset them because they resented having to lie and pretend.

When couples fight about sexual initiation and intercourse frequency, it is easy for them to fall into the cycle of anticipatory anxiety, tense and negative experiences, frustration, embarrassment, and eventually sexual avoidance. Guilt and blame become the dominant emotions. This pattern was broken when Jill and Stefan had sex with the intention of conceiving their first child but quickly regressed after Jill became pregnant. After their daughter's birth, intercourse took place once or twice a month. Stefan stopped initiating because of his anger at being rejected. Jill felt that Stefan rejected her affectionate overtures and felt emotionally abandoned. Even though there was severe alienation, Jill very much wanted a second child.

The therapist found it hard being in the same room with Jill and Stefan. The tension was palpable. It was easier for them to socialize with other couples and do things as a family than to be a couple. Fortunately, neither was threatening divorce, which adds an additional destructive dynamic to a troubled relationship. In addition, Jill and Stefan shared life goals and religious values, parented well, and felt supported by family and friends—all of which reinforced marital stability. They thought of themselves as a viable couple, committed to their marriage. However, the sexual problem was tearing at and weakening their marital bond. Jill questioned her love for Stefan; she saw him as irrational and mean in regard to sex. Stefan confided to the therapist that he was thinking of beginning an affair. The therapist told Stefan that affairs often become more emotional and complicated than planned. Furthermore, affairs are much easier to get into than out of. Stefan committed to not having an affair while he and Jill were in couple therapy.

The first therapeutic task was to break the cycle of guilt and blame. Stefan and Jill began thinking of themselves as an intimate team, striving to revitalize marital sexuality. The therapist's optimism helped them craft an expectation that this was a changeable problem. ISD was the mutual enemy. Their renewed marital commitment was an excellent prognostic sign for revitalizing sexuality.

Marital sex for this couple had never gotten on track, and ISD was a growing threat to their bond. Building marital sexuality would take a great deal of communication and effort on both their parts. Good intentions were not enough. It was crucial to approach the problem as a couple, break the cycle of guilt–blame, and cease the attack–counterattack pattern that demoralized and drained them. Playing "who's the bad spouse?" was getting them nowhere. Stefan agreed to stop name-calling and blaming. Jill lowered her wall of alienation and emotionally reinvested in intimate sexuality. Reluctantly, she agreed to postpone pregnancy until healthy couple sexuality was reestablished and to use the vaginal ring contraceptive until a joint decision was made to become pregnant. Stefan was hesitant to agree to a temporary prohibition on intercourse, but doing so acknowledged the reality of their situation. With the performance pressure of intercourse removed, they had the freedom to explore touching as a means to feel connected and share pleasure. This was very inviting for Jill, who missed affectionate touch, sensual touch, and sharing intimate feelings.

Rebuilding intimacy and sexuality was a complex, difficult couple task. Without the support and suggestions of the therapist, they would have given up in frustration and reverted to the guilt–blame pattern. One of the major functions of therapy is to keep motivation high so that the couple perseveres through frustrations and setbacks to achieve the satisfaction of a pleasure-oriented couple sexual style. A breakthrough for Stefan occurred when he realized that Jill was not punishing him by withholding sex. Her anxieties and inhibitions were real, not manipulative. Most important, Stefan realized that his being an intimate spouse, rather than a coercive, angry person, helped reduce Jill's inhibitions. When Jill felt secure that she could veto a sexual activity and Stefan would honor her wishes, her anxiety was reduced and she felt less need to say no.

Jill found that sensual experiences led to sexual feelings and was receptive and responsive to manual and oral stimulation, which she preferred to call "erotic sex." Stefan's rigid view that "only intercourse is sex" melted under these new experiences. It was Stefan who began insisting that not all touching had to lead to intercourse, an insight Jill greatly appreciated.

Intercourse was reintroduced as a "special pleasuring experience." It became part of the pleasuring–eroticism process, not the pass–fail test of their relationship. A side effect of the pleasuring exercises was that Stefan became a slower, more sensitive lover, which made intercourse more appealing. Jill's sexual response was similar to that of the majority of women, for whom achieving orgasm is easier with manual or oral stimulation than during intercourse. With self-acceptance and partner acceptance, Jill and Stefan developed a comfortable, functional couple sexual style. Not all touching culminated in intercourse, which helped Jill build sexual anticipation and excitement. Playfulness and erotic unpredictability facilitated sexual desire.

Becoming pregnant with a planned, wanted child is a major impetus for sexual desire. This was true not only for Jill but for Stefan as well. Intercourse with the hope of a second child was a strong sexual motivator. In addition, they continued broad-based affectionate, sensual, and erotic experiences. This provided the foundation for a strong, resilient sexual desire.

A relapse prevention plan is integral to comprehensive sex therapy. Sexual desire cannot be taken for granted. Jill and Stefan were motivated to maintain and generalize sexual gains. They set aside couple time when their daughter was being watched by another person or was asleep. Jill's initiating sex was important to reassure Stefan that he did not always have to stay in the rigid role of the initiator. Equally important, Stefan learned to accept a "no" without withdrawing or punishing Jill. Stefan did not regress to coercing Jill or calling her names. Jill did not regress to hiding behind a wall of emotional alienation.

For Jill, the keys to generalizing sexual gains were to reinforce intimacy, be open to sensual touching, and enjoy erotic scenarios. These continued to be her bridges to sexual desire. For Stefan, the keys were feeling that he and Jill were an intimate sexual team, enjoying both erotic sex and intercourse, and accepting sexual disappointments as normal rather than a reason for defensiveness and blaming. Stefan and Jill agree to implement the therapist's suggestion that once a month they have a sensual date, during which orgasm and intercourse were prohibited. This allowed them freedom to enjoy touching and to play sexually.

functions of sexuality

At its essence, sexuality is a couple, not an individual, experience. That is another reason that ISD is best understood as a couple issue. Sexuality is best when both people feel free to initiate affectionate, sensual, playful, erotic, and intercourse experiences. Equally important, both feel free to say no or suggest an alternative way to stay connected. Ideally, both partners value sexuality as a shared pleasure. Couples who are comfortable with touching inside and outside of the bedroom, who are aware of the value and dimensions of pleasuring, and who realize that not all touching leads to intercourse have a solid base for sexual desire. Each component of the sexual prescription—an intimate relationship, nondemand pleasuring, and erotic scenarios and techniques—require couple involvement. Each person is responsible for her or his sexuality. To keep desire vital, the couple continues to share as an intimate sexual team.

Exercise: Sexual Desire as a Couple Issue

This exercise involves two steps. The first is for each spouse to write self-blaming or blaming-the-partner statements and then next to each statement write a healthy counterstatement that challenges irrational, self-defeating blaming. The second step is to discuss new, healthy understandings and awareness about sexual desire as a couple issue. Write down and save these understandings so that you can use them as a resource in the coming weeks, months, and years.

Examples of self-blaming and partner-blaming statements (with counters) include the following:

- **"It's all my fault."**—Sexual desire is complex; there is no angel and no devil.
- **"My spouse doesn't love me."**—Love and sexual desire are not the same.
- **"It's guilt from my Catholic background."**—Guilt inhibits sexual desire. However, Catholic spouses report high desire and satisfaction. The new Catholic teaching (almost all religions agree on this) is pro-sex in marriage.
- **"If only my spouse would change, my desire would be fine."**—You can only change yourself. You cannot change your partner, although you can encourage and support her or him in making changes.
- **"If only I hadn't gotten pregnant."**—"If only" thinking is self-defeating. Deal with the present; you cannot change the past.
- **"I can't enjoy sex until I lose 20 pounds."**—A positive body image is important, but sexuality should not be held hostage to weight or a perfect body image. Sexual desire is based in the relationship and on giving and receiving pleasure-oriented touching.
- **"Romantic love is gone; there's nothing I can do."**— Romantic love is very fragile; it seldom lasts more than 2 years and typically dissipates after 6 months. Sexual desire

is based on mature intimacy and valuing variable, flexible couple sexuality.

- **"The best sex is premarital or extramarital."**—Marital sexuality is special and can be high quality, vital, and satisfying.
- **"We've been trapped in a no-sex marriage for so long that it will never change."**—Chronic problems are difficult to resolve, but motivated couples do revitalize intimacy and sexuality.
- **"We have the only nonconsummated marriage in the city."**—Because of stigma and embarrassment, people do not discuss this problem. Nonconsummated marriages exist, and the problem is resolvable.
- **"Since my spouse had an affair, I will never trust her or desire to be sexual with her."**—Couples can and do survive affairs. Intimacy and sexuality facilitate the healing process and are an integral component in rebuilding the marital bond.

There are many more self-defeating cognitions, but happily, there are even more emotional and rational problem-solving counters to this negative thinking, which you will learn about in this book.

The second step is to discuss sexual desire as a couple issue to acknowledge and reinforce crucial insights. Together, write down two to five statements about ISD as a way to acknowledge and reinforce crucial insights. Be sure these statements are clear and genuine. New understandings and awareness facilitate self-acceptance, partner acceptance, and being an intimate sexual team.

- "There is no good guy or bad guy; ISD is the common enemy. We will confront it together and revitalize marital sexuality."
- "Our love for each other and commitment to the marriage will help us overcome ISD."
- "We are good people and a good couple and deserve to enjoy our sexuality."

- "The sexual problem has been a drain, and we have been terrible to each other. But now we are committed to being an intimate sexual team and developing a vital, satisfying sexual relationship."
- "We want to have sex and a baby. We are going to support each other in reaching this goal."

Your list of emotional problem solving will allow you to maintain an intimate sexual team approach even when you encounter the inevitable frustrations, disappointments, and setbacks.

confronting desire problems as an intimate sexual couple

When Barry treats demoralized couples who have chronic ISD and marriages in which there has been no sex for years, the concept of being an "intimate sexual team" is what keeps the partners motivated. A crucial aspect of the team concept is not to turn on or attack your spouse. You win or lose as a team. You acknowledge sexual successes and share intimate feelings. When you fail, support and encourage each other; do not engage in blaming. Learn from the problem and plan for the next encounter. Trust that your spouse has your best interest in mind and wants you to enjoy healthy sexuality individually and as a couple. The most powerful aphrodisiac is to have the arousal of each partner play off the other partner's arousal, creating an erotic flow. This is a natural extension of the "give to get" pleasuring guideline.

Sexuality works best when each person is open and receptive. This is the opposite of the self-defeating pattern in which one partner demands and the other feels coerced and avoids (the pursuer–distancer dynamic). Each partner's sexual desire and bridges to desire are acknowledged and accepted. Both the higher desire and lower desire partners think and talk about sexuality as a couple issue, with the shared goal of establishing a sexual relationship that energizes their bond. It is not "his way" or "her way"; it is finding "our way." The quality of intimacy and sexuality is more important than the quantity of intercourse. A comfortable, vital couple sexual style is more important than individual sexual prowess. The focus is on sharing pleasure, not on individual intercourse performance. Confronting and changing the no-sex relationship are challenges you meet as an intimate sexual team. When your sexual relationship is disappointing or gets off track, you view this as a lapse. Remaining on the same sexual team ensures that it does not turn into a relapse.

Establish positive, realistic expectations for marital sexuality. Sex is not the most important factor in marriage. Sex is not even the most important aspect of intimacy. Emotional closeness and giving and receiving nondemand touching are the core components of the intimate bond. Eroticism, intercourse, and orgasm are special, energizing experiences. When sex works well, it plays a 15 percent to 20 percent role in relationship vitality and satisfaction. Unfortunately, ISD is more powerful as a relationship stress than good sex is as a relationship enhancer.

Sexual intimacy includes emotional closeness, trust, affection, sensuality, playfulness, eroticism, intercourse, orgasm, and bonding. The most satisfying couple sexuality integrates intimacy and eroticism. Does this mean that the individual loses his or her sexual autonomy? Not at all. Each person remains responsible for his or her desire, pleasure, eroticism, and satisfaction. Being an intimate sexual team does not mean giving up autonomy or blurring personal boundaries. Healthy sexuality involves developing and maintaining a comfortable, intimate, and satisfying couple sexual style.

Should every sexual experience be functional and satisfying? This is an unrealistic expectation that will result in relapse. A positive, realistic expectation is that 40 percent to 50 percent of sexual encounters will be mutually satisfying; 20 percent to 25 percent will be good for one spouse and okay for the other; 20 percent to 25 percent will be good for one spouse with the other going along for the ride; and 5 percent to 15 percent of encounters will be mediocre, unsatisfying, or dysfunctional (Frank, Anderson, & Rubinstein, 1978). This is a very different image than the one portrayed in movies, on talk shows, and in novels. Acknowledging the reality of mediocre, unsatisfying, or dysfunctional sexual experiences is particularly important. This is the kind of sex where one spouse looks at the other and says, "I hope you are enjoying this; it's for you." The other person replies, "I thought this was for you." The couple who can laugh or shrug off these experiences and get together at a later time when they are more awake, aware, desirous, involved, and responsive has the right attitude. The couple who is frustrated, angry, panicky, or blaming is likely to relapse. Occasional mediocre or poor sexual experiences are normal.

summary

Conceptualizing ISD as a couple problem has great advantages—specifically, in breaking the guilt–blame cycle. The one–two combination of personal responsibility and being an intimate sexual team is key. Develop a couple sexual style that sets the framework for satisfying marital sex. Being an intimate couple allows you to confront the no-sex marriage and to revitalize sexual desire.

Key Points

- ISD is best understood, assessed, and treated as a couple issue.
- Becoming stuck in negative patterns such as pursuer–distancer or demander–withdrawer damages each partner and the relationship. The healthy strategy is to take personal responsibility for sexuality and become an intimate sexual team.
- The challenge for couples is to transition from the romantic love–passionate sex–idealization phase to valuing intimate, interactive couple sexuality.

CHAPTER 3

Turnoffs: Poisons for Sexual Desire

T HE TERM *inhibited sexual desire* (ISD) reflects the core issue of identifying and assessing factors (we call them *turnoffs* or *poisons*) that block sexual desire. Sexual desire is easy to kill. The potential for desire and pleasure is natural for both women and men, but it also is vulnerable. A myriad of psychological, biological, and relational factors can poison desire. The previous chapter explored the psychobiosocial model of understanding, assessing, and changing couple sexuality. This chapter focuses on the psychological and relational poisons that threaten desire. Chief among these are anger and other negative emotions, including depression, guilt, anxiety, inhibitions, obsessions, compulsions, and shame. To understand what causes and maintains ISD, you need to identify individual and couple poisons.

Desire is the easiest dimension of sexuality to disrupt. Positive anticipation is the key to desire. If that key is turned off, it affects the entire sexual process. Sexuality is natural, but it has to be nurtured and reinforced. All of us deserve sexual desire and satisfaction. However, when conflicts, inhibitions, and avoidance dominate, sexual desire is undermined. This is especially true when hurt and anger override desire.

when premarital sexual experiences and expectations poison marital sex

A depressing reality is that "hot" couples are particularly vulnerable to ISD once they cohabitate or marry. Why? The factors that drive premarital sex—newness, illicitness, risk taking, winning the partner over, romantic love, passion, idealization, and exploring sexual boundaries—are unstable. By their very nature, romantic love and passionate sex (labeled the *limerance* phase) erode with time. Ideally, hot sex is replaced by the integration of intimacy, pleasuring, and eroticism. Yet, too often, sex becomes routine, low quality, and infrequent. Typically, this occurs even before marriage. The joke is that marriage kills sex, but unmarried couples who have been together more than 2 years have higher rates of no-sex relationships than do married couples. The challenge for couples—whether straight or gay, married or unmarried—is to integrate intimacy and eroticism into a serious, ongoing relationship (Perel, 2006).

Romantic-love couples meet for weekends and special occasions. They have time, energy, and enthusiasm for each other. They ignore the real world of jobs, laundry, and schedules. The person and the relationship are idealized. Once married or cohabitating, they spend every night together and have to deal with the nitty-gritty tasks involved in sharing their lives. Within this context, sex is no longer idealized or supercharged. Healthy sexual couples value both planned and spontaneous sexual experiences. Unfortunately, for too many couples the reality is that sex becomes the last thing they do at night after putting the children to bed and watching the news or a comedy program.

Premarital sex is a self-defeating and unrealistic standard of comparison. Barry tires of couples complaining that sex was best during the first 6 months of their relationship. The decrease in sexual frequency and romance frustrates, embarrasses, and angers the couple. Do not make premarital sexual comparisons. This poisons marital sexuality. Couple sexual desire is based on a dramatically different way of thinking, feeling, and being a couple. Couple sexuality involves dealing with the whole person and sharing the complexities of your lives, including emotional and sexual intimacy. Premarital and marital sexuality comparisons involve "apples and oranges." They offer no help in resolving sexual issues and only cause blame and frustration. Disappointment, resentment, and feeling tricked or manipulated poison couple sexuality. The premarital comparison interferes with developing a couple sexual style that enhances intimacy, desire, pleasure, eroticism, and satisfaction.

Let us examine some other psychological and relational poisons that threaten desire.

anger

Anger has an extremely corrosive effect on couple sexuality. People can and do use sex to make up after an argument. This works as long as it is not associated with emotional abuse or physical coercion. However, chronic anger poisons both emotional and sexual intimacy. Key elements in intimacy are feeling emotionally attached and trusting. Chronic conflict and anger break this emotional bond. Your partner is no longer your trusted, intimate friend but an untrustworthy critic who could hurt or even destroy you.

Feeling attacked or put down is the main precursor of anger. This is especially impactful if the attack involves your body or sexuality. For example, a woman intent on hurting her male partner complains that his penis is smaller than an ex-boyfriend's. Later, she apologizes and says she did not mean it, but he continues to ruminate and feel put down. Anger and alienation build. The therapist explains that in any case, penis size does not reflect sexual prowess, nor does it affect female sexual response. Although this reduces myths, it does not reduce anger. Anger can destroy intimacy and fuel sexual avoidance.

Women feel anger, usually unexpressed, at "intimate coercion," which is a major cause of female ISD. The man who pushes sex despite the woman's reluctance and verbal protestations is an example of winning a sex battle but losing a satisfying intimate sexual relationship. Intimate coercion is different than marital rape. Marital rape is a repetitive pattern that destroys trust in voluntary, pleasure-oriented sexuality. Intimate coercion is an intermittent pattern that does not involve force but is destructive to intimate sexuality. The essence of coercion is that it is a demand for sex at this time and in this way; if these demands are not met, there will be negative consequences for the partner, such as harassment, put-downs, or not providing money or help around the house.

The man and woman perceive intimate coercion in dramatically different ways. He denies that it occurs or says it is not his fault and is shocked by her anger. His perception is that he is seducing or coaxing her, similar to premarital scenarios. She feels pressured and violated. Her preferences and desires do not matter; he puts his sexual needs over her emotional needs. Involved, mutual, pleasure-oriented sexuality decreases. She feels that for him frequency of intercourse is more important than her emotional and sexual feelings. She feels taken advantage of and abused. Intimate coercion must be confronted and this poison eliminated.

Another source of anger involves the aftereffects of an extramarital affair. Men react more angrily than women. The wife's affair is a reversal of the double standard. The most common female affair is a "comparison affair" that meets her emotional and sexual needs instead of these being satisfied in the marriage. She compares her lover with her spouse. Even when the affair is over, her husband feels judged and insecure, which is expressed as anger. Angry thoughts feed the cycle, especially when he is alone and ruminating. Some men react by shutting down sexually. Others forcefully initiate sex as if to avenge the affair. Angry sex kills loving feelings, alienating the wife and poisoning her desire.

The wife's response to the discovery of her husband's affair is angry withdrawal. This anger builds a wall of resentment that brooks no touching, affection, or caring. Anger and alienation build on themselves and poison desire.

Couples can and do recover from an extramarital affair. This involves the participating partner taking responsibility for the affair and apologizing and the couple creating a genuine narrative about the causes of the affair and its meaning for the marriage, rebuilding the trust bond, and developing a new couple sexual style (McCarthy & Wald, 2013; Snyder, Baucom, & Gordon, 2007).

Sexual issues are not the only, or even the chief, reason for marital anger. Major causes are hurt from and disappointment in your spouse, the marriage, or both. Hurt is caused by one partner saying derogatory things about the other, discussing the other's weaknesses with a relative or friend, putting the spouse down in front of others, revealing a secret he or she had promised to honor, telling a joke at the partner's expense, using a slap or a threat of force during an argument, or reneging on a financial agreement. Disappointment is caused by finding that your spouse is less successful than claimed, that the in-law's family is fraught with conflicts and not the loving family depicted, that the move to a safer neighborhood is not financially possible, that caring and attentiveness has given way to compulsive TV watching, and that promises of intimacy have been replaced by a marginal relationship.

Anger is a secondary emotion; hurt and disappointment are the primary emotions. Anger, whether caused by sexual or emotional factors, is a sexual turnoff. This is true for both men and women. In porn videos, anger is portrayed as a sexual turn-on, but that is not how anger works for the great majority of couples. Anger is best dealt with outside of the bedroom. Talk out issues over the kitchen table, on walks, or in a therapist's office. The bedroom is the worst place for anger. Being nude and prone increases personal vulnerability. It is too easy for arguments to degenerate into "atomic bomb" attacks on your partner, the marriage, or sexuality. Deal with conflicts clothed and sitting up. Argue your points, but do not put your partner down or fall into the "attack–counterattack" mode.

guilt

Guilt is a self-defeating emotion. When you feel guilty, you lower your self-esteem and are likely to repeat the same destructive behavior. For example, the man sneaks off to a strip bar and spends the $50 he planned to use for a couple night out. He keeps this secret and avoids his wife. He is afraid that if she knew, she would think he was "scum." As his self-esteem decreases, he feels guilty and lonely and returns to the strip club, which reinforces the self-defeating cycle.

For women, a major source of guilt is fantasizing about another man or having an affair. Sometimes the affair does not involve intercourse but does include flirting, kissing, hugging, late-night calls, fondling, caressing, or stimulation to orgasm. Feelings of adventure, illicitness, and attraction are powerful. Ambivalent feelings, fear of discovery, or disruption of a work situation or a friendship burden the affair, whether consummated or not. When the relationship ends, especially if it ends badly (as it usually does), feelings of guilt poison sexual desire. The bad feelings generalize to marital sexuality. Your spouse's reaction of blaming or anger feeds the guilt and is a further turnoff.

Guilt disrupts the process of sharing intimacy and pleasure by causing the person to put herself or himself down and isolate from the partner. To confront guilt, you need to take responsibility for your behavior; apologize; make amends; and most important, use all your resources to be sure that the problematic behavior does not continue.

anxiety

Sex and pleasure belong together. Sex and performance are a poisonous combination. Anxiety is the emotion associated with performance. The type of anxiety that most interferes with sexual desire is anticipatory anxiety. Desire is facilitated by positive anticipation but subverted by anticipatory anxiety. Approaching sex with fear of failure, procrastination, fear of embarrassment, or wanting to get it over with is a turnoff. It is like being burdened by a 100-pound weight before you dive into the swimming pool.

Performance anxiety has a negative effect on arousal and erotic flow. The man views erection and intercourse as a pass–fail test. Sex is not the sharing of pleasure but an individual performance where fear of failure predominates. Performance anxiety also affects women, interfering with subjective arousal and lubrication. When arousal and orgasm are taken out of the context of sharing pleasure and made into a performance goal, anxiety increases and desire decreases.

inhibitions

Sex is fun. Allow yourself to experience pleasure-oriented sexuality. What types of inhibitions interfere with a natural progression of desire, pleasure, eroticism, and satisfaction? Inhibitions include psychological, relational, or sexual factors that block pleasure. Typical inhibitions are poor body image, reluctance to initiate, unwillingness to let go sexually in front of your partner, embarrassment at being nude, self-consciousness about making sexual requests, reluctance to try an erotic scenario, and fear of embarrassment or rejection. Inhibitions take the fun out of sexuality and result in rigid sex roles and stereotypical sexual expression. Sex becomes mechanical and stale, draining desire. For example, the couple has sex late at night, with no lights, after the male's nonverbal initiation, with limited touching, in the missionary position, with perfunctory afterplay. Even if functional for both partners (it is less likely to be functional for the woman), how much fun is it? Few people look forward to that predictable scenario. Inhibitions rob sexuality of its vitality.

Inhibitions are a psychological form of withholding. You are not free with yourself or with your partner. Psychologically and sexually, you are hiding behind a wall; you are guarded and inhibited. Allow sexuality to be open, flowing, and free.

obsessions and compulsions

Obsessions and compulsions are sexual turnoffs. Sometimes they are a symptom of obsessive–compulsive disorder, but usually the problem is linked specifically to sexual expression. Obsessive thoughts interfere with spontaneity and communication. For example, the husband who is obsessed by a fetish is shut off from his spouse. A woman who obsesses that a mother should not receive oral sex blocks pleasure.

Compulsive behavior is off-putting. Washing genitals can increase sexual comfort, but compulsive, ritualistic washing is a turnoff. Compulsive behaviors such as counting intercourse strokes, using three different forms of birth control, or immediately jumping up to wash off semen are turnoffs.

Obsessive–compulsive behavior is based on the irrational fear of dirtiness and contamination. In fact, genital secretions are healthy. There are more germs in your mouth than on your genitals. An advantage of a monogamous relationship is that you can enjoy sex without fear of sexually transmitted infections (STIs) or HIV/AIDS. Sexual obsessions and compulsions rob the couple of healthy, vital sexuality.

shame

The sad reality is more than 90 percent of women and men have been subject to negative sexual experiences in the past (Rind, Tromovitch, & Bauserman, 1998). This refers not only to the major traumas of child sexual abuse, incest, and rape but to being sexually humiliated, feeling guilt over masturbation or fantasies, being sexually rejected or ridiculed, having a sexual dysfunction, dealing with an unwanted pregnancy or STI, being exposed to or peeped at, receiving obscene phone calls, or being sexually harassed. Unfortunately, it is common to have confusing, negative, traumatic, or guilt-inducing incidents in childhood, adolescence, or adulthood. This is not the way it should be, but it is an unfair fact. These experiences can be confronted and dealt with. Accept your sexual history; do not treat it as an embarrassment. The worst thing about a traumatic incident is that it becomes a shameful secret that controls sexual self-esteem.

Shame has no positive function. Shame involves negative thoughts and feelings that dominate the person's self-esteem. This is irrational because people blame themselves for something they did not intend or cause. Shame is worse than guilt. Guilt involves reaction to an experience, whereas shame involves a self-definition. Why "blame the victim"? You dealt with the abusive situation as well as you could given your awareness and resources at the time. You can feel pride in having survived. Guilt lies with the perpetrator; there is no reason for the survivor to feel shame. The adage "living well is the best revenge" is an optimal way to think about negative sexual experiences. Do not blame yourself; take pride in being a survivor. Express sexuality in a manner that reinforces self-esteem and your intimate relationship. Be a proud survivor, not a victim controlled by anxiety, anger, or shame (Maltz, 2012).

confronting and changing sexual poisons

Realizing that you have felt controlled by a sexual poison need not cause embarrassment or depression. Knowledge is power. Becoming aware of the poison and its self-defeating effects is a first step. Accept rather than deny or minimize. With increased awareness, you reduce the poison's control. You can replace this "trap" with sexually healthy ways of thinking, acting, and feeling. For example, if the poison is guilty withdrawal after an incident of masturbating to a "900" phone fantasy, share that information with your partner within 72 hours so that it does not become a shameful secret. You might agree to a negative contingency (such as cleaning the bathrooms for a month or sending a $25 check to a cause you vehemently oppose) each time you use the "900" line. Rather than taking a "time out" after an incident, you are urged to engage in an intimate date. This challenges the poison so it no longer controls couple sexuality. The one–two combination confronts the poison so that it is eliminated (or at least is no longer controlling) and helps reassert a healthy role for couple sexuality.

RICH AND ROBIN

Rich and Robin began dating as high school seniors. The "two Rs" were envied by friends as a happy, stable couple. They dated through college with only two minor breakups and married exactly a year after graduation. When they entered therapy, they had been married 4 years and had an 18-month-old daughter. Rich was successful in computer marketing and was actively involved in the care of their daughter. This enabled Robin to pursue her academic career as a doctoral student in literature. They were viewed by family and friends as a model couple, moving ahead with individual, couple, and family lives. Rich and Robin were affectionate in public, and because they had a baby people naively assumed that they were a sexually active couple. People do not realize the difficulties and pain that occur behind a bedroom door.

Rich and Robin were controlled by turnoffs and poisons, including several remnants from their premarital relationship. Robin felt very guilty about contracting an STI during the time she had broken up with Rich. She transmitted chlamydia to Rich, who had been furious and blaming. Rich was viewed by friends as easygoing, but Robin knew how angry he could be. He never hit her but had thrown things and put his fist through a wall. Robin was intimidated by his anger. Early in the relationship, they used sex to calm Rich's anger. Robin came to resent this, especially Rich's demand for oral sex. Robin viewed fellatio as Rich's pacifier, and giving oral sex had become a turnoff. Even before marriage, sexual frequency and quality (especially the latter) dramatically decreased.

The honeymoon had been a disaster. Rich demanded and forced fellatio after heavy drinking at the wedding reception. This was their only sex during the 2-week honeymoon. Awkwardness and resentment built, especially after Rich's hostile satire of them as the only husband and wife in America who had not consummated their marriage. (In fact, approximately 1.5 percent of marriages are not consummated within the 1st year.)

Robin wanted to get pregnant, so they developed a pattern of having sex in the middle of the night. Their daughter was conceived through intercourse at 2:00 a.m. Although they seldom discussed the no-sex state of the marriage, each of them was privately ashamed and embarrassed. Robin blamed Rich's angry, demanding approach and unwillingness to share feelings. Rich blamed the problem totally on

Robin, seeing her as sexually cold and inhibited. Rich felt that Robin had lied during the premarital years when they had felt romantic love and shared enthusiastic sex.

What brought the chronic problem to a crisis was that Robin discovered Rich was purchasing oral sex at a massage parlor on a weekly basis. Although he paid in cash, Robin became suspicious because debt was mounting. When confronted, Rich tried to finesse and minimize the problem. He finally admitted the paid sex incidents but blamed them on Robin for withholding sex. He assured her that he was safe, but she insisted that they both do an STI screen and an HIV test. Fortunately, the results were negative. The physician suggested consulting a marriage therapist with a subspecialty in sex therapy.

Robin and Rich were extremely uncomfortable during the first therapy session. They believed the cultural myth that couples in their 20s do not have sexual problems. In reality, sexual problems are the main cause of divorce during the first 5 years of marriage. When they realized they were not alone, feelings of stigma were reduced. The therapist put the problem in perspective: Like many married couples, Robin and Rich had not developed a comfortable, functional couple sexual style. Treating sexuality with benign neglect often results in a no-sex marriage.

After the initial couple meeting, individual psychological, relational, and sexual histories were scheduled. Each person had an opportunity to review positive and negative dimensions of his or her sexual development without the spouse present and to explore attitudes, behavior, and emotions. The therapist asked each partner to focus on his or her role rather than blame the spouse. Secrets, turnoffs, and poisons were carefully assessed.

In the couple feedback session, the therapist observed that when Rich and Robin began as a couple, they felt open and caring. Over the years, frustrations, secrets, resentment, bitterness, and poisons built and compounded. Respect, trust, and intimacy eroded. Living incongruent lives increased emotional stress. It is draining to appear to be a happy couple while in reality feeling alienated and trapped in a no-sex marriage. A goal of sex therapy is to confront personal, relational, and sexual poisons and to revitalize the intimate sexual bond. This entails dealing with secrets and turnoffs and breaking down walls of alienation and avoidance. Rich and Robin needed to begin thinking, talking, acting, and feeling like an intimate sexual team.

The therapist pointed out "traps" that each needed to be aware of and confront. Robin had to stop seeing sex as Rich's domain, instead valuing sexuality for herself and their marital bond. She needed to confront anger and resentment, not use sex as a way of withholding or getting even, although she could use her veto power to stop a sexual activity that she experienced as aversive. She reduced her guilty feelings about the STI and did not allow them to control her sexual self-esteem. Rich was understanding and supportive of these changes but reluctant to confront his traps. His biggest issue was his pattern of angry sexual demands and intimate coercion. To eliminate this, the therapist advised instituting a 72-hour prohibition on sexual activity after an angry incident. In addition, Rich had to stop judging and blaming Robin.

Rebuilding the marital bond and revitalizing sexuality are not easy. Rich and Robin were committed to their marriage and family, but the poisons were severe. They had to confront these poisons and commit to eliminating (or at least significantly reducing) them. Each person had to assume responsibility for his or her behavior. Gradually, they began feeling and acting like an intimate sexual team. The marital bond of respect, trust, and intimacy was badly frayed but still intact and open to being revitalized.

The change process was uneven—two steps forward and one step back. It is easier to confront a poison before it takes hold, but Rich and Robin's poisons were chronic. They liked the analogy of marriage as an emotional bank account. Premaritally, they had made big deposits and few withdrawals. Since marriage, there had been few deposits (their child was the main one) and many withdrawals, especially in the sexual area. They had to conscientiously make small, steady intimacy deposits and guard against poisonous withdrawals.

The change process was arduous and required a great deal of psychological energy. But it was worthwhile. Robin assertively vetoed what she found uncomfortable. Rich stopped intimate coercion. They trusted that each of them was dedicated to revitalizing their intimate sexual bond. If an incident got them off track, the person who was responsible assured his or her spouse that it was not intentional, which took away the poison.

Rich was surprised at how much he enjoyed sensual, nondemand touching. Robin joked that they were better at pleasuring than at sex. The therapist reinforced the importance of emotional intimacy and nondemand pleasuring as a solid basis for couple sexuality. At the same time, he urged them to confront poisonous attitudes and behavior. Sexuality could not bloom if poisonous feelings and turnoffs were present, like weeds overrunning a flower garden.

It was Robin who initiated the return to intercourse. She requested that they maintain the prohibition on quickie intercourse as well as fellatio to orgasm. Rich agreed to honor this. He was enthusiastic about intimate, interactive sexual experiences. Robin's taking the role of requestor and guiding this transition to intercourse was a significant breakthrough. Equally important was monitoring turnoffs. For example, if Rich became frustrated and angry, rather than acting out, he called a time-out. They left the bedroom, brewed herbal tea, and talked for half an hour over the kitchen table. Robin listened empathically and validated his feelings even if she did not agree with his proposed course of action. They went to sleep as intimate friends, with the agreement that they would discuss the problem during therapy if they could not resolve it by themselves.

At therapy termination they planned follow-up meetings and relapse prevention strategies. Poisons are never totally gone. You have to monitor poisons and be committed to avoid falling into old traps. Individually and as a couple, you must value and nurture emotional and sexual intimacy.

confronting and reducing sexual turnoffs

Changing behavior is seldom easy, nor is it total. Even people who have successfully stopped smoking and have not had a cigarette in years still experience the urge to smoke. It is easier to totally cease a behavior than to moderate it; for example, it is often easier to stop drinking entirely than to drink moderately. Intimacy and sexuality are areas where balance and moderation are the norm, which makes the change process challenging.

Couples with a no-sex marriage struggle to revitalize intimacy and desire. Some poisons can be totally eliminated, but others need to be monitored. For example, a couple with a history of physical and verbal abuse who commits to abstain from abusive behavior can totally eliminate the poison of intimate partner violence but needs to manage differences and conflicts. If conflicts and anger intensify, there is fear of regression. Partners need to utilize emotional-regulation skills and the time-out technique. Fears and resentments never disappear, but they no longer control the couple.

Individually and as a couple, you can confront marital and sexual turnoffs. They do not deserve power over your life or sexuality. Do not allow them to control your present or future. The person with obsessive thoughts about an STI or an affair accepts the reality of the past but does not let this control the present. You cannot change the past (although you can learn from it). Take responsibility for yourself in the present. Do not remain stuck in the victim role. You are a survivor who is aware of poisons and is committed to not repeating self-defeating behavior. You are empowered to view sexuality as a positive, integral part of your personality and express this sexually so that it enhances your life and relationship.

Exercise: Identifying and Changing Sexual Poisons and Turnoffs

This exercise involves a concrete, personal assessment of sexual poisons and turnoffs. Develop a realistic plan to eliminate or drastically reduce them. Do the assessment phase separately, then work as an intimate sexual team on the change phase.

Begin by first listing personal poisons and turnoffs, then couple poisons and turnoffs. Focus on your own poisons and turnoffs; do not second-guess those of your partner. Examples of individual poisons include dwelling on angry thoughts, resentment over a sexual incident, inhibition about making sexual requests, avoidance of sexual topics, a secret arousal pattern, obsessive–compulsive reaction to vaginal secretions, irrational fear of pregnancy, making yourself unattractive to avoid intimacy, feeling controlled by childhood sexual trauma, overscheduling so there is no time for intimacy, making sexual demands or threats, being afraid to try new erotic scenarios, and feeling that you do not deserve sexual pleasure. Make two columns. In the first column, list what you feel are the advantages of maintaining each poison. Be honest. Perhaps you maintain the poison because it protects you from anxiety or fear of failure, is a way to control or punish your partner, gives you a sense of power, or serves to maintain the status quo. Are these in your best interest? In the second column, write how your life and marriage would be better without these poisons. What would you be free to try? Would this facilitate sexual anticipation and desire? You owe it to yourself and to the relationship to challenge and reduce poisons and turnoffs.

What is your role (not your partner's) in maintaining couple poisons? Examples include your role in the pursuer–distancer dynamic and the intimate coercion process, avoiding couple time, not making sexual requests yet resenting your spouse's insensitivity, maintaining an extramarital affair or a secret sexual life, comparing your partner with a person you fantasize about, or blaming problems on your partner's family of origin. Next to each couple poison, draw two columns. In the first column, list what you consider as the advantages of maintaining this poison. For example, it maintains the status quo, it is easier to blame your partner than to take personal responsibility, it allows you to avoid initiating and to maintain emotional and sexual distance, it is based on your fear that if the issue is addressed it will destroy your relationship, it allows you to maintain secrecy or get sympathy from friends and family. Is that what you really want? Is that healthy for your marriage? In the second column, list the advantages of resolving the sexual problem for you and the marriage. What will it take to confront couple poisons? How much time and energy? What attitudes and behaviors need to change? Do you value the benefits of a secure, satisfying, sexual marriage? Be specific and concrete about the challenges and rewards of the change process.

Exchange lists as you enter the change phase. It is easy to become defensive and counterattack when reading your spouse's material; that is counterproductive. The key to change is approaching sexuality as an intimate team. You trust that your spouse is on your side and will help you confront poisons. Sexuality is a team sport; do not turn against your intimate partner. Stay away from the "guilt–blame game." Your partner is being vulnerable in disclosing turnoffs. Honor that vulnerability; do not turn it against him or her. Listen to your partner's requests regarding how you can support the change process. Overcoming turnoffs and poisons is a one–two combination: (1) each person takes responsibility for changing his or her attitudes and behavior, and (2) the partners work together to eliminate the poisons and revitalize marital sexuality.

Develop a specific, clear plan to confront and reduce individual and couple poisons. Each partner states how he or she will be supportive. What specifically will you do to promote change? What behavior is your partner committed to stopping so that the process is not subverted? No change plan is perfect, but it will be successful if the plan is clear, positive, gradual, and you are willing to emotionally problem solve when you encounter difficulties.

Change is a couple task. Sexuality is a shared, intimate process. You cannot force or coerce your spouse. This exercise and the follow-up experiences give you practice at being an intimate sexual team. Instead of denying poisons and turnoffs, focus on changing so that poisons no longer control your marriage and sexuality.

summary

There are a myriad of personal and couple turnoffs that can poison your sexual relationship. When poisons are identified and confronted, they lose power. Change is well on the way when you assume responsibility for your own turnoffs, recognize that each person has a right to express feelings, share problems with your partner, remain aware that your partner's intentions are not to poison the relationship, and work as an intimate sexual team to confront and eliminate or reduce these problems. Successfully confronting poisons is a source of pride.

Removing poisons is necessary, but not sufficient, for revitalizing couple sexuality. Intimacy, nondemand pleasuring, and erotic scenarios are integral to healthy sexuality. Affirming sexuality as a shared pleasure, a way to reinforce intimacy, and a tension reducer allows sex to play a positive role in your relationship.

Personal and couple poisons need to be monitored so that they do not regain power. You have devoted time and energy to identifying and eliminating poisons, but you cannot stop there. Keep aware and vigilant so that negative attitudes and habits do not return. It is normal to have lapses; do not allow them to become a relapse. Marriage cannot rest on its laurels. Be willing to address personal, relational, and sexual issues so that your relationship remains free of poisons.

Key Points

- Sexual desire is easy to subvert and kill. Each person needs to take responsibility for individual and couple poisons and work as an intimate sexual team to confront and change these negative behaviors.
- Differences, disappointments, and conflicts are normal and can be dealt with through emotional problem solving. When that doesn't occur, the poisons and turnoffs again dominate the sexual relationship and subvert desire.
- The best way to change poisons and turnoffs is to adopt healthy sexual attitudes, behavior, and emotions.

CHAPTER 4

The New Male Sexuality: Confronting Myths of Autonomous Sex Performance

Do DESIRE PROBLEMS cause sexual dysfunction or does sexual dysfunction cause desire problems? For the great majority of males, the causation is clear—sexual dysfunction causes inhibited sexual desire (ISD). The main male sexual dysfunctions are premature ejaculation (PE), erectile dysfunction (ED), and ejaculatory inhibition. For males, sexual desire problems are almost always secondary. In other words, the man once had desire, but it is now inhibited, low, or nonexistent. The destructive cycle is anticipatory anxiety, performance anxiety resulting in dysfunctional sex, and sexual avoidance due to embarrassment and failure.

There is a second pattern—variant sexual arousal, which affects approximately 10 percent of men. This can involve compulsive masturbation (often accompanied by the use of "900" numbers, online sex, or porn), a fetish (based on fantasy) arousal pattern, or an issue of sexual orientation. There is high desire for the variant arousal but low interest in couple sexuality.

Young males learn that desire, arousal, and orgasm are easy and automatic. Most males masturbate by age 16, usually beginning between ages 10 and 14. The combination of masturbation experiences and the fact that masculinity and sexuality are so closely tied reinforces sexual desire for the adolescent and young adult. These experiences are valuable but pose vulnerabilities when sexual function becomes less predictable. Ease and quantity of sex are not solid foundations for sexual desire. For example, an 18-year-old ejaculates, has a short latency period before he is receptive to sexual stimulation, and then can have another orgasm. Is this the best measure of sexual function and satisfaction? The easy, automatic, autonomous, quantity approach to sex sets the stage for sexual problems as men age.

By their mid 30s or early 40s, most men find that arousal is no longer autonomous; they need partner involvement and stimulation. About 1 in 3 men find this transition difficult and develop arousal (erection) problems (Metz & McCarthy, 2004). Valuing quantity over sexual quality is self-defeating. The focus on performance rather than on pleasure makes the male vulnerable to dysfunction. The worst sexual learning is that easy, predictable sex is better than intimate, interactive couple sexuality. Over time, especially in marriage, intimacy and pleasuring are key bridges to sexual desire. The prescription for sexual desire is integrating intimacy, nondemand pleasuring, and eroticism. Traditional male sexual socialization emphasizes only the erotic component.

A common male fear (which becomes a self-fulfilling prophecy) is that reducing self-confidence and goal orientation begins a "slippery slope" of becoming sexually self-conscious and losing erectile confidence. In other words, the cycle of positive anticipation, enjoying intercourse, and frequent sex will disappear, replaced by anticipatory anxiety, tense and failed intercourse, and sexual avoidance. What accounts for this self-defeating cycle? Self-consciousness and performance anxiety. Sex is an active, involved, participatory activity—not a spectator sport. The couple enjoys the erotic flow, in which each partner's desire, receptivity, and responsivity enhances that of the other. This pattern is referred to as *partner interaction arousal*, which is the basis of the "give to get" pleasuring guideline. At its core, sexuality involves giving and receiving pleasure-oriented touching. If the female partner is turned on, it is a turn-on for the male partner. Sexual desire is integrated into their relationship and is not something "magical." Each person's arousal plays off and enhances the partner's arousal. Distraction and self-consciousness break the erotic flow. When sex becomes a pass–fail performance test, conditions for dysfunction and ISD are created.

The answer to the anticipatory and performance anxiety cycle is not a return to the youthful pattern of easy, autonomous erections. Once sensitized to sexual difficulty, especially ED, a man cannot pretend nothing happened and resume automatic functioning. By the time he seeks help, the anxiety–failure pattern has become well established, resulting in secondary ED and ISD. Sex is now a source of anxiety, frustration, and angst instead of pleasure, eroticism, and satisfaction.

Sexual anxiety and avoidance are stigmatizing because sexuality is viewed as a measure of masculinity. The performance myth is that "a real man can have sex with any woman, any time, any place." You and your penis are human, not a perfect performance machine. How can you challenge this trap? The key strategy is to adopt the Good Enough Sex (GES) approach and discard the perfect, autonomous sex performance demand (Metz & McCarthy, 2007). GES includes establishing positive, realistic sexual expectations; viewing your partner as your intimate sexual friend; enjoying nondemand pleasuring that flows into erotic scenarios and feelings; enjoying your own and your partner's arousal; viewing intercourse as a special pleasuring and erotic experience, not a performance test; letting eroticism naturally flow to orgasm; and enjoying afterplay.

At its essence, sexuality is about intimacy and pleasure, not pressure and individual performance. Desire and satisfaction are more important than arousal and orgasm. Sex is more than the penis, intercourse, and ejaculation. The man can learn to value intimacy and partner involvement rather than automatic, autonomous functioning. Sexuality is about sharing pleasure and eroticism. Males have been socialized to function in a sexually autonomous manner and only turn to the woman when there is a problem. This is the porn model. The man becomes turned on by external visual stimuli, not by intimate, interactive couple sexuality. Being open to stimulation and arousal by the female is key to regaining erectile comfort and confidence.

GES concepts are particularly valuable for low desire, ED, and ejaculatory inhibition and less so for the most common male problem, PE. Even with PE, it is crucial to view your partner as an intimate sexual friend who can help you learn ejaculatory control to enhance sexual pleasure.

premature ejaculation

Most males begin their sexual lives as premature ejaculators. As they gain comfort and experience, most develop ejaculatory control. However, 3 in 10 adult males experience PE. The average time for intercourse from intromission to ejaculation is 2 to 9 minutes. Contrary to male braggadocio, the great majority of males ejaculate in less than 12 minutes.

Some define PE in terms of time (a minute after intromission), some in terms of activity (fewer than 20 strokes), and some in terms of whether the woman is orgasmic during intercourse (an extremely poor criterion because a significant number of women are orgasmic during erotic sex but not during intercourse). A reasonable approach is that if the couple is engaging in nongenital and genital pleasuring and the man's ejaculation is earlier than both partners wish and interferes with pleasure, then they can benefit by improved ejaculatory control. Learning ejaculatory control will increase sexual pleasure for the man as well as for the couple. Enhanced pleasure facilitates sexual desire.

PE is usually a primary dysfunction, although some men (especially when sex is infrequent or tension filled) develop secondary PE. The two most commonly used male strategies make the problem worse. The first is using "do it yourself" techniques to reduce arousal. These include the man biting his lip, wearing two condoms, or thinking of the money he owes. The outcome of distraction techniques is reduced sexual pleasure, not greater ejaculatory control. He risks creating ED, ISD, and couple alienation. The second strategy is to replace quantity for quality. This means having a second intercourse as quickly as possible. Second orgasms are usually less satisfying for the man, and the woman is more likely to feel like a sex object than a desired partner. This negatively impacts the sexual relationship, and desire decreases because of low satisfaction.

Learning ejaculatory control is a three-phase process. First, identify the point of ejaculatory inevitability, after which ejaculation is no longer voluntary. Second, use the stop–start technique as you approach the point of ejaculatory inevitability. The man signals his partner to stop stimulation as he approaches ejaculatory inevitability. Stimulation stops for 30 to 60 seconds until he no longer feels the urge to ejaculate. The couple then resumes pleasurable and erotic touch. This enhances awareness while maintaining pleasure and arousal. Both phases are practiced with manual or oral stimulation and involve communicating to the partner when to stop stimulation. The third phase involves learning ejaculatory control with intercourse. The couple practices intercourse in the female-on-top position, using slow, long stroking controlled by the woman. She stops stroking as he approaches the point of ejaculatory inevitability. As control increases, they slow down movement rather than stop. The couple experiments with intercourse positions, types of stroking, and rhythm of stroking. The hardest situation for ejaculatory control is with the man on top, using short, rapid thrusting.

Some men prefer to utilize medication to improve ejaculatory control. Antidepressant medications usually help delay ejaculation. The preferred strategy is to take daily small doses, although some men use a moderate dose 4 hours before intercourse. The problem is that when the medication is stopped, PE returns (a rebound effect)—sometimes more severely. For most men, the recommended technique is to practice the ejaculatory control psychosexual skill exercises while taking medication, then gradually phase out the medication.

Learning ejaculatory control is a couple task, requiring time, practice, and feedback. Ejaculatory control is not about the man performing to a standard or proving that he can "give" her an orgasm during intercourse. The focus is on mutually satisfying, pleasure-oriented intercourse (Metz & McCarthy, 2003).

A common mistake is for sex to end with the man's ejaculation. Many women enjoy manual or rubbing stimulation after intercourse—either for orgasm or to share closeness. Afterplay is the most neglected dimension of sexuality. Yet it very much affects the couple's (especially the woman's) sense of satisfaction.

Learning ejaculatory control is like learning any skill. It is a gradual process, requiring practice, feedback, and working as an intimate sexual team.

erectile dysfunction

Far too much of a man's self-esteem and sense of masculinity are tied to his penis. ED, commonly called "impotence" or "not getting it up," is a major male fear. A well-hidden fact is that by age 40, about 90 percent of men have experienced a problem with achieving or maintaining an erection adequate for intercourse at least once. By age 50, more than half of men report mild to moderate erectile difficulty. So a man's major fear is, in fact, an almost universal experience. Men are notorious liars and braggarts about sexual prowess. They deny sexual doubts, questions, or difficulties. The myth-based performance criterion of the ability and willingness of a "real man" to have sex with any woman, anywhere, at any time puts tremendous pressure on the man, especially on his penis.

For men under 40, most erectile problems are caused by psychological or relationship problems rather than by physical or medical factors. Physical vulnerabilities do increase with age. Common physical causes include alcohol abuse, smoking, drug abuse, side effects of medications (especially hypertensive and psychiatric medications), spinal conditions, prostate surgery, chronic illness, poorly controlled diabetes, and vascular insufficiency. Common psychological and relational causes are anticipatory anxiety, performance anxiety, distraction, self-consciousness, viewing intercourse as a pass–fail test, reluctance to request partner stimulation, and anger at the spouse. If an erection problem does not remit within 6 months, the man (and the couple) becomes trapped in the cycle of anticipatory anxiety, intercourse failure, frustration, embarrassment, and eventually avoidance. No matter what started the problem (alcohol, side effect of medication, fatigue, alienation, depression, anger, or trying to force sex), this self-perpetuating anxiety cycle maintains ED.

The hormonal, vascular, and neurological systems must be functional for adequate erectile response. Beginning in the mid 30s, there is a gradual decline in the efficacy of these physical systems. That is why there are few professional athletes beyond age 40; the body is a less efficient performance machine. Testosterone affects sexual desire, which indirectly affects erectile function. An erection involves increased blood flow to the penis (*vasocongestion*), which fills the tissues and increases the size of the penis. As arousal builds, rigidity (hardness) increases—a neurological response. These systems remain functional when we get older but are no longer at optimal efficiency. Psychological, relational, and psychosexual skill factors become crucial for erectile response after 35 to 45 years of age.

Erection is vulnerable to distraction and anxiety. Intimacy, nondemand pleasuring, and erotic scenarios and techniques are necessary factors. A 50-year-old man is not the easy, automatic, autonomous, sexual functioner he was at 20. Sexual response becomes less predictable. Both partners can accept sexual variability and flexibility while maintaining positive sexual feelings and expectations—the essence of the GES approach.

If you have questions about physical or medical aspects of your sexual functioning, consult an internist, urologist, or a sexual medicine specialist. Although not considered a male sex doctor, the urologist functions much the way a gynecologist does for women. Be sure the physician is interested in doing a comprehensive assessment, not in promoting Viagra, penile injections, external pumps, or surgery.

The most important assessment question is whether the man is able to get erections during self-stimulation, with manual or oral stimulation by his partner, during sleep, or on awakening. If so, it is likely that the physical factors are functional, although operating less efficiently. Anxiety, distraction, fatigue, and negative emotions are major factors interfering with sexual function. Psychological factors of comfort, involvement, intimacy, and openness are necessary to regain erectile confidence, especially after age 45 or 50. These include communication with and trust in the spouse, being turned on by her arousal, being open to her stimulation, and making sexual requests. Erotic factors, especially penile stimulation; her guiding intromission (i.e., guiding his penis into her vagina); awareness of personal and couple turn-ons; and enjoying orgasm with erotic, nonintercourse sexuality are crucial. If the couple chooses to use medical interventions such as Viagra or Cialis, injections, or an external pump, the partners have to communicate about how best to integrate this into their couple sexual style.

Guidelines for treatment of ED emphasize intimacy; nondemand pleasuring; erotic scenarios and techniques; and positive, realistic expectations. As with other sexual problems, seeking the counsel of a sex therapist is superior to working on your own or expecting that a stand-alone medical intervention will return you to autonomous, totally predictable erections.

The foundation for regaining erectile comfort and confidence is nongenital and genital pleasuring. A crucial technique is that the man (and woman) becomes comfortable with the waxing and waning of erections. Men are used to going to intercourse and orgasm on the first erection, so when an erection fades, they panic. The man is afraid that the sexual opportunity is lost. Most men strongly prefer to proceed to intercourse on their first erection. This is only a problem if it involves a performance demand. In fact, continued involvement, mindfulness, relaxation, and erotic stimulation ensure that the erection will wax again.

The process of waxing and waning of an erection can occur two to five times in a 45-minute pleasuring session. The next step is to be orgasmic at least twice while erect during erotic, nonintercourse sex (manual, oral, or rubbing stimulation). This increases awareness and comfort with the interplay between subjective and objective arousal. During the free flow of erotic stimulation (without switching to intercourse), he can reach orgasm. Subjective arousal (feeling turned on) usually precedes objective arousal (becoming erect). Without the worry of intercourse failure, eroticism and orgasm flow. The next step is for the woman to play with the penis around the vagina to desensitize performance anxiety and give her practice at stimulating and guiding the penis. She decides when to transition to intercourse and what position to use and guides intromission. During intercourse, the couple is encouraged to use multiple stimulation (he touching her breasts, she stroking his testicles, kissing, fantasizing), which heightens erotic flow.

Since 1998, an increasing number of men have been using Viagra or Cialis to improve erectile function. Viagra is the first user-friendly medical intervention; men take a pill approximately an hour before initiating sex (Goldstein et al., 1998). Viagra and Cialis have two advantages. First, they are vasodilators that enhance blood flow to the penis and allow retention of the erection. Second, they serve as a positive psychological stimulus (a placebo response) to reduce performance anxiety. The partners need to be comfortable and open when integrating proerection medication into their intimacy, pleasuring, eroticism style (McCarthy & Fucito, 2005).

Men who overcome ED do not go back to easy, automatic erections. They are more aware, better lovers who have comfort and confidence with achieving erections and appreciate variable, flexible sexual experiences. Approximately 85 percent of their sexual encounters flow into intercourse, while another 5 percent to 10 percent are sensual or erotic experiences. Mediocre or disappointing sexual experiences are accepted. Neither the man nor his partner overreacts. If sex gets off track, it is seen as a lapse, not a relapse. Embracing the GES approach to ED and male and couple sexuality is a wise decision that will allow you to be sexual into your 60s, 70s, and 80s. Men (and couples) who can shrug off or laugh about disappointing or unsuccessful sexual experiences are in a solid position to generalize erectile comfort and confidence.

ejaculatory inhibition

This is the least known male sexual dysfunction. The old terms *retarded ejaculation* or *ejaculatory incompetence* had a negative, put-down connotation. *Ejaculatory inhibition* (also called *delayed ejaculation*) refers to the man wanting to reach orgasm but being unable to because his sexual response is blocked (inhibited). The most severe form, primary ejaculatory inhibition (inability to ejaculate by any means), is very rare. Among young men, the most common manifestation is the inability to ejaculate during intercourse, although they do during masturbation (and usually with partner manual or oral stimulation). This can continue for years without being addressed until the couple wants to become pregnant. This occurs in less than 2 percent of young males.

Ejaculatory inhibition is most common in its intermittent form, affecting as many as 15 percent of men, especially after age 50. Difficulty in ejaculating stems from a range of inhibitions—the inability to let go, beginning intercourse at low levels of subjective arousal, not being comfortable requesting additional erotic stimulation, fear or ambivalence about couple sexuality, or feeling sexually guilty.

Some males reach orgasm with a very narrow type of stimulation—rubbing against bed sheets, a fetish arousal pattern, or self-stimulation using porn. They feel inhibited during intimate, interactive couple sex. Sexuality is a cooperative, sharing experience between two people who are actively involved in giving and receiving pleasure. With ejaculatory inhibition, this process is blocked. Rather than orgasm being the natural culmination of erotic flow, it becomes an anxiety-provoking goal the man fails to achieve.

As with other sexual dysfunctions, ejaculatory inhibition is best viewed as a couple issue. The couple—not just the man—needs to increase involvement, pleasure, and eroticism, which allows arousal to naturally flow to orgasm. You cannot will or force an orgasm. The key is to increase eroticism, especially subjective feelings of being involved and turned on. Erections (objective arousal) can occur at low levels of subjective arousal, so the woman mistakenly believes that the man is highly aroused. A common inhibition is feeling shy about requesting additional erotic stimulation during intercourse, believing that thrusting should be enough. Males with ejaculatory inhibition can have intercourse for half an hour, an hour, or longer. Those suffering from PE or couples worrying about ED envy these men. What nonsense! This type of intercourse is mechanical (and sometimes aversive), not pleasure oriented. Involvement and arousal do not increase. Intercourse is to service the partner rather than to give and receive pleasure.

Two techniques facilitate orgasm during intercourse—multiple stimulation and using orgasm triggers. A guideline is not to initiate intercourse until the man's subjective arousal is at least a 7 and preferably an 8 on a 10-point scale of subjective arousal. Another is to request stimulation to increase eroticism. This can involve fellatio while he moves rhythmically, the woman stroking the man's buttocks or testicles during intercourse, or combining kissing and giving manual stimulation throughout intercourse. Requesting multiple stimulation during intercourse enhances involvement and erotic flow. Why should multiple stimulation cease when intercourse begins? Erotic scenarios involve giving, as well as receiving, stimulation. You can switch intercourse positions. She does chest or anal stimulation while he gives breast or clitoral stimulation. He verbalizes sexy feelings, fantasizes, or tells erotic stories.

Orgasm triggers are idiosyncratic. One of the best ways to identify orgasm triggers is to tune into the touches, thoughts, fantasies, and movements you utilize during masturbation right before the point of ejaculatory inevitability. Transfer these to partner sex. Orgasm triggers include verbalizing or making sounds, moving your body, focusing on a fantasy, giving stimulation, watching your partner, and enhanced rhythmic thrusting. Use orgasm triggers to move from erotic flow (an 8 or 9) to letting go and coming.

sexual dysfunction and inhibited sexual desire

Sexual dysfunction, especially ED and ejaculatory inhibition, usually results in secondary ISD. Sex is no longer an anticipated pleasure. It becomes a source of disappointment and frustration and is something to be feared and avoided. This is exacerbated when the man employs do-it-yourself techniques such as using two condoms or a desensitizing cream for ejaculatory control, using a "cock ring" or an injection for erection problems without telling his spouse, or buying an herb or potion that is supposed to force ejaculation. These either do nothing or cause more severe sexual or relationship problems. Sex is a team sport. You need to communicate and work as an intimate sexual team to resolve the problem. Focus on rebuilding comfortable, functional, satisfying couple sexuality. It is a gradual process, not a miracle cure. Couple sex therapy is more successful than trying it on your own. There is a positive reciprocal relationship between sexual pleasure and sexual desire. ISD and performance anxiety subvert pleasure for both people.

variant sexual arousal

Approximately 2 percent to 4 percent of males have a variant arousal pattern. The most common types are fetish arousal, cross-dressing, using "900" numbers with a specialty in "kinky" fantasies, cybersex, and dominant–submissive scenarios. Another type is a deviant arousal pattern (this is rare, occurring in fewer than 1 percent of men) that is abusive and illegal. Deviant arousal includes exhibitionism, voyeurism, frotteurism, obscene phone calls, and pedophilia (Fedoroff, 2010).

Variant arousal is very narrow but very powerful. It combines high secrecy, high eroticism, and high shame—a poisonous combination. It is quite difficult, and for many men impossible, to transfer variant arousal to couple sex. Premaritally and early in the marriage the man might be functional, but over time he develops ISD because there is low desire for intimate, interactive couple sex. Sexual desire is trapped in the narrow dead end of secret variant arousal.

This problem absolutely requires clinical intervention. Typically, the man is in denial or minimizes the impact of the variant arousal. He is intent on keeping this from his spouse. This secret is exposed when he is arrested (for deviant sexual behavior) or there is a very high Internet bill (for variant arousal). This is a major crisis for the man and the marriage. Therapeutic intervention is preferable to crisis management. This problem will not be resolved unless addressed therapeutically.

Let us first consider the more serious problem of deviant arousal, which is both illegal and harmful to others. The pattern develops in childhood or early adolescence and is reinforced by thousands of experiences of masturbating to images of deviant arousal. It is best thought of as an impulsive, compulsive behavior that serves as the man's "secret sexual world." He distorts reality by thinking it is his special turn-on and does not harm others. Couple sex cannot compete with this distorted fantasy and secret sexual world.

Fetishism, cross-dressing, masturbating to porn, going to massage parlors or prostitutes, and telephone or online sex do not involve illegal activity or harm to others. However, they are very impactful on the marriage, subverting couple intimacy. The woman feels relieved when the problem is revealed because she has blamed herself or felt "crazy" because she didn't know what was wrong. Rather than feeling involved and turned on during partner sex, he tries to shut her off and focuses on the variant fantasies. Most men, and many women, use fantasies as a bridge to desire and arousal, a healthy form of multiple stimulation. However, variant fantasies serve as a wall to block out the partner. Intimacy is a victim of variant sexual arousal.

A common therapeutic strategy is a one–two combination of the male confronting and stopping the variant arousal pattern and the couple developing an intimate, interactive sexual style. The woman is not responsible for changing the man's variant arousal; he is. However, it is a joint responsibility to develop a comfortable, functional couple sexual style. Other therapeutic strategies involve accepting or compartmentalizing the variant arousal. This approach requires the couple to consult with a therapist to ensure that accepting or compartmentalizing variant arousal will not subvert their emotional and sexual relationship.

sexual orientation issues

Sexual orientation issues are extremely disruptive to the man and a major threat to the marriage. This type of issue is a powerful secret he tries to hide from his wife. Emotionally and sexually, he is leading a double life.

Sometime in their lives (most often in adolescence or early adulthood), approximately 1 in 5 men have sexual experiences with other men. Sexual fantasies or experiences with men do not mean the person's orientation is homosexual. Sexual orientation involves an emotional and sexual commitment to a woman for heterosexuals or to a man for homosexuals (Diamond, 2003). In clinical practice, Barry has seen a range of situations, from someone who is clearly gay and uses the marriage as a convenient cover, to a man who is aroused by being fellated in an anonymous encounter but is not emotionally or sexually attracted to men, to men who are passive in anal intercourse (the most dangerous behavior for HIV/AIDS), to men who obsess about and are afraid of being homosexual yet are clearly heterosexual, to men who use sex with males as a way to get back at their spouse or as a tension reducer to compensate for an emotional problem. In cases where the husband's orientation is gay, trying to convert him to heterosexuality for the sake of the marriage or children is self-defeating. Most of these marriages will end in divorce, and that is for the best. Trying to pretend about a desire that is weak or nonexistent is in no one's interest. Because of emotional closeness, concern for children, practical factors, or any combination of these, some couples choose to stay in a no-sex marriage (often with one or both people having affairs). These decisions are best made in the context of couple or individual therapy.

Where the man is ambivalent about sexual orientation, the treatment of choice is individual therapy, with couple therapy occurring concurrently or sequentially. Sexual orientation is a major life commitment. Although it is possible to be sexual with both men and women, this does not mean the person's orientation is bisexual. If bisexuality is defined as equal emotional and sexual commitment to both sexes, the number of bisexuals is small. However, the number of men (and women) who can function bisexually is much greater. To rebuild desire, the man's sexual commitment must be to a genuine marital sexuality. He cannot pretend or try to convert to heterosexuality to save the marriage.

Exercise: Confronting Male Sexual Problems

This exercise has two components. The man honestly and objectively examines past and present sexual functioning in regard to PE, ED, ISD, and ejaculatory inhibition. Is sex functional or dysfunctional? How does this affect sexual desire? The man should not blame his spouse but take responsibility for his sexual attitudes, behavior, and feelings.

The second component is sharing understandings with his partner. He proposes a strategy to address the sexual problems, whether through individual therapy, couple therapy, sex therapy, or a self-help approach. The man is clear about how he plans to change and what he needs from his partner.

If there is a problem with a variant arousal pattern or sexual orientation, this exercise might cause it to surface for the first time. It has been the man's shameful secret, which he needs to confront rather than deny or minimize. Is he open to change? Is he willing to seek therapy? Does this problem mean the marriage is not viable? Is he motivated to resolve the problem and develop a new couple sexual style? What is a healthy role for the woman?

In sharing information about sexual dysfunction or other sexual problems, the woman has an opportunity to present her perceptions and feelings and add a helpful perspective. She can suggest alternative ways to approach the problem or support his proposed strategy. She clarifies what she is willing to do, as well as her limits. How can she be an active, intimate team member in confronting the sexual problem and revitalizing couple sexuality?

DOUG AND ALICIA

Doug married Alicia at 27, joking that he finally got caught. In reality, he was glad to be married and looked forward to a secure marriage. Although Doug had engaged in sex with more than 20 women, he never discussed the problem of PE. He focused on sexual quantity rather than quality, lasting longer the second time.

Alicia had not raised the issue of PE either. Alicia had fewer pre-marital partners, but her relationships were longer. In her experience, ejaculatory control usually improved after some months. She naively hoped this would happen with Doug.

The "magic" of romantic love and passionate sex lasted 8 months, ending 4 months before marriage. Doug and Alicia admitted that the quality of their premarital sex was not high but fondly remembered very special sexual experiences. Romantic love fades even among the most loving, sexually functional couples. Unless it is replaced by mature intimacy, the sexual relationship is vulnerable. Three months before their marriage, Doug threatened to call it off because Alicia was saying no to sex with increasing frequency. Rather than deal with the issues of sexual desire and PE, Alicia tried to placate Doug.

This proved disastrous. Alicia felt sexually anxious and pressured. Increasingly, she resented Doug, feeling more alienated and less sexually receptive and responsive. Alicia's desire and orgasms decreased. Doug felt it was on his shoulders to keep sex alive, and his focus was frequency.

Doug and Alicia fell into the traditional trap. He wanted to ignore or minimize his sexual problem and she wanted to cure it for him. When this did not happen, Alicia became angry and Doug's worst critic. A year and a half into the marriage, the problem of PE was raised, this time with more vehemence and less empathy. After a frustrating experience, Alicia accused Doug of being uncaring and sexually selfish. Impulsive sexual fights in bed while nude and lying down are volatile and counterproductive. Doug was shocked and offended, counterattacking by calling her a "frigid bitch." Alicia saw him as mean, and she withdrew.

Doug decided that he would show her by achieving ejaculatory control on his own. He used as his resource an advertisement in a men's magazine for a desensitizing cream with a money-back guarantee. All it did was irritate his penis. Doug then consulted a male sex clinic that prescribed an antidepressant medication and penile injections. He did not tell Alicia about this, but was pleased that his ejaculatory control improved and that he stayed hard even after he ejaculated. When Alicia found the medication, she was very concerned that Doug was depressed about his sexual function. This made him so self-conscious that he threw out the pills and stopped the penile injections. PE returned with a vengeance. Medication can serve as a resource in learning ejaculatory control, but it is not a miracle cure. If incorporated into a couple's ejaculatory control program, medication can be a valuable adjunct. However, if done as a stand-alone intervention, especially if kept secret from one's spouse, it is likely to backfire and cause sexual alienation and ISD for one or both partners.

Doug's strategy had been to do it himself, reduce arousal, and prove something to Alicia. Unfortunately, he wound up with a worse problem—erectile anxiety. He inserted as soon as he became hard, ejaculated at or right after intromission, and blamed it on Alicia's sexual lack of interest. This is an example of the iatrogenic effect of focusing on sexual performance; it creates more severe sexual and relational problems. It was not long before Doug and Alicia were avoiding not only intercourse but affectionate touch. They were stuck in the cycle of emotional alienation, ISD, avoidance, and a low-sex marriage.

It was Alicia who challenged the cycle by suggesting couple sex therapy. Alicia had been in individual therapy as a college student and had benefited from 2 years of group therapy as an adult. Doug was distrustful of general psychotherapy but open to sex therapy.

Regaining comfort and confidence with pleasure, eroticism, and erection was the initial therapeutic focus. Doug began to treat Alicia as an intimate sexual friend with whom he could share sexual concerns and anxieties and make sexual requests. Alicia was a willing and supportive sexual ally. Pleasuring exercises made Alicia feel very good, and her sexual enthusiasm transferred to Doug. This is a common pattern: Women find sex therapy concepts and techniques easier to accept than men. Intimacy and nondemand pleasuring greatly enhanced Alicia's sexual anticipation and desire. Her openness and desire increased Doug's involvement and arousal. With manual and oral stimulation, Doug was surprised at how quickly his confidence with erections returned. Sex was no longer a race toward intercourse and ejaculation. Slowing down the process, while increasing erotic stimulation, improved ejaculatory control.

A breakthrough occurred when they began the stop–start technique. Alicia used manual stimulation, and when Doug approached the point of ejaculatory inevitability he signaled her to stop. They did this for 10 to 12 minutes, openly communicating and enjoying erotic feelings. Although Alicia found it less fun after the first week, they knew they could master ejaculatory control if they worked together. Being intimate sexual friends, with each spouse's arousal enhancing the other's, was particularly valuable. Doug was not performing for Alicia; they were sharing pleasure and eroticism.

For the transition to intercourse, Alicia guided intromission. She began with slow, long thrusting. They used the stop–start technique before and during intercourse. What worked even better was changing the type and rhythm of coital thrusting, especially using circular thrusting. Alicia could be orgasmic with both intercourse and erotic stimulation, and Doug particularly enjoyed Alicia being orgasmic during intercourse. Doug was learning ejaculatory control not for Alicia to have orgasms during intercourse but to make the sexual experience comfortable, pleasurable, and satisfying for both.

function and desire

The man (and the couple) can enjoy the process of desire, pleasure, eroticism, and satisfaction. A sign of healthy male sexuality is replacing unrealistic demands to be a perfect sex performer with a mutual pleasure orientation. Adolescent and young adult sexual experiences take place in a double-standard context, which ultimately undermines male sexuality—especially after age 40 and in marriage. Easy, automatic, autonomous sex functioning can transition into valuing intimate, interactive, variable, and flexible GES sexuality. ED or ejaculatory inhibition is a sign that this transition has been unsuccessful. This sets the stage for a relapse into ISD and avoidance. Male ISD is more likely than female sexual problems to lead to a no-sex marriage. Male sexual problems that interfere with intercourse are more disruptive to the relationship and require comprehensive treatment, specifically couple sex therapy.

Male sexual dysfunction is best conceptualized and treated as a couple issue. The woman's role as the intimate sexual friend is crucial. The man takes responsibility for changing his sexual attitudes, behavior, and feelings, but the partners work together to develop a comfortable, functional, and flexible couple sexual style. This will inoculate the man and the couple against a no-sex marriage as he and the relationship age.

summary

Male sexual dysfunction usually precedes ISD. The man feels embarrassed and humiliated because he cannot meet the rigid performance demands he grew up with. He retreats into blaming himself, blaming his spouse, and sexual avoidance. The key to change is to adopt a broad, flexible, pleasure-oriented approach to sexuality—the GES approach. The couple is an intimate sexual team that develops a comfortable, satisfying sexual style. The man trying to change on his own is likely to cause more serious relational and sexual problems. Couple sex therapy facilitates the change process. When the problem involves a secret sexual life, therapy is vital.

Key Points

- Wise men adopt the GES approach of sharing sexual pleasure and eroticism and discard the individual pass–fail intercourse performance approach.
- Healthy male and couple sexuality is enhanced by turning to your partner as your intimate and erotic friend.
- You need to confront secrecy, shame, and rigid performance demands. Embrace intimacy, sharing pleasure; genuine eroticism; and the positive, realistic GES approach.

CHAPTER 5

Finding Her Voice:
Female Sexual Equity

Women have the same right to desire, pleasure, eroticism, and satisfaction as men do. The biggest mistake people make is to define female sexuality narrowly and mechanically. Sex does not equal intercourse. Sexual satisfaction does not equal orgasm. The myth is that if a woman has an orgasm, she will not have inhibited sexual desire (ISD). We are strong advocates for female orgasm, but this is not the cure for ISD.

Sexuality includes desire (anticipating being sexual and feeling that you deserve a healthy sexual relationship), pleasure (receptivity and responsivity to nongenital and genital pleasuring resulting in feeling turned on and vaginally lubricated), eroticism (letting go and allowing erotic flow to naturally culminate in orgasm), and satisfaction (feeling good about yourself, your partner, and your intimate bond).

The most common female sexual dysfunctions (in order of frequency) are

- secondary ISD,
- primary ISD,
- secondary nonorgasmic response during partner sex,
- painful intercourse,

- arousal dysfunction,
- primary nonorgasmic response during partner sex, and
- primary nonorgasmic response.

A primary sexual dysfunction means that there has always been a problem (e.g., primary ISD means the female has never felt deserving of sexual desire and pleasure). Secondary dysfunction means that she was once sexually functional but has become dysfunctional (e.g., secondary ISD means she once anticipated and enjoyed sex but now has little or no desire). Some women experience arousal and orgasm but are trapped in ISD. More typically, arousal and orgasm problems involve secondary ISD.

It is crucial to resolve the dysfunction when that is the main factor inhibiting desire. For example, if the female has a history of sexual desire but develops pain during intercourse and secondary nonorgasmic response, these are the focus of treatment. Comfortable, orgasmic sex is likely to result in increased desire. On the other hand, when the desire problem is primary and chronic (whether or not the woman experiences orgasm), desire is the focus of treatment. For most women, both desire and dysfunction issues need to be addressed, but desire is the primary issue (Basson, 2007).

As with desire problems, arousal and orgasm dysfunction are best considered a couple issue. The traditional trap was to label the woman "frigid." Happily, this term has fallen into disrepute. While the old trap was to blame the woman, the new, "politically correct" trap is to blame the man: "Males are selfish, lousy lovers." It is a cop-out to label the woman frigid or the man a lousy lover. Blaming and shaming make the sexual problem worse.

The therapeutic strategy is the one–two combination of the woman increasing awareness and taking responsibility for her sexuality and the couple working as an intimate sexual team. She can increase feelings of comfort, deserving, and anticipation and take an active role in the pleasuring process. Keys to arousal are receptivity and responsivity to genital and erotic stimulation. The female communicates and guides her partner (either by putting her hand over his or making verbal requests), showing him what turns her on. They learn to talk, feel, problem solve, and share as an intimate sexual team. He is open to her requests and guidance instead of playing the "macho" role of the sex expert. They are trusting, equitable partners (Hall, 2004).

In the traditional scenario, the woman remains passive while the man "services" her during foreplay to get her ready for the main event of intercourse. Although some women prefer this scenario, most prefer intimate, interactive pleasuring. *Pleasuring* refers to giving and receiving sensual and erotic touching, especially the "give to get" pleasuring guideline that encourages couples to enjoy each other's sexual responsivity. The woman's arousal plays off and builds on that of her involved, caring partner. Pleasure and eroticism are good in and of themselves; they do not have to be goal oriented (i.e., culminate in intercourse). Unfortunately, our culture labels erection as the measure of male sexuality and orgasm as the measure of female sexuality. These rigid performance criteria subvert sexual desire and satisfaction.

Major misunderstandings are rampant concerning female pleasure, eroticism, and orgasm. Old myths involved female passivity and less sexual capacity. Women felt pressure to be like men and have one orgasm during intercourse. Old repressive myths have given way to new performance myths. These include the belief that the woman must have an orgasm during each sexual encounter, that orgasm is the only measure of satisfaction, that a "G-spot" orgasm is the ultimate, and that being multiorgasmic is superior to having a single orgasm.

The scientifically valid concept is that female sexual response is more variable, flexible, and complex than is male sexual response. Male response is more predictable and stereotypical (i.e., he has one orgasm during intercourse). The woman can be nonorgasmic, singly orgasmic, or multiorgasmic, which can occur in the pleasuring phase, during intercourse, or through afterplay. Variable and flexible does not mean better or worse.

There is no "one right way" to experience orgasm. Only 1 in 4 women follow the male model of a single orgasm during intercourse without multiple stimulation. The most common pattern for "Jane and Joe Average" is for Jane to be orgasmic with manual or oral stimulation, or both, during pleasuring and for Joe to be orgasmic during intercourse. Although most women can be orgasmic during intercourse, many find it easier and more satisfying to be orgasmic with erotic sex or with multiple stimulation during intercourse. Most women do not have an orgasm at each sexual encounter. The most common pattern is for the female to be orgasmic in approximately 70 percent of couple encounters. Approximately 20 percent of women have a multiorgasmic response pattern. If she has six orgasms, does that mean she is six times more satisfied? There is no evidence that women who are multiorgasmic feel more satisfied than do women who are singly orgasmic. The healthy concept is to develop a pleasure–eroticism pattern that allows the woman to enjoy the sexual experience and be orgasmic when her erotic flow leads naturally to orgasm. The woman, as well as the couple, can enjoy the variability and flexibility of female sexual response (Foley, Kope, & Sugrue, 2012).

What does this mean for desire, pleasure, eroticism, and satisfaction? The key is to accept and enjoy variability and flexibility. Competing with a male performance standard subverts female desire, pleasure, and satisfaction. Each woman and each couple need to develop their sexual style, in which differences and preferences are respected and accepted. The woman—not the man or an arbitrary performance criterion—is the expert on her sexuality.

orgasm during intercourse

Freud made the distinction between "vaginal orgasm," which he labeled as "mature, normal, and occurring during intercourse," and "clitoral orgasm," which occurred during self-stimulation or with manual, or oral stimulation by the female's partner. Freud labeled clitoral orgasm as "immature and less satisfying." Scientific research by Masters and Johnson (1970) and research and clinical work by sex therapists found this to be inaccurate. A rigid performance criterion is scientifically incorrect and psychologically self-defeating.

Physiologically, an orgasm is an orgasm, whether resulting from masturbation, partner manual stimulation, intercourse, cunnilingus, vibrator stimulation, or rubbing stimulation. There are subjective differences in women's preferences and satisfaction. The woman should develop a pleasure–eroticism–orgasm pattern with which she feels comfortable and satisfied. This may or may not include being orgasmic during intercourse.

Nonorgasmic response during intercourse is *not* a sexual dysfunction—it is a normal variation of female sexuality. If she is aroused and orgasmic during partner sex and enjoys intercourse, this is optimal for her. A third of women never or almost never experience orgasm during intercourse. There is nothing "better" or "more mature" about orgasm during intercourse. Women who are orgasmic during intercourse typically utilize multiple stimulation—their own or their partner's manual clitoral stimulation, vibrator stimulation, or indirect clitoral stimulation provided by intercourse positions and movements. This is neither superior nor inferior to women who are orgasmic with manual, oral, vibrator, or rubbing stimulation. It is neither superior nor inferior to women who are orgasmic with only intercourse stimulation. Orgasm is not a competitive performance. Orgasm is a natural result of involvement, pleasure, eroticism, and letting go emotionally and physically (Heiman, 2007).

Let us review the most common female arousal and orgasm dysfunctions.

secondary nonorgasmic response during partner sex

Secondary nonorgasmic response during partner sex has increased in the past decade and is a major cause of secondary ISD. The woman with secondary nonorgasmic response has been orgasmic but no longer or rarely is (fewer than 20 percent of encounters). Part of the problem is performance anxiety and unrealistic expectations caused by the media's emphasis on the "big O." Orgasm has received inordinate focus—more than any other area of female sexuality. It is as if the test of female sexuality is orgasm. It has become a measure of the man to ensure that his partner has an orgasm (ideally during intercourse). This performance focus is self-defeating, resulting in secondary orgasmic dysfunction leading to ISD.

Orgasm is integral to the comfort–pleasure–eroticism cycle, not something separate from it. Orgasm is the natural culmination of involved emotional and sexual stimulation. Women have fallen into the male trap of pressuring themselves to be orgasmic each time and to feel that sex is a failure if they are not.

You do not need the "right" orgasm to prove something to yourself or to your partner. Orgasm is the natural result of the erotic flow process. It entails feeling comfortable with your body, taking responsibility for your sexuality, being receptive and responsive to pleasure, and letting go and allowing erotic flow to culminate in orgasm. Personal responsibility includes making sexual requests and guiding your partner. Your partner cannot make you have an orgasm, nor is he responsible for your orgasm. However, he can be caring, cooperative, and sharing—your intimate sexual friend.

Common causes of secondary nonorgasmic response are performance anxiety, anger, and emotional alienation. As is usually the case, sexual technique issues are easier to deal with than are emotional inhibitions or conflicts. The strategy is to increase sexual comfort, pleasure, and eroticism while decreasing performance pressure. This begins with nondemand pleasuring and can include a temporary prohibition on intercourse. Put intimacy, pleasuring, playfulness, and eroticism back into sexuality. Nondemand pleasuring is the underpinning of sensual and sexual response.

Allow sensual and erotic touching to move at your pace, rather than following the man's lead. Make requests and allow your partner to be open to your guidance. For example, some women prefer to begin genital touching with breast stimulation, others with vulva stimulation. This is not a matter of right or wrong. Identify your receptivity–responsivity patterns and share them with your partner. Most women prefer indirect rather than direct clitoral stimulation. A common female complaint is that the male tires of slow, rhythmic stimulation and switches to stimulation that meets his needs. This breaks your erotic rhythm. The strategy for dealing with this is communicating your requests and utilizing multiple stimulation before and during intercourse.

Arousal involves maintaining rhythmic clitoral stimulation while adding varied erotic scenarios—including manual and oral breast stimulation, stimulation of the mons or anal area, kissing and caressing, intravaginal finger stimulation, vibrator stimulation, or rubbing his penis against your breasts or vulva. Some women enjoy passively accepting stimulation (*self-entrancement arousal*), but most prefer actively giving and receiving (*partner interaction arousal*). Examples of being active include touching and stimulating your partner, focusing on a sexual fantasy, moving your body rhythmically to increase sensations, giving and receiving oral stimulation simultaneously, assuming a standing or kneeling position that allows erotic touch and movement, and engaging in multiple stimulation during intercourse. Increasing involvement, pleasure, and eroticism encourages orgasm.

Letting go and allowing arousal to flow into orgasm involves psychological and relational factors as well as psychosexual skills. The more the problem is caused by emotional and relationship inhibitions, the more the couple has to function as an intimate sexual team. The change process is complex and is undermined by miscommunication, misunderstanding, and frustration. When psychological and relational factors are the predominant cause, you are strongly encouraged to seek couple sex therapy rather than attempt change by yourself.

Anger, more than anxiety, interferes with sexual receptivity and responsivity. The woman who has turned off sexually because of anger or alienation finds it difficult to think of herself as part of an intimate sexual team. Anger is a powerful inhibitor of sexual desire. Negative emotions such as depression, boredom, sadness, frustration, and distraction, block sexual response. Relational factors that inhibit sexual desire include lack of couple time, conflict over money, irritation concerning personal habits, disappointment in your spouse or marriage, repeating negative patterns from your family of origin, and conflict over intimacy. Situational factors—such as lack of privacy, the phone ringing, the kids coming in, no lock on the bedroom door, an uncomfortable bed, no time to be sexual, work stress, drug or alcohol abuse, and side effects of antidepressants and other medications— interfere with sexual response. The psychological, relational, and situational changes that are necessary to enjoy pleasure, eroticism, and orgasm are doable but require persistence, feedback, and commitment. The couple can lose motivation and focus. The longer the secondary nonorgasmic dysfunction exists, the more likely it will result in ISD.

arousal dysfunction

The problem can be lack of subjective arousal, objective arousal, or both. *Subjective arousal* refers to being involved and feeling turned on. *Objective arousal* includes vaginal lubrication, increased muscle tension, blood flow to the vulva, hardening of the nipples, and physical receptivity to intercourse. Some women are orgasmic at low levels of arousal, but typically arousal involves erotic flow culminating in orgasm. Arousal dysfunction can be primary but usually is secondary.

A common theme is higher arousal from erotic stimulation than during intercourse. Another theme is that premarital sex was more erotic than marital sex is. Some women feel more aroused with their clothes on. Others say sex was more fun in the back seat of the car. The focus on goal-oriented intercourse robs sexuality of playfulness, seductiveness, unpredictability, creativity, and eroticism.

A key to understanding arousal problems is recognizing the different sexual socialization of women and men. Males typically learn arousal and orgasm through masturbation. For men, arousal is easy and predictable. The man gets spontaneous erections, and arousal is autonomous; he needs nothing from the woman. Female arousal is variable, slower, and can be lost because of distracting stimuli. Some women learn to masturbate to orgasm in childhood or during adolescence. However, for many women, masturbation begins later or does not occur. Interestingly, rates of female masturbation increase after marriage. A significant number of women are unsure of their receptivity–responsivity pattern. It is hard to share if you are not aware of your body's response to pleasuring and eroticism.

For many women, experiences with manual, oral, and rubbing stimulation are unsatisfactory. The woman reacts to the man's sexual style and needs rather than establishing her own. The rhythm of touching is his, not hers. Few women experience autonomous sexual arousal. Arousal is an intimate, interactive experience involving receptivity and responsivity to your partner's touching.

The most common sexual block is poor pleasuring–eroticism technique. Rather than blaming your spouse or labeling men as uncaring or insensitive lovers, take responsibility for your pleasure–eroticism. This includes awareness of your conditions for good sex—psychologically, relationally, and situationally. One woman's arousal dramatically increased after she asked her husband to put a lock on their bedroom door, brush his teeth before kissing, and be sexual between 7:00 and 7:30 a.m. For some women, a prime condition for good sex is feeling emotionally close before beginning erotic touching. For others, kissing and touching promote intimacy. For still others, talking builds intimacy and arousal, whereas others feel that talking distracts from arousal. Be aware of your conditions for pleasurable, erotic sexuality and communicate these to your partner.

The woman's sexual feelings and needs are as important as the man's. When there is an arousal dysfunction, it is better for the couple to follow her rhythm of touching, pleasuring, and eroticism. Men make two main mistakes. The first is to focus on genital stimulation when the woman's arousal is low. This increases self-consciousness and decreases pleasure. The second mistake is that as arousal builds he increases the speed and hardness of stimulation. He does this not to subvert her arousal but because that is his arousal pattern. Women need to establish and communicate their rhythm of pleasure and arousal, focusing on steady, slow, gradually building erotic stimulation. Some women prefer receiving, while others find give-and-take stimulation most arousing. Many women find stimulating their partner arousing. Be aware of your psychological, relational, erotic, and situational conditions for good sex. Make clear, specific requests of your partner; you are an active member of the intimate sexual team.

medical interventions to enhance sexual desire and arousal

The physicians women turn to for sexual concerns are an internist, gynecologist, or endocrinologist. The most common concern is lack of vaginal lubrication, especially for perimenopausal and menopausal women. Yet there are women in their 20s who feel subjectively aroused but are poor lubricators. Gynecologists assess for underlying pathology, such as low estrogen, vaginal infections, or side effects of medications. The physician can prescribe estrogen-based creams or hormone replacement therapy. The most common intervention is an over-the-counter vaginal lubricant.

There are two new trends in the medical treatment of female sexual dysfunction. The first is to use supplemental testosterone therapy or other medications to enhance desire. This is especially helpful for those menopausal women who report a total lack of sexual thoughts, feelings, and urges. The second is the use of oral medications, creams, or sexual aids to facilitate arousal. As with any medical intervention, it is important to view this as an additional resource to promote desire and pleasure, not a magic cure or stand-alone intervention. Lubricants or medications need to be integrated into the couple's sexual style of intimacy, pleasuring, and eroticism.

painful intercourse

Painful intercourse (technical terms are *dyspareunia* and *vaginismus*) occurs on occasion for the great majority of women. Sexual pain is a chronic problem for 10 percent to 15 percent of women and increases with aging. It is crucial to consult a gynecologist or nurse practitioner with a specialty in sexual pain for a comprehensive assessment of hormonal, vascular, neurological, and structural factors. If a specific physical cause is not found, the woman concludes that it is all in her head and feels put down. Pain is real; it is in your vulva, not in your head. Pain is a complex psychophysiological process. Often, the best way to deal with painful intercourse is to utilize psychological and behavioral changes in addition to physical therapy interventions. Medication is most effective when there is an acute infection or specific deficit. There is a new specialty—physical therapy with a focus on pelvic musculature—that has proven quite effective in dealing with sexual pain.

Two techniques are especially valuable for pain occurring during intromission. The first is for the woman to initiate and guide intromission. This makes sense because she is the expert on her vagina. Guiding intromission will often reduce or even eliminate discomfort. The second technique is to use a lubricant to facilitate intromission and coital thrusting. Many women use K-Y Jelly because it is a sterile substance they are familiar with from gynecological exams. Other women prefer lubricants that feel or smell sensuous. Just be sure they are hypoallergenic to prevent infection. Favorites are Astroglide, abalone lotion, or aloe vera lotion. Lubrication aids are especially helpful for women who feel subjectively aroused but experience limited lubrication. There are a number of causes of decreased lubrication, including aging. Women who are 40 years old lubricate less than 20-year-old women, and women who are 60 lubricate less than 40-year-olds.

A common cause of painful intercourse is discomfort resulting from prolonged coital thrusting. The average time spent in intercourse is 2 to 9 minutes (the average time for the entire lovemaking experience is 15 to 45 minutes). Fewer than 10 percent of intercourse experiences extend longer than 12 minutes. Women who are orgasmic during nonintercourse sex do enjoy intercourse. However, involvement and arousal decrease after 10 minutes of thrusting, and vaginal irritation increases—especially if the man engages in hard, prolonged thrusting. This creates danger of irritation in the female, which can be painful as well as heighten the risk of tearing the vaginal walls, developing an infection, or both. It is important to communicate when discomfort begins so that you minimize pain.

One way to increase involvement and arousal is multiple stimulation during intercourse. Why should kissing, caressing, playful touching, and erotic stimulation stop when the man's penis enters your vagina? Touching during intercourse can include breast stimulation, buttock stimulation, and especially clitoral stimulation. Switch intercourse positions or types of stroking if there is discomfort. Many women find circular thrusting particularly pleasurable, or they enjoy longer, slower thrusting. Men prolong intercourse with the hope that the woman will reach orgasm, not realizing she is becoming less turned on. Communication and working as an intimate sexual team are crucial to sustain desire.

There are a number of gynecological interventions for difficult, complex, or chronic cases of painful intercourse. The most intrusive is surgery. Alternatives include psychosexual skill exercises to strengthen vaginal muscles, hormone replacement therapy, physical therapy interventions, and medications. Be sure you have a good rapport with your gynecologist or nurse practitioner and that she or he takes your pain problem seriously. Referral to a subspecialist in gynecological pain might be advisable. Ask your spouse to accompany you to appointments, especially if you consult a physical therapist. Be clear about the ways in which your partner can be helpful, practically and emotionally, in managing painful intercourse.

primary nonorgasmic response

Primary nonorgasmic dysfunction (also known as a *preorgasmic* condition) means the woman has never experienced orgasm by any means. This occurs in 5 percent to 10 percent of adult women. The more common problem is primary nonorgasmic dysfunction during partner sex, a complaint of 10 percent to 15 percent of women. The female has been orgasmic with self and/or vibrator stimulation but not during partner sex. Approximately half of young women learn to be orgasmic during masturbation, the other half with partner manual, oral, or rubbing stimulation. Fewer than 10 percent of women have their first orgasm during intercourse.

The treatment of choice for preorgasmic women involves increased sexual awareness, body exploration, mindfulness, and masturbation. This can be done individually, augmented by self-help materials and psychosexual skill exercises, or through a 10-session women's sexuality group. The group reduces stigma and provides practical and emotional support and motivation for change as women see other group members progressing. Masturbation as a treatment technique was revolutionary a generation ago (Barbach, 1975), but self-exploration and masturbation are now recognized as the easiest, most natural way of learning to be orgasmic. Men have few problems reaching orgasm, in part because of masturbation experiences. The woman who is aware of her arousal and orgasm pattern can transfer this knowledge to partner sex. Masturbation promotes a healthy, self-affirming attitude toward your body and personal responsibility for sexuality. Use of vibrator stimulation as an adjunct to masturbation has become popular in the past 25 years. The speed and intensity of vibrator stimulation breaks down inhibitions and self-consciousness and serve as an orgasm trigger. Although women fear becoming "hooked" on the vibrator, most find the transition to hand or partner manual, oral, or intercourse stimulation relatively easy. Women can use vibrator stimulation (either alone or during partner sex) as a special turn-on to facilitate erotic flow and orgasm.

Self-stimulation allows the woman to be aware of and use "orgasm triggers." This facilitates moving from high levels of erotic flow (an 8 or 9 subjective arousal on a scale of 0 to 10) to orgasm. Orgasm triggers are variable and individualistic. They include tightening leg or thigh muscles to build tension until it bursts forth in orgasm, verbalizing you are "going to come," doing breast and clitoral stimulation simultaneously as you move toward orgasm, and using vibrator or intravaginal finger stimulation to enhance erotic sensations. Erotic stimulation is focused and rhythmic. Reinforce orgasm triggers and transfer these learnings to partner sex.

Many women find it easier to learn to be orgasmic through masturbation than through partner sex. For some women, the transition to orgasm with a partner is easy; for others, it is more challenging. If nonorgasmic response during partner sex involves a specific sexual inhibition, it is simpler to resolve than if there is an emotional inhibition. The most direct technique is stimulating yourself to orgasm with your partner present. Sexually and emotionally, this is a major breakthrough. He can observe how you become aroused and reach orgasm (which is motivating and exciting). Then, with your guidance, he stimulates you to erotic flow and orgasm. For women who feel self-conscious, asking him to be vulnerable and doing self-stimulation first can be freeing.

Key concepts are for the woman to take the sexual lead, develop her "sexual voice," make requests, and set an erotic rhythm. The man should be open and responsive to her requests. A key component in a healthy relationship is the man's openness to the woman's influence. Discard the belief that it is your partner's responsibility to "make you come." This pressure wilts your sexual desire, pleasure, and eroticism. It also results in frustration and anger, which negates the man's role as an intimate sexual partner. Neither partner can force an orgasm. Orgasm is a natural result of erotic flow and letting go; it cannot be willed, forced, or coerced. Focus on the scenarios, positions, feelings, and techniques that heighten pleasure and eroticism. If you think of arousal on a scale of 0 (*neutral*) to 5 (*moderate*) to 10 (*orgasm*), many women find the real problem is going from 2 to 5. Neither cunnilingus nor intercourse is arousing unless feelings are at least at 5 before beginning erotic activities. Otherwise, erotic stimulation can be counterproductive, resulting in self-consciousness.

Traditionally, couples transition to intercourse at the man's initiative when he feels his partner is ready. Let the woman initiate the transition to cunnilingus or intercourse. Many women find it easier to be orgasmic with manual or oral stimulation. Being orgasmic is more than just prolonging stimulation. Moving from 5 to 8 on the arousal scale involves making verbal and nonverbal requests to enhance erotic feelings. This includes multiple stimulation such as combining manual clitoral stimulation, oral breast stimulation, and stroking your partner's penis; involving yourself in an erotic fantasy as you enjoy cunnilingus; switching positions to kneeling or standing while moving your body in rhythm with his stimulation; and rubbing your clitoris against his penis or thigh while he plays with your breasts or buttocks. Use of orgasm triggers allow eroticism to flow from 9 to 10. Orgasm triggers in partner sex are similar to or the same as orgasm triggers with masturbation.

Some women either prefer or need intercourse for orgasm. Female sexuality involves accepting and honoring individual differences. Starting intercourse at level 6, or preferably level 7 or 8, facilitates arousal during intercourse. You can set the rhythm of thrusting. This is easier in the woman-on-top or side-by-side intercourse positions. Use of additional clitoral stimulation by your hand, your partner's hand, or vibrator allows arousal to build toward orgasm. Asking him to make specific movements, controlling thrusting by putting your hands on his buttocks, or guiding his touching are valuable techniques. Communicate and experiment to develop a pleasure–eroticism pattern that allows you to enjoy orgasm during partner sex.

Vaginismus is a specific dysfunction that refers to the tightening or spasming of the vaginal opening (*introitus*), which makes intercourse impossible or very painful. A gynecological examination is necessary for diagnosis. Vaginismus requires sexual therapy or physical therapy using *in vivo* desensitization (often with vaginal dilators). The active involvement and support of your partner are crucial. The good news is that the likelihood of successful treatment is high; the bad news is that it is a gradual, sometimes frustrating process. Maintaining motivation and working as an intimate sexual team are crucial but can be emotionally taxing. Couples do best when they are open to sensual and erotic nonintercourse scenarios. Physical and emotional intimacy makes it easier to rebuild desire. Couples who have stopped physical contact are faced with the double task of rebuilding connection and confronting painful intercourse.

Often what motivates the ISD couple is a desire to become pregnant. The need for intravaginal ejaculation challenges the pattern of avoidance. Although gynecologists can do insemination with the husband's sperm, most couples prefer trying to become pregnant naturally—that is, through intercourse. Desire for a child is a powerful impetus. The couple works as an intimate team, using the resources of a gynecologist or nurse practitioner, a couple therapist, and a physical therapist with a specialty in female pelvic musculature. The woman increases awareness and control of her vaginal muscles. She gradually guides intromission. Use woman-on-top intercourse with slow, comfortable thrusting. One benefit of treating painful intercourse is that it increases the woman's awareness, responsivity, and valuing of sexuality. This inoculates her against desire problems in the future.

FAITH AND SAM

Faith and Sam had been married 4 years and 6 months. They were convinced that they were the only couple in America who had been married that long and not consummated their marriage. Faith's vaginismus had been diagnosed by a gynecologist before marriage, but he had not made a treatment recommendation. The minister who married them counseled love and patience but said nothing specific about sex. Premaritally, Faith and Sam had been sexually active, utilizing oral and rubbing stimulation. Unfortunately, their enjoyment of erotic, nonintercourse sexuality decreased over time.

Faith developed secondary arousal dysfunction, secondary orgasmic dysfunction, and secondary ISD. Sam remained sexually functional but was hostile and emotionally distant. He had two one night affairs and threatened an ongoing affair. Faith felt that would be devastating and would throw the marriage into crisis. She manually stimulated Sam to orgasm one or two times a week, but it was uninvolved sex in which she "serviced" him. These experiences further reduced Faith's sexual desire. Sam enjoyed orgasm but felt emotionally isolated. It was a self-defeating cycle. This pattern kept them from addressing the ISD and painful intercourse issues.

The motivation that led to therapy was a shared desire to have a child. Sam viewed a baby as a bond that would hold the marriage together—a questionable rationale, but motivating for Sam and Faith. Children were an integral part of Faith's life plan and a strong motivation to resolve the intercourse avoidance problem. The gynecologist recommended bypassing the sexual issue by using artificial insemination. Neither partner was enthusiastic about the technological solution, so the physician made a referral to a female sex therapist with expertise in treating painful intercourse.

Sam and Faith were relieved to learn that other couples have nonconsummated marriages and that painful intercourse is a treatable problem with a good prognosis. The fact that Faith's desire, arousal, and orgasm dysfunctions were secondary was a good prognostic sign. Faith had the ability to enjoy pleasure and eroticism.

Inadvertently, Sam's sexual attitudes and behavior exacerbated Faith's sexual difficulties. Sam was surprised when the therapist asked if he wanted to be Faith's intimate sexual friend or her sexual critic (the role he now played). Desire had been subverted by frustration; they were working at cross-purposes. Each had to take responsibility for his or her behavior. Sam had to begin thinking, acting, and feeling like an intimate sexual spouse. Faith had to reinvolve herself in intimate, interactive sexuality and realize that she deserved desire, pleasure, eroticism, and satisfaction. Faith set the pace for approaching vaginal intromission. Sam was her active supporter and "cheerleader."

With Faith taking initiative, Sam as the sexual ally who enjoyed giving, and performance pressure reduced, Faith again enjoyed being sexual. The transition to rubbing stimulation for eroticism and orgasm was relatively easy. Viewing erotic videos and Sam verbalizing sexual scenarios significantly enhanced Faith's arousal. At a different time, they did the slow, painstaking psychosexual skill exercises to confront painful intercourse. Working with the physical therapist, Faith learned general relaxation techniques, mindfulness, specific pelvic relaxation, pubococcygeal muscle control, use of dilators for vaginal insertion, and movement with fingers and dilators.

With the guidance of the couple sex therapist, Faith used psychosexual skill exercises, especially playing with Sam's penis around her vagina, to desensitize her anxiety. Faith felt in control of the process. Fear and discomfort gradually decreased, and Faith was open to intravaginal sensations. Once intromission occurred, Faith and Sam did not immediately proceed to thrusting but became comfortable with intercourse sensations and minimal movement (the "quiet vagina" exercise). Faith had to experience intercourse as functional before she could perceive it as pleasurable. Luckily, they were a couple that easily became pregnant (in the 4th month of trying). Faith did not begin to enjoy intercourse until 6 months after the baby was born. Sam and Faith developed their couple sexual style, which integrated manual, oral, rubbing, and intercourse stimulation.

Exercise: Identifying Sexual Problems and Deciding How to Proceed

This exercise is for you to do alone and then share with your partner. Do an honest, objective assessment of past and present sexual attitudes, behavior, and feelings. Write this down to make it concrete. Create four categories: desire, pleasure, eroticism, and satisfaction. Consider self-stimulation experiences as well as partner experiences. When has sexual desire (anticipation and deserving) felt the highest? When have you most enjoyed sensuality and pleasuring? When have you felt erotic and orgasmic (by self, partner manual stimulation, cunnilingus, vibrator stimulation, rubbing stimulation, intercourse, afterplay)? When have you felt the most satisfied, emotionally and sexually?

Do not be surprised if your answers reflect different times and different circumstances for each dimension. Some women remember experiences when desire was high, even though they were not orgasmic. Some find they were sexually responsive in a previous relationship, even though, in retrospect, it was an unhealthy one. Be especially aware of times when arousal was high and you were easily orgasmic. If this has never occurred, then the dysfunction is primary. If it has occurred, the dysfunction is secondary. This is a good way to assess whether the arousal or orgasm dysfunction preceded or followed the desire problem. The woman who is regularly orgasmic but experiences ISD is in a different position than the woman whose desire decreased after developing an arousal, pain, or orgasm dysfunction.

How do you feel about desire, pleasure, eroticism, and satisfaction at present? Do you view desire and orgasm as your responsibility, your partner's, or a joint responsibility? Taking responsibility is very different than blaming yourself or blaming your partner! When conveying your insights to your partner, be clear in differentiating the past and present. Share understandings about your sexual function and dysfunction; do not do an assessment of your partner's sexuality. This allows him to be nondefensive and give feedback on how he perceives and feels about your sexuality and your sexual relationship.

Most important, propose how to address the problem. Our usual recommendation is couple sex therapy. Consider other alternatives, including a self-help individual or couple program, individual therapy, a woman's sexuality group, consulting a gynecologist or endocrinologist, or talking to a minister or marriage therapist. Tell your partner about the alternatives you have considered and why you chose the one you did. Some women discuss two or three alternatives. His perceptions and feedback are a vital part of the problem-solving process. A self-defeating reaction is to give up and do nothing. Benign neglect results in sexual problems becoming chronic and severe.

Decide on a strategy to address the sexual problem and make a good-faith effort to promote change. If this does not help after a reasonable amount of time and effort, explore a different alternative. Couples often decide to address the problem themselves, but if it does not change in 3 to 6 months, then seek professional intervention. Remember, sexual problems are changeable. Enhanced sexual desire and function increase personal and marital well-being.

summary

The woman should value sexuality for herself and the marriage. The bad news is that rates of sexual dysfunction are higher for women than for men. The good news is that successful resolution of sexual problems is easier for women. Women do better in, and feel they get more from, couple sex therapy (Brotto & Woo, 2010). There is no direct relationship between sexual function and sexual desire. Usually, both issues have to be addressed, along with the broader issues of intimacy, eroticism, and your couple sexual style.

Key Points

- Developing your sexual voice, which affirms your erotic scenarios, is a worthwhile challenge.
- Accepting your sexual feelings and needs, including your balance of intimacy and eroticism, is healthy for your relationship.
- Don't fall into the trap of orgasm as a pass–fail performance test. Develop and enjoy your preferred pleasuring–eroticism–orgasm pattern.

PART 2

Change

CHAPTER 6

Being an Intimate Sexual Team: Discovering Your Couple Sexual Style

T WO MAJOR CONTRIBUTIONS from the sex therapy field to the study and treatment of couple problems are the use of psychosexual skill exercises and the concept of a couple sexual style distinct from the general relational style. Discovering the couple sexual style has two dimensions (McCarthy & McCarthy, 2009). The first is how to balance each person's sexual autonomy (*sexual voice*) with being an intimate sexual team. The second is how each couple sexual style integrates intimacy and eroticism.

The most common couple sexual styles in order of frequency are the following:

1. Complementary (mine and ours)
2. Traditional (conflict minimizing)
3. Soul mate (best friend)
4. Emotionally expressive (fun and erotic)

Each couple sexual style has its strengths and its vulnerabilities. Sexually, one size does not fit all. The emotional–behavioral challenge for the couple is to discover and choose the sexual style that fits each partner's feelings and needs and facilitates sexual desire. Your chosen sexual style ensures that you can build and maintain a way of thinking, feeling, and initiation so that sex plays an energizing 15 percent to 20 percent role in your relationship. A mutually acceptable sexual style reinforces initiation and touching to confront and change inhibited sexual desire (ISD) and the no-sex marriage.

Determining your couple sexual style is a joint decision that breaks the traditional power struggle over intercourse. Sexual power struggles are poisonous for the couple and sexual desire. The key is to reach an emotional–attitudinal–behavioral commitment to a couple sexual style that facilitates healthy sexuality. You can discover the sexual balance and integration that best fit you. Play to the strengths of your chosen couple sexual style. However, it is also important to understand the potential vulnerabilities of your chosen couple sexual style, with a commitment to be aware of and actively monitor these potential traps.

The traditional belief was that the more intimacy and communication, the better the sex. This "common sense" approach has misled millions of couples. Although sex therapists are in favor of good communication and genuine intimacy, this is only one component of healthy sexuality. A sole focus on intimacy can actually cause ISD (Sims & Meana, 2010). Healthy couple sexuality requires finding a mutually comfortable level of intimacy; valuing nondemand pleasuring; adding erotic scenarios and techniques; and establishing positive, realistic sexual expectations.

The key is to find a mutually comfortable, functional couple sexual style that promotes desire, pleasure, eroticism, and satisfaction. The couple sexual style allows each person's sexual voice to be heard as part of an intimate team that integrates intimacy and eroticism in a manner that promotes sexual desire and satisfaction. We will carefully examine the strengths and vulnerabilities of the four primary couple sexual styles to help you choose which one is the best fit for your relationship.

complementary couple sexual style

This is the most commonly chosen couple sexual style, especially among couples who attend therapy. The strength is that each person has a positive sexual voice within a securely bonded relationship. The complementary sexual style follows the therapeutic model of personal responsibility for desire, pleasure, and eroticism while being part of an intimate sexual team. Both partners value intimacy and eroticism. You are not clones of each other, but you are aware of your partner's feelings and preferences, especially in terms of sexual initiation. A particular strength of this sexual style is "his," "hers," and "our" bridges to sexual desire. This style values both autonomy and being a securely bonded couple.

The prime vulnerability of the complementary couple sexual style is treating your sexual relationship with "benign neglect," allowing sex to operate on automatic pilot. To maintain desire and satisfaction, your sexual relationship needs new inputs and continual energy. Value couple sexuality that is open to change and growth.

traditional couple sexual style

The major strengths of the traditional couple sexual style is that both partners accept the traditional gender roles upon which their sexual relationship is organized. It is the man's role to initiate intercourse with a focus on sexual frequency, while intimacy and affection are the woman's domain. With this clarity, sex is not a source of conflict, nor does it require thought or negotiation. This style emphasizes marriage, children, family, and religion, resulting in a stable marital bond. There are many supports for your marriage, including same-gender friends who make jokes about the foibles of the opposite sex. If the traditional couple becomes non-sexual, this is accepted as normal with aging and is not a threat to the marriage, especially if the partners remain an affectionate couple.

There are two major vulnerabilities of the traditional couple sexual style. The first is that, with aging, the man's ability to achieve predictable, autonomous erections becomes problematic. The second vulnerability is that the woman feels her needs for attachment and affection are negated and overwhelmed by the intercourse focus. In both cases, the couple does not function as a supportive, intimate sexual team.

soul mate couple sexual style

In the past, the soul mate couple sexual style was thought to be the ideal. The key ingredients were high levels of intimacy, communication, and mutuality. These are the closest, most intimate couples. Being emotionally attached is more highly valued than sexual frequency. This couple sexual style can be highly validating. You feel accepted for who you really are and trust that your partner "has your back."

Unfortunately, there are several vulnerabilities with the soul mate sexual style. The major issue is that the couple feels so close that sexual desire is smothered and they "de-eroticize" each other. Another vulnerability is that the overemphasis on mutuality causes low sexual frequency because sexual feelings and desires are not the same. A particular vulnerability is that soul mate couples do not recover from an extramarital affair. They stay stuck in feeling betrayed by their best friend rather than embracing the healing and recovery process. For many couples, the soul mate relational style is a good fit but the soul mate sexual style is not.

emotionally expressive couple sexual style

This is the most fun and erotic sexual style. Each partner has the freedom to set her or his own sexual rules. People envy this playful and sexually liberated couple's fun, vibrant approach to sexuality. Major strengths include freedom from traditional sexual constraints; valuing sexual play and eroticism; freedom to set your own sexual rules and expectations; and the embrace of role-enactment arousal—including playing out erotic fantasies, using erotic videos and sex toys, and engaging in sexual role playing. In addition, the emotionally expressive sexual style is the most flexible and resilient, including the ability to recover from affairs.

The emotionally expressive sexual style has a number of potential vulnerabilities, making it the least stable couple sexual style. In essence, there is too much emotional and sexual drama, which drains intimacy and security. Resilience is a strength. However, after healing from a number of sexual fights or affairs, the couple runs out of energy. Vital, passionate sex gives way to blame and bitterness. A particular vulnerability is that when hurt, angry, or drunk, one member of the couple may say or do something very damaging to the partner and relationship. This is the sexual equivalent of "dropping an atomic bomb." For example, the man says, "You lied about valuing sexuality. If I had known the truth, I never would have committed to being a couple," or the woman says, "You have the smallest penis of any man I've been with."

It is crucial that the emotionally expressive sexual couple have a firm commitment that, no matter what, they do not drop the "sexual bomb." Having clear emotional and sexual boundaries protects the couple against impulsive, destructive fights.

discovering the right couple sexual style for you

There is no "right" sexual style that fits all couples. Each couple creates a unique balance of autonomy and coupleness and develops a special blend of intimacy and eroticism. It is crucial to choose a couple sexual style that is comfortable and functional for both partners. Especially important is that the sexual style enhance strong, resilient sexual desire. If one partner advocates for the traditional sexual style and the other lobbies for the emotionally expressive sexual style, their sexual relationship will be stuck in a continual self-defeating power struggle in which no one wins and their sexual relationship loses.

Once you make an emotional commitment to your couple sexual style, play to the strengths of your chosen style. However, remain aware of potential vulnerabilities so you avoid those traps. Remember, the core concept of your couple sexual style is that desire, pleasure, and eroticism contribute 15 percent to 20 percent to relationship vitality and satisfaction.

Exercise: Choosing Your Couple Sexual Style

Start this exercise by individually writing answers to the following questions. Be honest and specific—don't give "socially desirable" answers or try to second-guess your partner.

1. How important is sex in your life? What do you value most about couple sexuality?
2. In terms of affectionate touch, do you prefer kissing, hugging, or holding hands?
3. Do you enjoy cuddling and sensual touch? Do you prefer mutual touching or taking turns? How important is nondemand pleasuring for you and your relationship?

4. What is the meaning and value of playful touching? Do you enjoy silly nicknames for genitals and sexual activities?

5. How much do you engage in and value erotic scenarios and techniques? Do you prefer focused stimulation or multiple stimulation? Self-entrancement arousal or partner interaction arousal? Do you like to use external stimuli? Do you value erotic sexuality as a path to orgasm or do you prefer that the erotic experience flow to intercourse?

6. What is your preferred intercourse position—man on top, woman on top, side to side, or rear entry? What type of thrusting is most arousing—in and out, circular, deep inside, fast or slow? Do you enjoy multiple stimulation during intercourse?

7. Do you enjoy and value afterplay as part of your couple sexual style? Do you share a sense of bonding and satisfaction?

Next, share your responses with your partner. Where there are differences or conflicts, carefully discuss the question and clarify practical and emotional dimensions of your responses. Remember, you are not clones of each other. You want to maintain your sexual autonomy (sexual voice) and affirm your sexual desire and feelings about intimacy and eroticism. Your preferences and sensitivities are part of who you are as a sexual person and must be integrated into your couple sexual style if you are to be truly satisfied.

To discover an intimate, pleasurable, erotic, satisfying couple sexual style, you need to take personal responsibility for sexuality as well as embrace being an intimate sexual team. As you review your answers, discuss what balance between autonomy and coupleness is right for you. The soul mate couple sexual style is the most intimate, whereas the traditional couple sexual style has the clearest gender roles and is the least emotionally intimate. The emotionally expressive couple sexual style is the most flexible and allows the greatest freedom to be sexually expressive. The complementary couple sexual style is the most commonly chosen because it balances individual sexual autonomy with being a securely bonded sexual couple. When choosing your couple sexual style, with your unique modifications and characteristics, do not be politically correct. What is the best fit for you?

The second prime factor is to determine the best integration of intimacy and eroticism for you as a couple. The emotionally expressive sexual style focuses on eroticism, whereas the soul mate sexual style focuses on intimacy. The traditional sexual style divides roles by gender: Eroticism is the man's domain, and intimacy is the woman's domain. In the complementary sexual style, each partner values both intimacy and eroticism. Again, the personally relevant question is what is the right integration for you as individuals and as a couple. Don't worry about what is "socially desirable." What is important is the integration that allows you to experience strong, resilient sexual desire. Obviously, both intimacy and eroticism are valuable for sexual desire. Focus on what works for you as a couple.

Discovering the right couple sexual style is about mutuality and a positive influence process. To be an intimate sexual team, avoid power struggles or "winning the battle but losing the war." We suggest that each partner have the ability to veto a sexual style that would be a bad fit. Even more important is to discuss the remaining sexual styles that could work for you. Then choose the couple sexual style that you feel best suits you.

playing to the strengths of your chosen couple sexual style

Choosing your couple style is the first step; implementing this style is the more important step. Each style has its signature strengths. Divide strengths into dimensions of initiation, pleasuring, eroticism, and maintaining desire. For example, a strength of the complementary sexual style is emphasizing "his," "hers," and "our" bridges to desire. A strength of the soul mate style is the emphasis on affection, pleasuring, and mutuality. A strength of the emotionally expressive style is creating vital eroticism, including role enactment scenarios. A strength of the traditional sexual style is clarity about male initiation with a focus on intercourse, so conflict and negotiation about sexuality is minimized.

List the strengths of your chosen couple sexual style with a focus on initiation, pleasuring, eroticism, and maintaining sexual desire. Talk about how to implement these aspects so you can enjoy the strengths of your chosen couple sexual style.

being aware of and monitoring potential traps

Each couple sexual style has vulnerabilities (*traps*). Your task is to be aware of these pitfalls. You owe it to yourself, your partner, and your relationship to create and maintain a healthy couple sexual style. Good intentions are not enough. You need to monitor potential traps at least twice a year so sexuality remains comfortable, pleasure oriented, vital, and satisfying.

The most common trap for the complementary sexual style is to treat sexuality as a "done deal" and not put energy, playfulness, or creativity into couple sexuality. Sexuality is not a passive activity. A strategy to keep sexuality energized and vital is to have each partner commit to developing a new sexual scenario every 6 months. This can involve a change in initiation patterns, a new bridge to sexual desire, a new lotion for pleasuring, an unpredictable erotic scenario, a different intercourse position or type of thrusting, or a lighthearted afterplay scenario.

The potential trap for the traditional sexual style is that the roles become too rigid. The man resents that he has to do it all sexually, and the woman resents that her needs for intimacy and touching always have to result in intercourse. A suggested strategy is that once every 6 months the man initiate a nondemand pleasuring date with a prohibition on intercourse and orgasm and that every 6 months the woman initiate a playful or erotic date that could lead to orgasm or transition to intercourse at her initiation. You can value traditional roles and the traditional couple sexual style while "spicing it up."

The potential trap for the soul mate sexual style is that there is so much emphasis on intimacy and mutuality that desire is smothered and sexual frequency is low. Too much closeness, predictability, and warmth robs sexuality of playfulness and vitality. The suggested strategy is that once every 6 months each partner initiates a selfish or playful sexual scenario. The advantage of an asynchronous scenario is that it challenges the "tyranny of mutuality" and allows sexual feelings of one partner free reign. The advantage of a playful scenario is that it confronts the trap that intimacy needs to be serious and meaningful at all times. A sign of healthy sexuality is that it is open to playfulness.

The trap for the emotionally expressive sexual style is very different than those for other sexual styles. Emotionally expressive couples are strong on fun, unpredictability, vitality, and resilience. The trap is too much emotional and sexual drama. These partners wear each other out and break personal and sexual boundaries. Because of this, the emotionally expressive couple sexual style is the most volatile and insecure. The suggested strategy is that each partner make a short list (two or three items) of potential "atomic bomb" sexual issues. No matter how hurt, angry, or drunk, the partners commit to not "dropping the bomb." The best example of a volatile situation is lying nude in bed after a negative sexual experience. An example of the "bomb" is when the man says, "You pulled a bait and switch; if I knew who you really were, I would never have married you." Or the woman says, "If you can't keep it up, why do you bother with sex at all?" Sexual fights bring out the most destructive emotional responses. The worst time to talk sex with your partner is in bed after a negative sexual encounter. Although this is true of all couples, it is especially dangerous for emotionally expressive couples.

The key guideline is to play to the strengths of your chosen couple sexual style and to make a clear commitment to stay away from the traps involved in the couple sexual style you've chosen.

KEN AND LUANN

A very common trap for couples caught in a no-sex relationship is to be stuck in a good–bad power struggle. You become so adamant about not being the sexual loser that you completely forget about the positive role of healthy couple sexuality. The longer you remain in the power struggle, the more chronic and severe the ISD.

Ken and Luann look back on the first 22 months of their sexual relationship with positive, powerful memories. However, after 8 years of a no-sex marriage, the good memories have faded, replaced by a blame–counterblame dynamic that dominates both the marriage and sexuality. Luann and Ken do almost no emotional problem solving and have given up trying to positively influence each other. They are stuck in the stubborn power struggle of not wanting to be labeled the "bad person" or the "sexual loser."

Luann had hoped for a soul mate sexual relationship, whereas Ken had assumed they'd adopt the traditional couple sexual style. Instead, they entered couple sex therapy as a demoralized, alienated couple whose intimacy and sexuality issues were draining their marital bond. The four-session assessment model (McCarthy & Thestrup, 2008a) was very helpful, especially the individual psychological–relational–sexual histories. Seeing each partner alone reduced defensiveness so the person could focus on his or her role in the sexual alienation and avoidance.

Luann felt hurt and confused by their no-sex relationship. Although she attacked Ken, she was unsure whether it was her fault, his fault, or a symptom of a fatally flawed marriage. Luann wanted to become pregnant but was frustrated by the sexual avoidance and did not want to be a divorced single parent. She felt Ken demonized her because she did not accept his intercourse initiations as her "wifely duty." She remembered an experience 3 months before their marriage: She had felt stressed and tired, but because Ken was desirous and aroused she orally stimulated him to orgasm and then spit out the ejaculate. Ken's reaction was extremely negative. He felt that she had doubly rejected him by refusing intercourse and then spitting rather than swallowing. Luann felt she was being a giving partner and that his reaction was childish. She thought that sexually he was a "spoiled brat." After that incident, the only "acceptable" sex was intercourse, which became tense and infrequent. All sexual activity had ceased 4 years previously. Luann felt intimidated and pressured by Ken. Although she masturbated two to three times a month, she experienced ISD regarding couple sex, especially intercourse.

Ken's story had a very different perspective. He blamed the no-sex marriage totally on Luann, and felt she enjoyed humiliating him sexually. Ken masturbated daily, finding this much easier and more predictable than tense intercourse sex. Ken bitterly complained that Luann was a "cold fish" who wouldn't accept his touch and wouldn't touch him.

The couple feedback session is a core component in the psycho-biosocial sex therapy model. It has three foci: (1) a new individual and couple narrative to identify psychological–relational–sexual strengths and vulnerabilities, (2) an emotional–behavioral commitment to a therapy plan and therapeutic goals, and (3) assignment of the first psychosexual skill exercise to be done in the privacy of the couple's home.

Luann and Ken needed to develop a new, genuine way of talking, feeling, and speaking the same emotional and sexual language. The therapist's analogy was that Ken was speaking German in a hostile, blaming manner and Luann was speaking Greek in a confused and alienated manner. They needed to be empathic, respectful partners and speak English about intimacy and sexuality. ISD and sexual avoidance was the common enemy. Confronting and changing this pattern was a couple challenge. Ken and Luann needed to be intimate sexual allies.

The therapist noted they had failed to transition from a romantic love–passionate sex–idealized couple to a mutually acceptable couple sexual style. They agreed to the therapeutic plan of a 6-month "good faith" effort to develop a new couple sexuality based on desire, plea-sure, eroticism, and satisfaction. Therapeutic goals included rebuilding the marital bond of respect, trust, and commitment; rekindling sexual desire by creating a mutually agreed on couple sexual style; and considering a planned, wanted child. The first psychosexual skill exercise to try at home was finding a "trust position" (McCarthy & McCarthy, 2012). This allowed them to break the cycle of avoiding touch.

The couple sex therapy program lasted for 7 months, with the focus on nondemand pleasuring, using touch to rebuild sexual anticipa-tion, and adopting the complementary couple sexual style. This is the sexual style choice of more than 75 percent of couples in sex therapy. Rather than one spouse having to give in, the complementary couple sexual style facilitates sensual, playful, erotic, and intercourse touching. Reducing stigma and rejection was empowering and motivating for Ken, who urged Luann to stop using birth control and enjoy "making a baby." Luann learned to trust that Ken was her intimate and erotic friend rather than a punishing critic. Couple sex therapy was a chal-lenging, complex process, but with an emphasis on touching and working together as a complementary sexual couple, Luann and Ken felt free of sexual poisons and open to embracing their new couple sexual style with strong, resilient sexual desire.

summary

When a couple becomes caught in the cycle of anticipatory anxiety that focuses on tense intercourse sex and frustration, embarrassment, and avoidance, the no-sex marriage becomes the dominating reality. One of the best strategies to confront and change this self-defeating pattern is to step up to the challenge of creating a new couple sexual style that promotes individual and couple sexual desire. The focus is on touch as the prime anti-avoidance technique. Your chosen couple sexual style allows you to balance personal autonomy (your sexual voice) with being a sexual team that integrates intimacy and eroticism.

Key Points

- There is no one right couple sexual style, but it is imperative to create a mutually acceptable sexual style that facilitates desire.
- Play to the strengths of your chosen couple sexual style while being aware of and monitoring its inherent vulnerabilities.
- Your couple sexual style allows you to balance your individual sexual voice with being a sexual team that integrates intimacy and eroticism.

CHAPTER 7

Building Anticipation: Bridges to Sexual Desire

P EOPLE THINK THAT sexual desire is something you are born with—and that it is unchangeable. You either have it or you do not. The belief is that those with low desire are deficient or abnormal, that inhibited sexual desire (ISD) is a character flaw. Our culture teaches that men are supposed to be the sex experts and initiators, thereby multiplying the stigma of ISD for men. No wonder so many men, women, and couples suffer in silence.

In truth, sexual desire is complex, with many causes and many dimensions. Desire involves psychological, biological, relational, cultural, value, and situational factors. Sexual desire can and does vary among individuals and couples—and even sexual encounters. Desire can be facilitated and strengthened—or it can be subverted and poisoned (McCarthy & Farr, 2012).

ISD is best thought of as a couple issue. Building bridges to desire is likewise best thought of as a couple process. Bridges to desire are ways of thinking, anticipating, and experiencing an encounter that makes touching and sexuality inviting. Ideally, each person develops individual as well as couple bridges to desire (McCarthy, 1997).

Not every bridge needs to be mutual. Sexual initiations and scenarios often work better for one partner than for the other; this is normal and healthy. For example, many men enjoy visual stimuli such as erotic clothing or an X-rated video to ignite desire. Many women prefer seductive initiation or a scenario of extended, involved pleasuring to build sexual anticipation.

Sexuality is a one–two combination. First, you are responsible for your own sexuality, including desire. Second, you are part of an intimate sexual team. Couple sexuality is about sharing, facilitating, encouraging, and supporting. It is not only normal but also preferable for each person to have his or her personal bridges to desire. Once the cycle of sexual avoidance is broken, having multiple ways to anticipate and initiate sexual encounters will allow desire to remain vital. You have a variety of ways to emotionally and physically connect. Choice, rather than obligation, enhances desire. When sex degenerates into "Are we going to have intercourse or not?" the relationship is in trouble. When one spouse demands intercourse and the other wants to avoid this pressure, the result is a power struggle and a no-sex marriage. Sexual power struggles are poisonous for the man, the woman, and the couple. It is important to identify personal and couple poisons that subvert desire but even more important to develop healthy attitudes, initiation patterns, and feelings that promote sexual anticipation and desire.

core strategies

Strategies to facilitate sexual desire include the following:

- nurturing anticipation;
- owning your sexuality;
- feeling that you deserve sexual pleasure;
- enjoying erotic, orgasmic sex; and
- valuing intimate, interactive sexuality.

Desire is the core factor in sexuality. The prescription for sexual desire is positive anticipation, an emotionally intimate relationship, nondemand pleasuring, erotic scenarios and techniques, sharing orgasm, feeling emotionally bonded and satisfied, and maintaining a regular rhythm of sexual activity. Sexuality is a core means of expressing intimacy, but feeling intimate and connected is not dependent on intercourse. Touching can occur inside and outside the bedroom. Not all touching has to, or should, lead to intercourse.

nurturing anticipation

Anticipation is the central ingredient in sexual desire. Anticipation cannot be willed, forced, or coerced, but it can be facilitated and nurtured. You undermine anticipation by bowing to internal and external pressure and faking sexual desire when you do not feel it.

There are two main ways you can build sexual anticipation. First, look forward to sexual encounters in the same way that you look forward to a sporting or musical event. Our culture idealizes romantic, spontaneous, swept-away, nonverbal sex. This makes for sexy movies and love songs but is not helpful to married couples, especially those with jobs and children. Romance and spontaneity are fine, but being dependent on these is too limiting. Intentional, planned dates can generate anticipation and desire. Be open to both planned and spontaneous sexual encounters. Set aside time, and anticipate being sexual. Afterward, acknowledge and savor the experience. This establishes a positive feedback cycle—anticipation, satisfying sex, and enjoying a regular rhythm of sexual experiences. Unless you set aside couple time, sex becomes relegated to late at night in bed, which can be functional but is unlikely to be energizing or vital. Being awake and aware facilitates anticipation.

A second way to build anticipation is feeling free to make requests of your partner, particularly for special scenarios and turn-ons. Requests improve sexual quality, increasing pleasure and eroticism. Two minutes of foreplay, 5 minutes of intercourse, and 30 seconds of afterplay does not promote anticipation. Sex that has settled into a mechanical routine is not inviting. Erotic scenarios and personal turn-ons add a special dimension. When you feel comfortable talking about sexuality, can make requests, value playful touch and unpredictability, and are free to try erotic scenarios, desire will be strong and resilient.

Anticipation is inhibited by routine and mediocre sex, lack of intimate communication, performance pressure, the assumption that all touching leads to intercourse, and sex in bed late at night with the lights out. You can enhance anticipation by setting aside couple time; planning sexual dates, making requests; allowing sexuality to be fun and pleasure oriented; feeling free to play out erotic scenarios and turn-ons; and valuing flexible, variable, and unpredictable couple sexuality that includes but is not limited to intercourse.

own your sexuality

You are responsible for yourself as a sexual person. It is not your partner's job to make you desirous or turn you on. This is more easily
accepted by males because men and women experience such different sexual socialization. The media emphasizes how different sex is for
women than for men. In truth, there are many more sexual similarities
than differences between adult women and men. Psychological and
relational factors are more important than physiological or hormonal
factors in sexual desire (Hyde, 2005).

One gender difference involves experience with masturbation.
More than 90 percent of males have masturbated to orgasm by age
16. Female rates are less than half that, and a significant number of
women do not masturbate until after marriage. Masturbation has been
a source of guilt or embarrassment, but that view is based on ignorance.
In truth, masturbation is normal, natural, and healthy. It helps men and
women own their sexuality, be aware of their receptivity–responsivity
pattern, learn their arousal and orgasm preferences, and be in a better
position to make requests and guide their partner.

You deserve sexual self-esteem. Sexuality enhances your life and
relationship when it is comfortable, pleasure oriented, and mutual.
Owning your sexuality and feeling personal responsibility enhance
desire. You feel free to assert your sexual rights (including freedom
from unwanted pregnancy, sexually transmitted infections [STIs],
HIV/AIDS, and sexual coercion). You are free to discuss sexual desires
and wants, make requests, share vulnerabilities, disclose personal
turn-ons, and feel accepted rather than criticized or judged.

It is crucial to accept your sexual past, including negative or
traumatic experiences such as child sexual abuse, incest, rape, being
exhibited to and peeped at, receiving obscene phone calls, dealing with
an STI, having an unwanted pregnancy, being sexually humiliated or
rejected, having a sexual dysfunction, being sexually harassed, being
caught masturbating, or feeling guilt over sexual fantasies. Negative
sexual experiences are almost universal phenomena for both females
and males. Sadly, it is normal to have negative sexual experiences—
whether as a child, adolescent, young adult, or adult. You can accept
these experiences and integrate them into your sexual self-esteem.
You are a survivor, not a victim. Feeling controlled by guilt because

of past trauma cheats you of sexual self-acceptance and enjoyment of couple sexuality (Cohn, 2011).

you deserve sexual pleasure

The essence of sexuality is giving and receiving pleasure-oriented touching. A focus on pleasure rather than on performance facilitates desire. Sexual performance to prove something to yourself or your partner or to meet the demands of your spouse subverts sexual desire. You deserve to feel good about yourself as a sexual person and to enjoy couple sexuality. Your sexual feelings, preferences, and desires count. *Sexual pleasure is an inherent right for women, men, and couples.*

Males are socialized to focus on performance, especially intercourse and orgasm, rather than be pleasure oriented. The most common cause of male ISD is a sexual dysfunction, especially erectile dysfunction and ejaculatory inhibition. The male feels that if he does not function perfectly he does not deserve to enjoy being sexual, and so avoids sex. Another male performance trap is to focus on his partner's sexual performance—believing that she needs to be orgasmic each time and that he is responsible for her orgasm. Performance orientation (whether his or hers) turns sex into a pass–fail test. This sets the stage for failure, frustration, embarrassment, ISD, and avoidance. It is healthier for both the man and the marriage to adopt a pleasure orientation and view your wife as your intimate sexual friend.

Feeling deserving of pleasure is particularly important for women. Our culture has not supported female sexuality, especially women valuing eroticism. Traditionally, female sexuality has been contingent on romanticism, love, and body image. It is easy for the woman to fall into the trap of feeling that she does not deserve sexual pleasure, thus turning herself off. It is as if sex is a reward for being a perfect woman in a perfect relationship. Loss of sexual pleasure is a punishment for any deficiency. You deserve to feel good about your body; to enjoy sensual and sexual touch; to have sexual thoughts and fantasies; to embrace eroticism; and to anticipate sexuality because you are a woman, noncontingent on any other factor. Women who are overweight deserve to feel sexual, nonorgasmic women deserve to feel sexual, and women in conflictual marriages deserve to feel sexual. Feelings of being undeserving subvert self-acceptance and exacerbate ISD.

enjoy erotic, orgasmic sex

Sometimes ISD exists by itself; more often, a desire problem coexists with an arousal or orgasm dysfunction. This is especially true of males with erectile dysfunction (ED). Sexual comfort and confidence are important for both men and women. Sexual confidence requires changing attitudes and emphasizing a broad-based, flexible approach to sexuality—the Good Enough Sex (GES) approach. Sex is so much more than intercourse. If desire is contingent on each experience being an "A" performance, you are vulnerable to ISD. When sexuality is broad based, with a variety of bridges and pleasure-oriented scenarios, desire will be robust and resilient.

We are proponents of eroticism, orgasm, and intercourse, but there is more to sexuality than that. The seductive but false assumption is that if both partners had guaranteed orgasms there would not be a desire problem. Once they become involved, many people reach orgasm; the problem is anticipating and initiating sex. They "want to want to have sex" but do not.

You can increase awareness of your emotional and practical conditions for good sex, enhance intimacy, build sexual comfort, and be responsive to your partner's feelings and requests. This provides a solid basis for couple sexuality, but even this is not enough. Eroticism is key. To build eroticism, partners can increase manual and oral stimulation, experiment with erotic scenarios and techniques, utilize multiple stimulation during intercourse, and vary intercourse positions.

Some people prefer taking turns, while others like mutual stimulation. Some find intercourse most arousing; others prefer manual or oral sex. Some couples find focused stimulation most erotic; others value multiple stimulation. Be aware of and communicate your preferred pleasure–eroticism pattern(s).

Orgasm involves letting go and allowing arousal to naturally flow to climax. Men find it easiest to be orgasmic during intercourse. Female orgasmic response is more variable and individualistic. Some women find it easier to be orgasmic with manual stimulation, some with vibrator stimulation, others with oral stimulation or intercourse stimulation. You can develop a mutually satisfying pleasure–eroticism–orgasm couple style.

value intimate sexuality

Intimacy is a major bridge to sexual desire. Couple sexuality involves integrating intimacy and eroticism. Traditional socialization taught men to value sex and women to value intimacy. Sexual desire is robust when each partner values both emotional intimacy and erotic sexuality. The traditional adage that 90 percent of women prefer affection to intercourse does not promote sexual communication or understanding. Ideally, both men and women value intimacy, affection, pleasuring, eroticism, intercourse, orgasm, and afterplay.

Not valuing pleasuring is primarily a male trap. Males learn about sex as a short; intense; easy; and, unfortunately, autonomous function. Most men under 30 need little from their partner to experience desire, arousal, and orgasm. This does not serve men well after age 40, especially in marriage. If sexual desire is to remain vital, the man needs to be open to and value intimate, interactive sexuality. An involved, aroused partner is the main aphrodisiac for both men and women. Valuing emotional attachment and sexual intimacy is easier for the woman. That is the mode in which she learned to be sexual. It is a more challenging transition for the man. According to male mythology, a real man can have sex with any woman at any time. He has to confront this self-defeating attitude and learn to value intimate, interactive couple sexuality. He is used to being the giving sexual partner, receptive to her stimulation only after he is aroused. He assumes a predictable, automatic erection and worries that he is a "wimp" or "impotent" if he wants or needs her help in the pleasuring–eroticism process. The "give to get" pleasuring guideline has been one-way rather than mutual.

The man needs to become aware that his partner receives pleasure from playing with and arousing him. He must learn to value intimate sexuality, see her receptivity and responsivity as a cue for his arousal, be open and responsive to her manual and oral stimulation, and regard her as his intimate sexual friend. Desire is inhibited by self-consciousness, competitiveness, and a performance orientation. Desire is enhanced by intimacy, freedom, playfulness, unpredictability, creativity, giving and receiving erotic stimulation, and embracing a pleasure orientation.

VICTOR AND LYDIA

Like many couples in a no-sex marriage, Lydia and Victor were trapped in the cycle of embarrassment, guilt, blame, and resentment. Lydia's simple explanation was that Victor's incessant sexual pressure turned off her desire. Victor's explanation basically was that Lydia had sexually rejected him, and it was all her fault. Attack–counterattack and blaming increased emotional alienation. Affectionate touch was abandoned. They traded divorce threats.

Lydia consulted their minister, who wisely noted that this was a serious problem that required referral to a specialist who could treat both relationship issues and ISD. Victor reluctantly agreed. When they presented at the therapist's office, they were a demoralized couple who easily fell into the traps of anger and blaming. The therapist was empathic and respectful and helped them confront these traps. The clinician asked each partner to say what he or she most feared. Under the anger was a great deal of hurt and fear. Anger and blaming protected them from experiencing feelings of sadness and loneliness.

In individual meetings to assess each person's psychological–relational–sexual history, the therapist encouraged self-focus. Sexual initiation was difficult for each spouse, although for different reasons. Victor was shy and unassertive. His nonverbal initiations occurred late at night. Lydia desired romantic, seductive initiations and wanted them to come from Victor. She was put off by his initiation style, but she felt uncomfortable initiating. Unfortunately, the rigidity and passivity she had learned in premarital experiences plagued marital sex. Lydia felt trapped in a no-sex marriage. She felt hopeless about breaking the pattern and was the one most likely to leave the marriage.

In the couple feedback session, the therapist empathized with their feelings and frustrations but confronted them about the need to end the blame–attack cycle. Lydia and Victor agreed to a 6-month good-faith effort to revitalize marital sexuality and build bridges to sexual desire. They ceased threats of divorce and stopped refighting old battles. If they wanted to discuss past issues, they agreed to do so in the therapist's office. At home, Victor and Lydia focused on increasing emotional and sexual intimacy and engaging in psychosexual skill exercises to rebuild sexual desire.

Lydia found the structure of the sexual exercises helpful; they promoted a comfortable way to initiate touching and break the avoidance cycle. Reintroducing nongenital touch and valuing sensual experiences increased motivation and positive feelings. This became Lydia's favorite bridge to sexual desire. Nondemand touching tapped her need for closeness and intimacy. Victor enjoyed showering with Lydia and found touching in the shower erotic. This became his favorite bridge to sexual desire. Both realized how much they missed touching. Realizing that sex was not a "good guy–bad guy" conflict opened the door to renewed intimacy. Victor's verbalizing that he loved and valued her meant a great deal to Lydia. Her initiating spontaneous affection in public helped them feel like a loving couple. Affectionate touch was an affirmation that theirs was a viable marriage and that sexuality could be revitalized.

The value of couple therapy, as opposed to trying to resolve problems on your own, is that when the inevitable stresses and disappointments occur, the therapist helps to assess them in a problem-solving manner so that the partners do not fall into old traps. The therapist helped Victor and Lydia remain motivated and not feel overwhelmed by difficulties and setbacks. In movies and sitcoms, change is intense and dramatic; love conquers all. Lydia and Victor found that reestablishing desire and healthy sexuality was gradual and often difficult. The therapist's support, insight, processing exercises, suggestions, and exploration of couple dynamics were vital in the change process.

Seeing desire as a couple issue and working as an intimate sexual team were key for Lydia. She became comfortable with sexual initiation and found that touching was a bonding, energizing experience. It was through Victor's initiation of sex play in the shower that Lydia accepted that her orgasm pattern involved manual and rubbing stimulation, not intercourse. Lydia's favored term was "erotic play." Interestingly, Victor found it more arousing to give cunnilingus than Lydia found in receiving oral sex. Lydia enjoyed cunnilingus and intercourse, but her arousal was highest and orgasm most likely with Victor engaging in rhythmic two-finger stimulation around her clitoral shaft or with Lydia rubbing her vulva against his thigh. Victor took great pleasure in Lydia's arousal. He accepted and enjoyed her style of orgasmic response. Lydia felt sexually validated by Victor, which increased her desire. Another bridge to desire for Lydia was dancing. She loved to dance and much preferred home to crowded, smoky bars. Combining dancing with seductively touching and undressing Victor was an inviting bridge to desire.

Victor's initiation repertoire and bridges to desire expanded. He liked planned sexual scenarios, which Lydia accepted as long as he did not spell them out in detail. She found this clinical and off-putting, telling Victor, "Doing it is more fun than listening to you plan it." An inviting bridge for Victor was being sexual early in the morning after he showered. Another bridge was touching Lydia while viewing an R-rated movie and being sexual afterward.

After they had reestablished a regular rhythm of affectionate, sensual, playful, erotic, and intercourse touch, Lydia felt closer to Victor. Victor's feeling good about their sexual relationship brought out the closeness and couple attachment Lydia valued. These were very different feelings from the sexual pressure and power struggles of the past. Victor was pleasantly surprised by the flexible, varied sexual style they adopted, which was not the "meat and potatoes" intercourse sex he was used to. Victor read that broad-based sexuality would inoculate him against sexual problems as he aged. This was reassuring. However, it was a dividend, because he very much enjoyed the sexuality they were currently experiencing.

A special scenario was that once a month Lydia and Victor set aside time for a sexual date, with an agreement that it not culminate in intercourse. Sometimes it was a sensual evening with dancing and playing. Most of the time it involved high levels of eroticism, resulting in orgasm for both. Lydia found it especially satisfying to bring Victor to orgasm orally because he felt so uninhibited. Lydia enjoyed intercourse, but when it came to high-intensity sex nothing beat erotic sexuality.

Lydia and Victor now realize that not every bridge to sexual desire would work every time. They feel secure enough to accept occasional mediocre sexual experiences or lack of desire by one or both. Lydia and Victor are aware that they cannot be complacent about sexuality. Sexual desire must be nurtured and bridges to desire expanded and reinforced.

anticipation as the key to desire

For many couples, sex is tied to romantic love and passion. The best sex is new and sweeps the partners away. By its nature, romantic love/passionate sex is a fragile, time-limited phenomenon that seldom survives more than 2 years. For romantic-love couples, sex ends with time and marriage. What a self-defeating approach!

Sexual desire can remain a vital part of marriage. You can enhance desire by developing one or two favorite bridges, varying bridges depending on your mood, creating special bridges for special occasions, and devising exotic bridges with which to experiment. The function of bridges to desire is to build anticipation. Some bridges are planned, others spontaneous; some are mutual, others preferred by one partner; some are complex, others simple; some require accoutrements, others just the two of you. What fits your couple sexual style?

Be sure the bridge facilitates sexual anticipation. Some couples enjoy a romantic country inn. Others prefer their own bed and lighting a fragrant candle as a cue. For some couples, a regular Friday night or Sunday morning sexual date facilitates anticipation. For others, having varied days and times enhances excitement. Some couples enjoy being sexual once or twice a week. Others find desire high one week (they will be sexual four times) and then will not be sexual again for 10 days. What facilitates your anticipation and desire?

Exercise: Building Bridges to Sexual Desire

There are many sources of sexual desire, including (but not limited to) sharing pleasure, feeling "horny," reinforcing intimacy, using sex as a way to connect, being turned on by a fantasy or movie, using sex as a way to relax before sleep, taking advantage of time away from children, sharing loving feelings, having a special date for a birthday or anniversary, indulging in the novelty of staying at a hotel, making up after an argument, and feeling erotic after sensuous caressing. Be open to a variety of individual and couple bridges to sexual desire.

A persistent myth is that your partner should be the source of all sexual desire. According to this myth, if you have fantasies of another person or a movie star, you are being disloyal. In truth, fantasies and other external stimuli (movies, TV, novels, people on the street, sexy pictures, Internet stimuli, erotic videos, songs) can be major sources of sexual desire. Few people fantasize about intercourse in bed in the missionary position with their spouse. Erotic imagery involves nonsocially desirable acts, people, and situations. If individuals were prosecuted for their sexual thoughts and fantasies, almost everyone would be in jail. Sexual fantasies are a natural, healthy bridge to desire. They spice up and invite desire as well as increase responsivity during partner sex.

For this exercise, each person lists at least three and up to 10 bridges to sexual desire. Share two or more of these with your partner, but keep at least one to yourself. Sexual desire is subverted by sharing all and describing everything in detail. Share erotic turn-ons and scenarios, but remember to keep seductiveness, unpredictability, and playfulness alive in your relationship. Instead of "meat and potatoes" ways of having sex, think of erotic scenarios and techniques you would like to experiment with.

One of the most interesting things about being a sex therapist is discovering the range of experiences that individuals and couples find erotic. There are the traditional romantic scenarios of dressing up and having a gourmet dinner that includes wine and candles, ending with tender, loving, and prolonged sex on silk sheets. There are the traditional erotic scenarios of going to a motel, watching X-rated videos, dressing in sexy lingerie, and having intercourse under a mirrored ceiling. For some people, the key is location: being sexual in front of a blazing fire, in the shower, on an antique bed at a historic inn, or on a deserted beach. For others, the key is external stimuli: erotic dancing, sex videos, covering each other's genitals with lotion, feeding your partner gourmet snacks in bed, or reading erotic stories aloud. Some couples emphasize sexual technique: simultaneous fellatio and cunnilingus (69), vibrator stimulation during intercourse, one-way sex to arouse the partner to total abandon, multiple stimulation during intercourse, switching intercourse positions three times, or using light bondage as an erotic stimulus.

Anticipation of a sexual encounter is a powerful bridge to desire. Rather than waiting for desire to occur "naturally" or expecting all desire to come from your partner, use fantasies or a planned erotic scenario to facilitate desire. For example, if you have a sexual daydream or see an attractive person in a store, allow that image to "simmer" through the day so that at night it serves as a bridge to sexual initiation. If a favorite erotic scenario is surprising your sleeping partner by taking off your top and rubbing your breasts on his face, think of this after you put your children to sleep. Erotic cues and scenarios facilitate anticipation and desire.

maintaining sexual desire

Maintaining sexual desire is not the same as building sexual desire. You can reinforce anticipation by establishing a rhythm of pleasure-oriented sensual and erotic experiences. The excitement of discovering new bridges is replaced by the challenge of maintaining vital marital sexuality. The difference is analogous to starting a new business and maintaining an ongoing business; the circumstances require different attitudes and skills.

Routine, mechanical sex subverts desire. After you have devoted the time and energy to exploring and developing bridges, do not negate these gains by treating sex with benign neglect. Both the man and woman should affirm the value of intimate, erotic sexuality. The most powerful bridge is anticipating an experience in which both partners are involved, giving, and responsive. Couples who anticipate giving and receiving pleasurable and erotic touch maintain a vital, satisfying sexual relationship.

The more varied the bridges, the easier it is to maintain desire. A variety of turn-ons, initiation patterns, times, and places facilitate robust sexual desire. The more each partner feels that he or she deserves sexual pleasure and anticipates a satisfying experience, the stronger the desire. A key element in maintaining desire is a regular rhythm of sexual contact—whether three times a week or every 10 days. Sexuality is like anything else; if it is neglected or unused, you lose enthusiasm. When you attempt sexual activity, you feel awkward and self-conscious, which interferes with pleasure and erotic flow. A prime way to maintain desire is through touching, both inside and outside the bedroom. Not all touching can or should lead to intercourse. Touching is a way to stay connected and serves as a bridge to desire, pleasure, and eroticism.

Desire and satisfaction are more important than arousal and orgasm (McCarthy & Wald, 2012). Quality of the sexual experience is more important than quantity. These two guidelines help you maintain a vital, satisfying sexual bond.

reinforcing old bridges, building new ones

Sexual desire needs continual nurturing; it cannot be taken for granted. Emily's father was a factory foreman who emphasized the importance of preventive maintenance rather than letting machinery rust or holding off on making repairs until it broke. This is the strategy we advocate for couple sexuality.

Keep your desire bridges in good repair and spice them up so that they remain vital. What worked in previous months or years becomes less inviting if you do not vary sexual scenarios. For example, one couple found that being sexual before or after a nap on the weekend served as a bridge for desire. With time, this became a mechanical routine rather than an exciting cue. To revitalize this bridge, the man purchased body lotion and awakened his partner with a sensual massage. Or she awakened him by covering his stomach and inner thighs with "fish kisses." They were creative, enjoying wine and munchies in bed as an appetizer, with sex as the main course. Putting energy, creativity, and playfulness into a tried-and-true bridge can revitalize sexual vitality.

Building new bridges is particularly important. A favorite analogy is between sex and ice cream. Some people have two or three favorites, at times will try another, and for special occasions will experiment with an exotic flavor. Other people want to try all 33 flavors, look forward to the flavor of the month, and invent their own flavors. For those with the latter preference, building new bridges and erotic scenarios is critical. Their partner accepts this rather than being defensive or resistant. Be open and receptive to each other's sexual preferences and feelings.

You have a right to veto anything that is uncomfortable or opposed to your values. Intimate coercion has no place in your relationship. Coercion does more than inhibit sexual desire; it kills it. Sexual scenarios should not take place at the expense of your spouse or the marriage. Within this guideline, both people are free to play, experiment, and enjoy erotic scenarios and techniques. Some bridges are better for one partner than for the other, which is fine. Sexual desire is about sharing and playing. Sex is not a competition, nor is it a zero-sum game. Develop at least one new bridge each year that is inviting for both partners.

summary

Building bridges to sexual desire is a powerful strategy to break the cycle of the no-sex marriage. Sexual desire is not a biological given. It is influenced by psychological, relational, and situational factors that can be nurtured and enhanced. Developing both individual and couple bridges facilitates anticipation and enhances strong, resilient desire.

Key Points

- Developing "hers," "his," and "our" bridges to sexual desire is a powerful strategy to create healthy, resilient couple sexuality.
- Both intentional and spontaneous pleasuring and intercourse experiences enhance sexual desire.
- Positive anticipation, a sense of deserving, freedom, choice, and pleasure orientation promote strong, resilient sexual desire.

CHAPTER 8

Attachment: Enhancing Intimacy

Desire for an intimate, secure relationship is a major force driving the decision to marry. An intimate marriage facilitates sexual desire. Intimacy is broad based; it is not limited to sexual intercourse or even sexuality. Intimacy involves both emotional and sexual dimensions. A prime function of sexuality is to reinforce and deepen intimacy. Intimacy is higher during pleasuring and afterplay, less so during intercourse itself. Traditionally, intimacy has been strongly valued by women and undervalued by men. In reality, intimacy is of as much value for men as for women. The role of emotional intimacy is to nurture your marital bond, while the role of sexual intimacy is to energize your bond.

The essence of intimacy is feeling emotionally open, securely attached, and valued. At its core, marriage is a respectful, trusting commitment. Intimacy enhances these feelings. People have emotionally close relationships with friends, siblings, parents, and mentors. The integration of emotional and sexual intimacy makes the marriage relationship special (Johnson, 2004).

No-sex marriages have a major negative impact on intimacy. Unfortunately, sexual dysfunction and conflicts have stronger negative effects on the marital bond than do the positive dimensions of healthy sexuality. Lack of intimacy drains loving feelings and threatens marital viability. Intimacy and sexuality play a significant, but not dominant, role in a good marriage, contributing 15 percent to 20 percent to marital vitality and satisfaction. Inhibited sexual desire (ISD) and other sexual problems have a major negative role. Sexual problems subvert the relationship, often resulting in separation and divorce, especially in the first 5 years of marriage.

The three most common sexual problems are sexual dysfunction, fertility problems, and an extramarital affair. Of these, an affair has the most impact on intimacy because it is a direct challenge to the trust bond. People do not choose to have a sexual dysfunction or a fertility problem, whereas an affair is at least partly a choice behavior. Affairs are a violation of the trust bond, subverting emotional and sexual intimacy.

Which is more important—emotional or sexual intimacy? This makes a great talk show debate or argument at a bar but is not helpful for the couple. Emotional intimacy and sexual intimacy are different but complementary. In a healthy relationship, both types of intimacy are well integrated.

Traditionally, men and women learn very different lessons about intimacy. Women are socialized to value feelings, emotional attachment, and an intimate relationship but to devalue sexuality, especially eroticism. Males are socialized to identify masculinity with sexuality and to emphasize sexual prowess, especially intercourse frequency. Men are not socialized to value emotional closeness, intimacy, or a committed sexual relationship. It is no wonder that with such different socialization and peer influences, men and women have a difficult time understanding and communicating the meaning of intimacy, touching, and sexuality.

There are more similarities than differences in intimacy needs between women and men, especially for married couples (Gottman & Silver, 1999). The idea of an innate "war between the sexes" or that men and women are from different planets is nonsense. Both women and men are capable of desire, pleasure, eroticism, and satisfaction. Both are capable of empathy, closeness, sadness, and anger. Gender struggles are not primarily based on biological differences, nor are they predestined. Misunderstandings and conflicts are primarily a function of socialization and media hype rather than genetic or hormonal differences.

Our premise, which has strong empirical support, is that an intimate, satisfying marriage recognizes shared feelings, capabilities, and values of both the woman and man (Metz & McCarthy, 2010). This promotes a respectful, trusting friendship, which is the foundation for a satisfying, stable marriage. Emotional and sexual intimacy generates special feelings and energizes the marital bond.

Healthy sexuality plays an integral role in couple satisfaction. The main functions of sexuality are as a shared pleasure, a means to deepen and reinforce intimacy, and a tension reducer to alleviate the stresses inherent in life and marriage. Intimacy and sexuality energize and strengthen your couple bond. When sexuality is problematic or nonexistent, it serves as a major drain, robbing the marriage of intimacy and vitality and threatening the viability of the relationship.

emotional intimacy

Emotional intimacy has a more subtle role in marital satisfaction than sexual intimacy, but it is just as important. Mature intimacy is quite different from the romantic love that initially brought the couple together. Romantic love is an intense emotional experience; your partner has chosen you. Romantic love usually dissipates by the time the couple is married or within the first year. When romantic love is replaced by mature intimacy, the marriage has a solid foundation. It is integral to emotional intimacy to feel cared for and care for your partner, share positive and negative feelings, acknowledge personal strengths and vulnerabilities, experience empathic communication, feel personally validated, enjoy a sense of "we-ness," establish closeness, and value your secure bond.

An emotionally intimate relationship brings out the best in each partner. Emotional intimacy blends autonomy and coupleness. Both emotional caring and a positive influence process are reinforced. There is a beneficial reciprocal relationship between emotional intimacy and sexual satisfaction. However, sexual problems subvert emotional intimacy. Decreased emotional intimacy makes sexual problems worse and sets the stage for a no-sex marriage. Emotional intimacy has value in itself. It is a major factor in both psychological well-being and marital satisfaction. Maintaining emotional intimacy is a positive prognostic sign for resolving sexual desire and dysfunction problems.

Unfortunately, *intimacy* is an overused term whose definition centers on "feeling good." Intimacy is more than positive feelings. Genuine intimacy includes the entire range of personal and couple feelings and experiences. In addition to positives and strengths, intimacy involves sharing a range of vulnerabilities, fears, and negative experiences—from anger, disappointment, boredom, and numbness to joy, excitement, closeness, and love. The core of marriage is respect, trust, and commitment. Without this, intimacy is vulnerable and unstable.

Throughout this book, we emphasize the necessity for partners to be an intimate sexual team. Intimacy does not mean giving up your personhood. You retain autonomy and individuality. The challenge is to achieve a healthy balance of individuality and coupleness. Either extreme can cause problems. People who are isolated or overly protective of personal boundaries are unable to feel close and share their lives. At the other extreme are enmeshed or fused couples. These couples are so reactive that they cannot make requests, incorporate negative feedback, or express sexual needs. They think of themselves as extremely intimate, but clinicians view this brand of closeness as a self-defeating pseudo-intimacy. Healthy intimacy allows for both individuality and coupleness (Lobitz & Lobitz, 1996).

Emotional intimacy includes freedom to express feelings without needing the approval of your spouse. It helps to have the partner's emotional validation, but the validation has to be genuine, not given to placate or accommodate. Healthy marriages accept differences in feelings, attitudes, and behavior without negating intimacy. Being an intimate couple does not mean being clones of each other. Intimate partners listen to and discuss feelings in a respectful, caring manner. Your partner does not have to agree with you. Each person has a right to his or her feelings and thoughts. A strength of intimate relationships is that your partner knows you psychologically and emotionally. You feel loved and accepted for who you are, for your strengths and vulnerabilities, competencies and idiosyncrasies (Doherty, 2013).

sexual intimacy

Ideally, emotional and sexual intimacy are integrated. Some couples have difficulty with emotional intimacy but do well with sexual intimacy. More typical is that couples enjoy emotional intimacy but are inhibited sexually. The most common pattern is that the couple has difficulty with both emotional and sexual intimacy. The traditional marriage therapy maxim was that if the couple resolved emotional and relationship problems, sex would take care of itself. Although this is true for some couples and some sexual problems, it is not the norm. Sexual intimacy, especially sexual desire, is a unique dimension that needs to be specifically addressed to flourish.

Sexuality is more than genitals, intercourse, and orgasm. Sexual intimacy is more than functional sex. The essence of sexual intimacy is openness and comfort, the ability to share your body—especially through sensual, playful, and erotic touch. People can be sexually responsive and functional with no intimacy. Consider the one-night stand or angry sex. Sex is at its most human when the relationship integrates eroticism and intimacy. Sharing yourself, your body, and your feelings is the essence of sexual intimacy. Partners share sexual thoughts and feelings, enjoy sensuality and nondemand pleasuring, give and receive erotic stimulation, come together during intercourse, allow arousal to flow to orgasm, and enjoy afterplay as a bonding experience.

The main functions of couple sexuality are sharing pleasure, deepening and strengthening intimacy, and reducing tension to deal with life and relationship stresses. Marital sex can mix and match these functions, depending on the couple's feelings, needs, situation, and time constraints. Sometimes sex is very intimate—tender, warm, extended, and loving. At other times, sex is short, intense, and lustful. Intimate sex can be loving, erotic, or both. Intimate sexuality involves awareness of feelings and needs in the moment. Intimacy includes freedom to take sexual risks and communicate desires. The prescription for vital sexual desire and satisfying couple sexuality is to integrate emotional intimacy, nondemand pleasuring, and erotic scenarios.

Nondemand pleasuring is key. Affectionate experiences (holding hands, kissing, hugging) and sensual (massaging each other, cuddling on the couch semiclothed, snuggling at night or in the morning) have value in themselves. Couples enjoy touching both inside and outside the bedroom. Touching can serve as a bridge to sexual desire, but not all touching can or should lead to intercourse. Touching also is a way to demonstrate attachment. Sometimes you want an orgasm; sometimes you want a hug. Men have a hard time asking for a hug, so they initiate sex. Women have a hard time saying they feel lustful, so they initiate a hug. Optimally, the woman and man are comfortable initiating nondemand pleasuring, erotic play, and intercourse.

Touching is a request, not a demand. Intimate coercion has no place in marriage or any relationship. Coercion poisons sexual desire. Intimate coercion includes the threat of an affair, withholding love or money, being angry or belittling, or using sex as a bribe. Genuine intimacy respects the autonomy and personal boundaries of each partner. Requests do not carry the implicit threat of a negative consequence if there is no sex. The partner has the right to accept, say no, or offer an alternative way to emotionally and physically connect. A demand says, "Do this my way now or there will be negative consequences." A request says, "This is how I feel and what I want; I am open to your feelings and needs. I want this to be enjoyable, or at least acceptable, for both of us." With demands, you win the sexual battle but lose the intimacy bond. With requests, both partners and couple intimacy are winners.

Exercise: Emotional Intimacy

In discussions of intimacy, the traditional focus is on the spontaneous expression of feelings. We are in favor of spontaneity and naturalness, but it is naive and self-defeating to believe that this alone will sustain a marriage, especially a marriage plagued by sexual issues. This exercise asks you to have a planned, intentional "intimacy date."

Traditionally, males have undervalued intimacy, so let the man be the initiator. Be sure you are both alert and awake, have time (at least a half an hour, although an hour is preferred), and will not be interrupted (the children are asleep or out of the house, the answering machine is on, and you do not answer the door). The man can enhance the milieu by pouring two glasses of wine and playing music in the background as you sit on the porch or in the family room. Initiation is personal and inviting, not "We have to do this exercise."

Discuss an experience when you felt especially emotionally intimate. Examples include walking on the beach and sharing affectionate touch, disclosing hopes and dreams, recalling your most intimate lovemaking, showing your spouse the neighborhood in which you grew up, discussing your best and worst childhood experiences, deciding you want to start a family, going on a picnic or hike and talking about your life plans, feeling romantic and loving after attending a friend's wedding, reacting to a loss and crying together, sharing excitement after a promotion, staying up all night to wallpaper your first apartment, walking in the rain, realizing after your first child was born that you are a family. Focus on feelings, not on the event. How open were you? How close did you feel? How trusting were you?

What is the current state of emotional intimacy in your marriage? Be honest and specific. What do you say or do that facilitates intimacy? How frequently does it occur? How genuine are your feelings? How do you feel after an intimate time together?

The next topic is sensitive and difficult. What attitudes, behaviors, and feelings inhibit intimacy? Focus on your personal feelings and behavior, not on what your partner does or does not do. It is a cop-out to blame your spouse. Take responsibility for your behavior. Specifically, what do you do or not do that blocks emotional intimacy? Is it intentional or unintentional? What are the advantages of maintaining barriers to intimacy? Are you willing to give up these barriers?

Make three specific requests of your partner that will enhance feelings of intimacy. Remember, these are requests, not demands. What do you want your partner to say or do that would increase your feelings of intimacy? Examples include talking by phone during the day (at least every other day); nondemand touching before going to sleep or on waking; taking a walk and talking about feelings at least once a week; disclosing a painful experience or feeling as your partner empathically listens; saying "I love you" in a genuine manner; going out for dinner or coffee once a week and discussing couple plans; putting on music and dancing after the children are asleep; making birthdays and your anniversary special celebrations; making a romantic gesture like bringing flowers or a personal gift; desisting name calling and not engaging in dirty fighting in the midst of a conflict; greeting your partner with a hug. Each spouse makes three specific, personal requests.

Intimacy does not mean you get everything you ask for or want. Each partner is his or her own person with separate feelings, perceptions, and needs. Your partner does not have to give you everything the way you want it. Losing personal autonomy or giving up a sense of self to please your spouse does not promote genuine intimacy. In fact, it subverts intimacy. Both partners commit to listening in a respectful, caring manner. Both are committed to increasing intimacy, expressing feelings, and being a respectful, trusting couple.

the interplay between emotional and sexual intimacy

Emotional and sexual intimacy are different but complementary. Emotional intimacy usually involves affectionate touch, sometimes sensual touch, but usually not erotic touch. Sexual intimacy focuses on erotic touch and usually, but not necessarily, includes intercourse. Women often say they need to feel emotionally connected before having sex. Men often say that sex facilitates emotional connection. Ideally, the woman and man value both emotional and sexual intimacy. These are not dichotomous dimensions; nor are they gender specific. Emotional intimacy can be as valuable for the man as for the woman. He has a right to emotional closeness, a hug, a supportive partner, just as she does. She has as much right to eroticism and orgasm as he does. Desire, pleasure, and orgasm promote her well-being as well as couple satisfaction.

Intimacy dates can be primarily touching or a blend of talking and touching. Although intimacy dates can evolve into intercourse, that is not their purpose. The primary function of intimacy dates is to enhance feelings of openness and attachment. Touching—whether affectionate, sensual, or playful—facilitates intimacy. Think of your spouse as an intimate friend who allows you to express a range of feelings and with whom you share good and bad times. Intimacy dates keep couples connected and set the stage for sexual desire.

Exercise: Sexual Intimacy

This exercise focuses on enhancing sexual communication and pleasure. Because the man traditionally initiates sexual activity, let the woman take the lead. Ideally, both the woman and man are comfortable initiating. Both feel free to say no to a sexual request and suggest an alternative means to physically connect. To establish a comfortable milieu, begin by taking a shower or bath together. Cleanliness (especially washing genitals) facilitates sexuality. Showering or bathing can be a sensual experience. If showering, experiment with types of spray or temperatures; if bathing, try a new bath oil or soap to increase awareness of sensual stimuli.

Start by soaping your partner's back. Trace muscles and contours; rub and gently massage, then ask him to face you. Soap his chest, stomach, genitals, hips, and legs. Let him soap and wash you. Many couples find sexual play in the shower particularly inviting. As you rinse off, play with his body, including his genitals.

Proceed to the bedroom, feeling natural being nude. Pleasuring and erotic scenarios are best done in the nude. Begin touching, using the giver–receiver format. Midway through, switch to mutual stimulation. Most couples enjoy both partner interaction arousal and self-entrancement arousal; be aware of your feelings and preferences. Explore and see what feels good.

What is the best way to transition from pleasuring to eroticism? The traditional sexual script was to move from "foreplay" to intercourse, with the man directing foreplay to get the woman ready for intercourse. Be intimate partners; engage in nondemand pleasuring; evolve into erotic stimulation, which can include intercourse but is not limited to intercourse.

In pleasuring, the woman enjoys touching for herself, without second-guessing his desires. The man is passive, with his eyes closed as he takes in pleasurable sensations. She mixes genital with nongenital pleasuring. Couples are used to short, intense male arousal. Experiment with moderate and fluctuating levels of pleasure for both of you. Be aware that subjective arousal waxes and wanes, as does his erection. This is a new experience for couples who always go to intercourse on the first erection.

Then switch roles. He can enjoy being the giver in a pleasure-oriented manner rather than regarding it as goal-oriented foreplay. Enjoy exploratory touching rather than focusing on "turning her on." Experiment with playful, teasing pleasuring, mixing nongenital and genital touching. Let her decide when to transition to mutual give-and-take erotic touching.

Experiment with multiple stimulation in the context of erotic, nonintercourse sexuality. Later you can experiment with multiple stimulation during intercourse. Examples include kneeling while facing your partner, who is also kneeling, and kissing while giving mutual manual stimulation, with the man doing oral breast stimulation; the woman standing, the man kneeling and giving manual vulva stimulation, combined with oral breast stimulation; engaging in mutual manual stimulation while the woman verbalizes a fantasy of him being her sexual slave; the woman lying on her side, the man kneeling, rubbing his penis against her breast as he manually stimulates her vulva; the woman lying on her back, the man between her legs, giving oral stimulation and simultaneously manual anal stimulation, while she caresses her breasts and verbalizes erotic feelings. If she desires, continue erotic stimulation to orgasm.

Let the woman initiate the transition from pleasuring to intercourse and guide intromission. Integrate multiple stimulation during intercourse. Traditionally, men focus solely on thrusting. Most women (and men) find that multiple stimulation during intercourse increases involvement and erotic flow. Here are some examples: From the man-on-top position, the woman caresses his testicles as he stretches and licks her breast; from the rear-entry position, the man caresses her vulva as she verbalizes erotic feelings and he fantasizes; in the woman-on-top position, he watches her arousal as he plays with her breasts and she uses circular thrusting; from the side-by-side position, she strokes his chest as he rubs her buttocks and they kiss each other's bodies.

Afterplay is an integral part of sexuality. Many couples feel emotionally closer after being sexual than at any other time. Strengthening intimacy is a prime function of sexuality. You feel emotionally bonded after a sexual experience. Afterplay is the most ignored element in sex. Do you like to lie and hold each other, sleep in your partner's arms, engage in playful tickling or share a warm kiss, take a walk, read poetry, nap and start again, or talk and come down together? Find one or two afterplay scenarios that are comfortable, satisfying, and bonding.

KATHARINE AND ERIC

When they first heard about the concept of an intimacy date, Katharine was thrilled, but Eric was put off. They'd had intercourse only four times since their son was born 18 months earlier. Eric worried that intimacy dates would be another way to avoid sex. Tension over their no-sex marriage had steadily built and was interfering with all aspects of the relationship, including parenting. Sexual tension was expressed through irritability, especially Eric's harping about Katharine's judgment and not trusting her. Although he considered separation, Eric was afraid Katharine would cut him off from their son as she had cut him off sexually. Katharine worried about Eric's anger and blaming and feared that he would withdraw financial support if they separated. Trust and intimacy were at a low ebb.

Intimacy requires willingness to be emotionally open and trust your spouse. Their minister suggested therapy, but Katharine was not willing to engage in sex therapy. Eric was willing to see a therapist about the sex problem but was not willing to enter marriage therapy. When Eric was 9, his parents had begun marriage therapy, but after several therapies and therapists, they divorced when Eric was 13. This made him cynical about the potential for marriage therapy to improve his and Katharine's relationship.

Their church sponsored a weekend retreat for couples, which the minister encouraged Katharine and Eric to attend. There they were introduced to the concept of intimacy dates as a way to reinforce emotional attachment. Over the next 2 months, Katharine and Eric adopted the structure of weekly intimacy dates, usually initiated by Katharine. Katharine made it clear that she did not want intimacy dates to turn into sexual dates. After initial resistance, Eric accepted this and learned to value these experiences. He especially enjoyed dates where they went for a walk while a neighborhood friend watched their son. Katharine valued this time with Eric, which allowed her to share feelings and discuss life issues. They had an understanding that they would not talk about sex, parenting, or money on these intimacy dates. Katharine's attachment to and trust in Eric increased. Eric did not see intimacy dates as a substitute for a sexual relationship, but they increased his desire to revitalize the marriage. An unexpected side effect was that they became cooperative and supportive parents. Emotionally and parentally, they were a team.

Instead of being angry and blaming, Eric shared with Katharine his puzzlement that emotional intimacy did not transfer to sexuality. Rather than feeling hurt and counterattacking, Katharine admitted that she shared his puzzlement. They agreed to again seek the minister's counsel. The minister congratulated them on the positive changes and growth in their relationship.

The traditional view is that if the couple deals with conflicts and reestablishes emotional intimacy, the sexual problem will naturally improve. Unfortunately, this is not true for the majority of couples, including Katharine and Eric. The minister strongly recommended they consult a female sex therapist whose core training was in pastoral counseling. This was the impetus Katharine needed to begin couple sex therapy. Katharine's trust and intimacy with Eric had grown; she felt comfortable seeing a female therapist and was reassured that the therapist utilized a spiritual-based approach.

The therapist was very supportive of intimacy dates and strongly encouraged continuing them. The clinician utilized feelings and insights from the intimacy dates to assess what was inhibiting sexual desire. During intimacy dates, Katharine was her own person. Eric accepted her and enjoyed being with her. In their sexual relationship, Katharine was not her own person. In the past, Katharine had been aroused and orgasmic, so Eric felt that there was no sexual problem except her withholding. Eric considered himself the sexually interested and sophisticated partner and saw Katharine as less sexual.

A core element in revitalizing marital sexuality was that Katharine needed to own her sexuality. She said, "I want to have my sexual voice." Eric needed to accept that her sexual desires and preferences were different than his. This did not make them inferior or better, just different. Learning to accept different preferences through intimacy dates made sexual differences easier for Eric to understand and accept.

In reviewing her sexual attitudes and experiences, Katharine realized that she had been primed to develop ISD. Katharine's dating and premarital experiences reinforced what she had learned from her mother and the church: Males were more sexually oriented than females. Katharine was surprised that arousal and orgasm were easy for her but felt that sex was driven by the man and that he got more from it. When Eric and Katharine began as a couple, this pattern was reinforced. Katharine felt attracted to Eric and from the beginning enjoyed emotional and sexual intimacy. However, Eric did not attend to Katharine's need for a relationship that integrated intimacy and pleasuring. After 2 months, they had stopped discussing sexual feelings and requests and each encounter ended with intercourse.

Eric felt that the sexual problem began after the birth of their son, but Katharine dated it to the pregnancy. For Katharine it was very special to have sex with the intention of becoming pregnant. She was put off that Eric seemed to care only about increased intercourse frequency. A major disconnect occurred after she became pregnant. Katharine was aware of changes in her body—from nausea to breast tenderness. Her sense of sexual excitement was mixed with worry when the baby moved. Eric seemed oblivious. He wanted to continue intercourse for the whole 9 months. It was as if Katharine's body and feelings did not count. They went to childbirth preparation classes together, and Eric was present at the birth of their son. However, Katharine did not see Eric as her intimate sexual friend.

After their son was born, Katharine felt even more emotionally and sexually alienated. Mothering and breastfeeding were a major transition, especially dealing with sleep deprivation. Katharine saw Eric as uninvolved and felt that he was as sexually demanding as the baby was physically demanding. One time Eric sucked on her breasts when they were full of milk. He thought it was funny, whereas Katharine thought it was gross. Eric had known that Katharine was upset but did not know why.

Awareness of what causes ISD is helpful but only if it facilitates positive changes in the couple's intimate sexual relationship, especially building bridges to sexual desire. Insight is counterproductive when used as ammunition for blaming.

Eric affirmed that Katharine's emotional and sexual needs were as important as his. He no longer pushed sex at the expense of her feelings. Katharine began to think of Eric as her trusted, intimate sexual friend. Eric was open to following her sexual lead. Katharine wanted to use intimacy dates as a transition to sexual dates. However, Eric needed to wait for her verbal invitation, not push. Eric preferred initiating sexual dates in a different manner but accepted Katharine's preferences. If she did not want a transition to intercourse, he could enjoy intimacy and sensuality. Eric had a hard time understanding that Katharine put less importance on orgasm, which for him was central. They had one intimate sexual experience where he was orgasmic and Katharine was not. Katharine felt she enjoyed and got more out of these intimate experiences than Eric. This helped him understand the multidimensional aspects of her sexual feelings and satisfaction.

Sexuality was a more satisfying part of their marriage than ever before. Katharine felt pleased with the quality of their sexual relationship. She and Eric were an intimate, equitable sexual team. Katharine believed that the key to maintaining gains was weekly intimacy dates. Eric committed to initiating an intimacy date if they went more than 10 days without a sexual encounter.

maintaining intimacy during hard times

Intimacy nurtures the marital bond. Yet it does more than that. Intimacy is easy when things are going well. A measure of marital viability is the ability to retain intimacy and stay emotionally connected during times of stress or conflict. Maintaining a view of your spouse as your intimate sexual friend even when there are disappointments or frustrations is a sign of mature intimacy and a healthy relationship. Conflict does not have to negate emotional intimacy. Anger need not be a reason to stop being sexual. Learn to deal with hurt and angry feelings—outside the bedroom. Sexually intimate couples who have confidence in their ability to resolve conflicts have an invaluable marital resource. Couples who do not sacrifice intimacy while dealing with conflicts and negative feelings are especially healthy.

What happens when anger and conflict center on sexual issues, especially an extramarital affair or a sexual secret such as compulsive use of porn? It is doubtful that what we say in this book will successfully address these problems. This type of issue usually requires professional therapy. Rather than letting the problem fester and destroy intimacy, it is a sign of good judgment to seek couple or sex therapy. (Appendix A offers suggestions and guidelines for choosing a therapist.)

summary

Enhancing emotional and sexual intimacy is a powerful means to build and reinforce sexual desire. Partners who reestablish intimacy are in a better position to challenge their no-sex marriage. Intimacy is a couple process; being an intimate couple makes it easier to deal with sexual problems. This does not take away personal responsibility. However, it does change the guilt–blame trap that paralyzes the couple.

Intimacy has the positive function of enhancing the marital bond and building feelings of caring and closeness. Just as important, the couple becomes aware of how draining the sexual problem is and is motivated to confront it. Both partners value an emotionally and sexually intimate relationship.

Key Points

- Emotional and sexual intimacy are different but complementary. Emotional intimacy nurtures the bond, while sexual intimacy energizes the bond.
- Intimacy is much more than a "feel good" concept. Acceptance of individual strengths and vulnerabilities promotes genuine couple intimacy.
- Intimacy provides a crucial relational resource in confronting and changing ISD.

CHAPTER 9

Nondemand Pleasuring:
Let's Play Touchy-Feely

THE ESSENCE OF sexuality is giving and receiving pleasure-oriented touching. Touch and sensuality are the foundation for sexual receptivity and responsivity. In many, if not most, relationships, when intercourse ceases so does affectionate and sensual touch. Revitalizing touch and sensuality is crucial in breaking the cycle of the no-sex marriage.

Nondemand pleasuring is integral to sexual desire. The prescription for vital couple sexuality is integrating intimacy, pleasuring, and eroticism. A couple pleasure orientation contrasts with individual performance orientation. *Foreplay* is used to get the woman (and, with aging, the man) ready for intercourse. *Pleasuring* includes affectionate touch, sensual touch, and playful touch, both inside and outside the bedroom. Pleasuring has value in itself, not just as foreplay. Not all touching is oriented toward intercourse. *Pleasuring confronts the rigid dichotomy in the no-sex marriage that it's all or nothing—either no touching or foreplay to intercourse. Nondemand pleasuring is a crucial bridge to revitalize sexual desire.*

Pleasuring is a couple concept. Affectionate touch (holding hands, kissing, hugging) and sensual touch (nongenital massage, cuddling on the couch semiclothed, snuggling at night or in the morning) have great value. Playful touch intermixes genital and nongenital touch (showering or bathing together, whole-body massages, romantic or seductive dancing, playing strip poker or Twister). Couples are open to and can enjoy a range of sensual and playful touching experiences. Pleasuring can serve as a bridge to sexual desire and intercourse, but that is not its chief function. Touch is not a pressure or demand for sex. Nondemand pleasuring is just as it sounds—a way of maintaining physical contact, feeling connected, and sharing pleasure. Each partner communicates his or her feelings and desire for touch and intimate attachment.

Nondemand pleasuring is in direct contrast to the game playing and miscommunication that characterizes so many couples. Pleasuring challenges the couple to communicate in a clear, comfortable, trusting manner. Touching can be a source of closeness, warmth, and intimacy rather than miscommunication, pressure, or conflict. Sometimes you want an orgasm; sometimes you just want to feel close and connected. Because many men have a hard time asking for a hug, they initiate sex; women often have a difficult time saying they want sex, so they initiate a hug. Through the process of nondemand pleasuring, each person becomes comfortable with feelings and the desire for affectionate, sensual, and playful touch. Optimally, both the man and woman are open to initiating pleasuring. Pleasuring is a valuable means to reinforce intimacy and attachment as well as a bridge to desire and intercourse.

requests, not demands

Touching is a request, not a demand. Intimacy and touching involve trusting your partner. Intimate coercion has no place in marriage or any other close relationship. Marital rape is the extreme of coercion in that it involves physical force. Intimate coercion does not involve force, but it does involve demands and pressure. Coercion says, "I want sex my way, at this time, and if you do not go along, then you will pay for it." This includes the implicit threat of an affair, withholding love or money if a specific sex act does not occur, being distant or angry if there is no sex, or using sex as a bribe. Coercion kills pleasure and desire.

Nondemand pleasuring involves requests and cooperation. You respect your partner's individuality and autonomy. Each person has a right to his or her feelings and to express desires and wants. The person has the freedom to enthusiastically accept, say no, or offer an alternative. A request says, "This is what I feel and want. I am open to your feelings and needs; you do not have to worry about negative consequences." Requests facilitate intimate communication. Demands set up an adversarial performance situation. With demands, you win the sexual battle but lose the intimate bond. With requests, both individuals and the relationship win.

Nondemand pleasuring facilitates sexual desire. Pleasuring forms a bridge between intimacy and eroticism. It is the vital link between an emotionally intimate and a sexually satisfying relationship. Replacing foreplay with pleasuring and goal-oriented individual performance with a pleasure-oriented couple focus facilitates sexual pleasure and satisfaction. Pleasuring requires the partners to be aware of and communicate how they are feeling and what they want. This replaces the rigid male–female sex roles we learned as adolescents. You engage as an equitable, intimate sexual team. Pleasuring challenges the rigid view that sex equals intercourse. The couple adopts a flexible, interactive approach to touching, sensuality, and sexuality. Rigid thinking and a dichotomous view of sex keep couples stuck in the guilt–blame power struggle. Pleasuring facilitates physical and emotional connection.

Couples with chronic inhibited sexual desire (ISD) are reluctant to experiment with nondemand pleasuring. Interfering factors include fears and inhibitions, but a prime factor is reluctance to reengage in touching. It is easier for the partners to avoid one another than to try again. The couple fears falling into the yes–no struggle of intercourse. One way to introduce nondemand pleasuring is through semistructured psychosexual skill exercises, with the clear understanding that there is a temporary prohibition on orgasm and intercourse. This provides a comfortable milieu in which to explore pleasuring.

Exercise: Nondemand Pleasuring

The focus of this exercise (preferably, a series of exercises) is to enhance communication and pleasure while reducing performance orientation. Both partners agree that this exercise will not lead to intercourse and orgasm. This facilitates awareness and helps both of you focus on feelings, touch, sensations, and sensuality. Sensuality is a core dimension that is reinforced by this exercise.

Because it is usually the man who initiates, let the woman take the initiative. Ideally, both partners feel comfortable initiating as well as feel free to say no and suggest an alternative way to experience physical connection. Begin by taking a shower or bath together because cleanliness (especially washing genitals) facilitates comfort and openness to touch.

Showering or bathing is a sensuous activity. Experiment with different types of spray and water temperatures or try a new bath oil or a bubble bath to increase awareness of sensual stimuli. Soap your partner's back. Trace the contours and muscles; rub and gently massage. This is not a rigorous back-rub, but a sensual exploration. Ask your partner to face you; look into his eyes. Eye contact facilitates closeness and trust. Soap his neck and chest. Move downward to his stomach. Soap and touch in a gentle, exploratory manner. Wash his genitals as you would any other body part. Genitals are an integral, natural part of his body. The focus is not on stimulation and arousal but exploration and pleasure. Touch and soap his hips and legs.

Now switch roles. Be open to his touching as he washes you, treating your breasts and vulva like any other body part. Be aware of what feels particularly sensual.

Dry each other. Take your time, be tender, stand still, and take a good look at your partner. Notice two or three physical attributes you find particularly attractive.

Proceed to the bedroom, feeling natural being nude. If you are not comfortable walking through the house nude, put on a robe or towel, but take it off when you reach the bedroom. Pleasuring is best done in the nude. In subsequent pleasuring experiences, you can experiment with sensual clothing or being semidressed. Keep the room at a comfortable temperature, with a moderate amount of light. If one person prefers to darken the room, that is fine, but be sure you can see your partner's body. To enhance the milieu, put on your favorite music, burn a candle with a pleasant fragrance, or both. Experiment with mood enhancers during subsequent experiences. For example, some couples find that classical music facilitates sensuality, others find that multicolored candles enhance the milieu, and still others use a lamp with a blue or red light.

Start with the giver–receiver format, and let the woman take the first turn as pleasure giver. Make sure that each partner has an opportunity to be both giver and recipient. In subsequent experiences, experiment with mutual pleasuring. A sexually satisfying relationship involves both partners being comfortable receiving and giving pleasure. Interestingly, men find it harder to receive than give.

The recipient in this exercise has three tasks. The first is to be passive and receive pleasure. The second is to keep your eyes closed, focusing on feelings and sensations. This also reduces the giver's self-consciousness. The third is to be aware of which parts of your body and what types of touch are sensual and pleasurable.

The following are guidelines, not hard and fast rules. Both partners are free to be creative and innovative.

The woman begins by looking at her partner's body in an open, exploratory manner. Feel free to play, giving a variety of sensual and playful touch. Rather than try to second-guess what he would like, engage in touching that you want to give. This is an opportunity to enjoy touching without being distracted by past frustrations or disappointments. Savor the simple pleasure of touching without trying to turn him on.

Have your partner turn over on his back and, keeping his eyes closed, get as comfortable as possible. Notice signs of relaxation in your partner and be aware of the differences between this and the tension experienced in prior sexual experiences. Continue gently massaging his forehead and outlining favorite facial features with your fingertips. Tenderly kiss his closed eyes, then kiss his face, ears, and neck. Massage his nipples. Does this touch feel sensual to him? Males inhibit their natural response because they think that men are not supposed to feel pleasure there. When exploring his chest, use smooth, tender strokes, covering the sides of his body as well. Lightly stroke his body hair and run your hands sideways around his stomach. How do his stomach muscles react to this touch?

Look at the front of his body. Does he have an erection? Accept his erection as a natural response to pleasure. Be aware of touching his penis when it is flaccid as opposed to when erect. Women view erections as a demand. Remember, there is a prohibition on orgasm. A common myth is that when the man has an erection, the woman must *do* something—have intercourse or at least bring him to orgasm. Interestingly, the man, too, believes that an erection must mean sexual arousal and rushes to intercourse even when he does not feel like having sex. Both partners can enjoy his erection as a natural response to touching and pleasure without feeling any demand.

Explore his genitals as you would other parts of his body. Be aware of his penis—glans, shaft, frenulum. As you explore his testes, notice which is larger and what the shapes remind you of. Notice how the testicles move inside the scrotum.

If he is circumcised (most American men are), trace the glans with your fingertips. If he is uncircumcised, move back the fore-skin and gently explore the glans. Massage and caress his inner thighs, perineum, and scrotum. Notice how the scrotum changes as he becomes responsive. When your touching stops, notice that his erection might subside. Erections naturally wax and wane (as does vaginal lubrication). Men become anxious when their erection wanes because they are used to going to intercourse and orgasm on the first erection. Waxing and waning of an erection is a natural, physiological response to prolonged pleasuring. During a 45-minute pleasuring session, his erection might wax and wane two to five times.

Awareness that sexuality is more than genitals, intercourse, and orgasm is crucial for both partners. Touch for yourself—enjoy rubbing, caressing, and playing. If at any point either you or your partner feels anxious or uncomfortable, do not stop or avoid each other. Lie and hold until you feel comfortable and secure. Then return to nondemand pleasuring. Proceed at your pace and comfort level.

Continue exploring his body, enjoying slow, tender, rhythmic, flowing touch. Enjoy his whole body, including his penis, as a natural part of him. When you feel comfortable with his body and sensual touch, switch roles with your partner.

Now it is the man's turn to give pleasurable touch. Find a comfortable position for giving, whether sitting, kneeling, or lying. Engage in touching and pleasuring for yourself. Do not try to repeat her pattern, second-guess what she wants, or turn her on. Traditionally, the man regards touch as foreplay to get his partner ready for intercourse. This exercise focuses on comfort, exploration, and sharing pleasure rather than intercourse. Your partner lies on her stomach, eyes closed, allowing herself to be open and relaxed. Touch and stroke the back of her body in a slow, rhythmic, and tender way. Do not rush the process. Explore from the top of her head to the soles of her feet, with a focus on pleasure and sensuality.

When it is time to turn over, gently help her move to her back. She keeps her eyes closed, focusing on feelings and sensations. Touch the front of her body, but do not zero in on her breasts or vulva. Integrate nongenital pleasuring with genital touch. Approach her breasts in a sensual manner. Explore a variety of touches while she remains aware of sensations and feelings. With the palm of your hand, start at her waist and move to her neck with one long motion. Be careful not to press hard; breasts can be sensitive. Sometimes the difference between pleasurable and irritating touch is less than an inch or a minor difference in pressure. Trace her nipples with your fingertips. Do they become erect?

Massage her torso and stroke her stomach, tickling and playing with her belly button. Explore her genitals. Run your fingers gently through her pubic hair and caress the mons. Spread the labia with your fingers. Become comfortable with the sight and feel of her genitals. Identify the clitoris and clitoral shaft by gently pulling back the clitoral hood. Look carefully at her labia, noticing how the labia surround the vaginal introitus (opening). As you explore her genitals, touch and stroke her arms, kiss her face, or both. Spread the vaginal opening with two fingers and notice the color and texture of the interior. Gently insert one finger into the vagina and notice the sensations of containment. This is not a medical exam, but a comfortable, gentle exploration. If at any time there is pain or either person becomes uncomfortable, stop touching, but keep contact by holding her. During intravaginal exploration, feel the warmth and dampness. Are you comfortable with the feel and smell of vaginal lubrication? This is a natural process that waxes and wanes in the same manner as erections. Touch and explore the mons and perineum. Move slowly and gently to ensure that touching and exploration are inviting and positive.

Explore her legs, thighs, and feet in a sensuous, unhurried manner. Do a whole-body massage, intermixing nongenital and genital touching. Be aware of favorite body parts and favorite touches. Focus on openness and pleasure, not on arousal or orgasm.

End this exercise by holding each other, experiencing warmth and closeness. Lie in bed and share feelings. What have you learned about sensuality and pleasure? Is once enough or would you benefit from repeated experiences with nondemand pleasuring? What can you enjoy in subsequent exercises? Verbally and nonverbally, guide your partner in the type of touching that is most pleasurable. Do you enjoy multiple stimulation or do you prefer one focused touch at a time? Does talking enhance intimacy or does it distract from pleasure? Is mutual touching more pleasurable than the giver–receiver format? Do you want more or less kissing? Is playfulness more pleasurable than slow, deliberate touching? How can you transfer what you have learned from nondemand pleasuring to lovemaking and intercourse?

the value of nondemand pleasuring in relation to intercourse

When sex becomes a pass–fail test of intercourse, your sexual relationship is vulnerable. This is true even if there is no sexual dysfunction. We are sexual beings, not perfectly functioning sex machines. If only perfect intercourse is acceptable, you are setting yourselves up for failure—if not this year, then 5 or 20 years hence. Orgasm and intercourse are a natural, integral part of sexuality. It is when intercourse and orgasm become a rigid performance mandate that problems occur.

Nondemand pleasuring puts intercourse into a healthy, integrated perspective. Not all touching is destined to end in intercourse. This frees both partners to enjoy touching—including erotic touch. The analogy we employ involves five touching gears, like a five-speed car transmission. Gear one is affectionate touching while clothed—hugging, kissing, holding hands; gear two is sensual, nongenital touching either nude or semiclothed; gear three is playful touching that combines nongenital and genital touch; gear four is erotic stimulation (at times to orgasm)—manual, oral, rubbing, or vibrator; and gear five integrates pleasuring and eroticism that flows to intercourse. To have an enjoyable ride, the experience does not always have to end in fifth gear.

Some couples have a pattern in which half of their nondemand pleasuring experiences transition past third gear. Of these experiences, 85 percent flow into intercourse. Those that flow into fourth gear (erotic stimulation) have a special sexual value. Couples who are aware of and comfortable with the concept that not all erotic activity has to culminate in intercourse have a flexible couple sexual style that helps prevent relapse. The key to successful transition from nondemand pleasuring to intercourse is not to treat this as a dichotomy. Be aware that you have sensual, playful, and erotic choices. This prevents you from falling into the "are we going to have intercourse or not?" trap. Intercourse is a valued option, not a demand. The healthiest way to view intercourse is as a special pleasuring–eroticism technique. This approach to valuing sexual variability and flexibility is the core of the Good Enough Sex (GES) approach, which is of particular value for couples after age 40 (Metz & McCarthy, 2007).

Intercourse is a natural extension of pleasuring and eroticism. It should not be treated as a test of sexuality. Cuddling in bed before sleep is an example of nondemand pleasuring. If both partners become erotically responsive and want to transition to intercourse, that is fine. If one partner becomes aroused and requests intercourse, that is also fine, as long as both partners treat it as a request, not a demand. Sometimes, for example, the woman prefers to stay with cuddling. At other times she suggests an erotic, nonintercourse experience (mutual or one-way). During some encounters she wants to create eroticism so that a mutual intercourse experience occurs. At other times she goes along for the ride, with sex being more for her partner. As long as there is a comfortable flow of touching and communication, this is a healthy process. If nondemand pleasuring becomes a sham—that is, if there is an overt or perceived demand for intercourse—it loses its value. In that case, the answer is a couple agreement that nondemand pleasuring *cannot* lead to intercourse. The partners close off a bridge to sexual desire and intercourse, but it is better to burn that bridge than to lose the value of nondemand pleasuring.

SYBIL AND MARTIN

Couples faced with chronic or intermittent sexual dysfunction find nondemand pleasuring of particular value in rebuilding sexual desire. Sybil and Martin had been a sexually active couple for 21 years (which included conceiving three children) until Martin began experiencing erectile dysfunction (ED) at age 47. Sybil blamed it on work, stress, and drinking. She told Martin not to worry. Martin responded that it was like trying not to think of a 500-pound yellow canary sitting on the side of the bed. After 2 months, Martin felt totally "impotent" and began avoiding sex. Sybil tried to minimize the problem by noting that Martin did obtain erections but lost them when they tried to have intercourse. Rather than being reassured, Martin stopped getting erections.

When faced with a sexual dysfunction that does not spontaneously remit within 6 months, the couple is well advised to seek sex therapy. The man can consult his internist or family practitioner for an initial screening for potential physical or medication factors affecting ED. We suggest seeing a sex therapist before or in tandem with consulting a physician.

Martin did the opposite of these guidelines. He avoided dealing with the ED for 3 years. Sybil stopped initiating because the situation was so tense and conflictual that she wanted to lessen the pressure. Sybil's intentions were good, but her withdrawal actually resulted in increased pressure on Martin. He was afraid she had given up and no longer valued him as a lover. Once a month, Martin initiated sex with the hope for a miraculous cure. Instead he felt embarrassed and humiliated when sexual intercourse failed.

Martin masturbated two to three times a week with good erections but felt ashamed. He eventually went to a men's sexual health clinic that advertised on sports radio. It guaranteed to restore potency or give a full refund. The technique used involved penile injections with a vasodilator, which increases blood flow. Martin had two injections at the clinic and was taught to do injections at home. He found self-injection awkward and at times painful. Martin felt self-conscious and worried about the clinical nature of the procedure. He told Sybil nothing about the injections.

The first time they tried intercourse after this intervention, Sybil was excited to see him erect. Martin did not want her to stroke him and went right to intercourse. Sybil lubricated, but her lubrication dried up because she felt that sex was uninvolved and mechanical. Although Martin was objectively aroused (had an erection), subjectively he did not feel turned on and was not enjoying intercourse. He did not reach orgasm, and Sybil experienced vaginal irritation. He pulled out and seemed very distressed but maintained an erection. Both knew something was amiss.

Sybil heard the story of the injection therapy from Martin 2 days later. She did not object to his consulting a urologist and trying the injections but was hurt that he did not tell her about them or suggest what she could do to help. For some couples, injection therapy can be valuable, but it needs to be integrated into their couple sexual style of intimacy, pleasuring, and eroticism. Sybil's not being allowed to touch Martin's penis and his fear that her stimulation might cause him to lose the erection were very distressing. They needed professional help. Martin was very reluctant to see a couple sex therapist, but Sybil insisted and made the appointment.

Sex therapists see many couples for whom a sexual dysfunction (especially ED) coexists with ISD. Erectile dysfunction is the most common cause of male ISD. Martin was anxious to find a quick solution. He hated the idea of being in therapy for months or years. Once Martin was in the therapist's office, Sybil wanted to talk about their relationship and focus on emotional issues. The therapist understood this gender split. He reassured Sybil that sexuality would not be dealt with outside the context of intimacy (the fatal flaw of the injection program). He reassured Martin that the prognosis for restoring erectile comfort and confidence was good. Erectile functioning is best dealt with as a couple issue. Both partners need to realize there is no miracle cure but that change is more likely if they focus on intimacy, pleasuring, and eroticism as a couple challenge.

After the assessment and feedback sessions, the therapist started Martin and Sybil with nondemand pleasuring exercises. When erection and intercourse are problematic, the couple reacts by decreasing or ceasing sensual and playful touch. Sybil missed touching more than intercourse. Martin associated anything other than kissing and hand-holding with a sexual demand and fear of failure.

Nondemand pleasuring exercises began with a temporary prohibition on orgasm and intercourse. With performance pressure reduced, Martin and Sybil focused on the feelings and sensations of sensual and playful touching. Sybil's reaction to pleasuring was quite positive. She felt more intimately connected with Martin than she had in the past 2 years. Martin's reaction was positive but mixed. He obtained erections but became discouraged when they dissipated. He missed the old days when sex, erection, and intercourse flowed easily and automatically. He enjoyed stroking Sybil but could not hold on to the good feelings. Sybil found it easier to initiate pleasuring than did Martin. Although he read and understood the concept of pleasuring and GES, he felt ambivalent and self-conscious.

The transition to genital pleasuring and erotic scenarios was easier for Sybil. Her desire, arousal, and orgasm flowed during these psychosexual skill exercises. Sybil, like many women, could be orgasmic with manual stimulation as well as during intercourse. Martin was perplexed as to why he was more involved and aroused when he was pleasuring Sybil than when she was stimulating him. Instead of feeling embarrassed and not saying anything, Martin expressed his puzzlement. He told Sybil that when the eroticism focused on her, his desire and pleasure were high, but when eroticism was reciprocal his desire and erection waned. With prodding by the therapist, Martin admitted that during masturbation he predictably experienced erection and orgasm. Martin feared Sybil's censure and was pleasantly surprised when she reported feeling hopeful because his "machinery worked." Sybil shared that she, too, masturbated and enjoyed predictable arousal and orgasm. Sybil wanted Martin to understand that although orgasm was easier and more predictable with masturbation, sexuality was more exciting and fulfilling with him.

The next day, Martin suggested that they take a walk—a good milieu for talking about their sexual relationship. He disclosed how self-consciousness and performance anxiety inhibited his pleasure.

Previously, he could not understand why he did better during masturbation and when being the pleasurer. Now he realized that it was
because there were no distractions or performance worries. He asked
that they start nondemand pleasuring over so that he could share
pleasure without self-consciousness or performance demands. Martin
felt freer emotionally and physically when he kept contact with Sybil
rather than being the passive, receiving partner. He was open to
experimenting with waxing and waning of erections. Martin learned
to be comfortable with pleasuring flowing into eroticism, erection, and
orgasm during erotic sexuality. This was a new experience. Previously,
Martin had been orgasmic only during intercourse. Sybil was open to
experimenting and sharing eroticism. Flexible, variable GES was good
for Sybil, and she wanted it to be good for Martin.

Eventually, Sybil and Martin developed three comfortable sexual
scenarios:

1. Nondemand pleasuring that focused on sensuality and playfulness (gears two and three)
2. Pleasuring that evolved into erotic stimulation, leading to
   orgasm for one or both (gears two, three, and four)
3. Pleasuring that evolved into erotic stimulation that flowed
   into intercourse (gears two, three, four, and five)

Martin valued gear five dates the most but learned to enjoy gears
two, three, and four. Sybil found gear four dates most sexually satisfying,
although she enjoyed all the sensual and sexual dimensions. Sexual
desire was expressed in a varied, flexible GES manner. Sex was less
predictable but more intimate, communicative, and of higher quality.
Nondemand pleasuring was key to revitalizing sexual desire.

how to keep the "demand" out

Nondemand pleasuring is more than a technique to recover from sexual dysfunction. It is a core strategy to maintain a vital, intimate sexual
bond. To maintain this intimate bond after they resume intercourse,
couples must keep the demand out of the pleasuring. Each partner is
comfortable initiating touching. Each communicates the type of touch
he or she wants. One might want sensual touch; the other says no to

that but is open to affectionate touch. One might want sensual touch, while the other prefers erotic touch. One wants intercourse, and the other prefers an erotic scenario.

Touching and sexuality are about pleasure and communication. They are about requests, not demands. When you remove prohibitions from orgasm and intercourse, you are opening new options for sharing instead of creating demands or putting pressure on each other. Keep the focus on awareness, comfort, mindfulness, communication, choice, and pleasuring. Do not fall into the traps of demands or performance orientation.

summary

Nondemand pleasuring is a vital component in couple sexuality. Pleasuring can include affection, sensuality, and playful touching. The essence of sexuality is giving and receiving pleasure-oriented touching. Nondemand pleasuring has value in itself, not just as a bridge to sexual desire and intercourse. Pleasuring includes touching both inside and outside the bedroom, with the understanding that touching is not always directed toward intercourse. Intimacy and nondemand pleasuring confront the rigidity of a no-sex marriage and help rekindle sexual desire.

Key Points

- Nondemand pleasuring is the foundation for a strong, resilient sexual desire.
- Nondemand pleasuring includes affectionate, sensual, and playful touch that occurs both inside and outside the bedroom.
- Nondemand pleasuring can be a major bridge to sexual desire, but it also has value in itself as a means to reinforce intimacy, attachment, and being a sexual team.

CHAPTER 10

Challenging Inhibitions:
Just Do It

B OTH WOMEN AND men have a healthy capacity to experience sexual desire and satisfaction. The essence of sexuality is giving and receiving pleasure-oriented touching. Each person deserves to feel comfortable with and enjoy touching and sexuality. You anticipate being sexual rather than feeling fearful, uncomfortable, or pressured. Awareness, comfort, anticipation, desire, pleasure, eroticism, intercourse, orgasm, and afterplay can flow as a natural process.

Inhibited sexual desire (ISD) means that this healthy process is blocked. It is both an individual and couple task to increase awareness of and challenge inhibitions. There are a myriad of possible inhibitions, which are divided into two broad categories—emotional and sexual. Emotional inhibitions include fear of intimacy, anger, poor communication, not valuing couple time, lack of respect because of job or money problems, disappointment with your partner or relationship, power struggles, role strain, a focus on parenting at the expense of being a couple, too much time and energy spent on work, being overly involved with your family of origin so that there is little emotional energy left for the marriage, being distracted by television or sports, being turned off by your partner's drinking or eating habits, depression or anxiety, and parenting conflicts. Examples of sexual inhibitions include anticipatory anxiety, performance anxiety, guilt or shame about past sexual experiences, embarrassment about sexual dysfunction, poor sexual communication, history of sexual trauma, aversion to kissing, self-consciousness about giving or receiving oral stimulation, fear of becoming pregnant, a history of sexual coercion, greater comfort with masturbation than couple sex, fear that a sexual secret will be discovered, a compulsive sexual pattern, poor body image, embarrassment over nudity, being uncomfortable making sexual requests, and feeling constrained about letting go and experiencing erotic flow and orgasm.

The least healthy way to confront these inhibitions is to feel guilt and shame and direct anger and blame toward your partner. What are psychologically healthy ways to address personal inhibitions? Your partner's inhibitions? A first step in addressing the problem is to confront denial. Be honest with yourself about inhibitions and how they interfere with sexual intimacy and desire. Disclosing your negative attitudes, feelings, and behaviors is an important step. These attitudes, feelings, and behaviors can come from abusive or traumatic childhood experiences, humiliation or rejection during adolescence, disappointment or anger about dating relationships during young adulthood, or frustrating and dysfunctional adult sexual experiences. You can discuss these with your spouse, a therapist, a sibling, or your best friend. You trust that your partner will be empathic and nonjudgmental and will not use this information to blame or belittle you. Self-disclosure is therapeutic. However, if self-disclosure is used against you, it adds to alienation and further inhibits desire.

The next step is assessing whether this inhibition can be overcome or lessened significantly or if it needs to be coped with and worked around so that it does not control your sexuality. This is a difficult assessment to make without the help of a therapist. Some inhibitions can be confronted and overcome. For example, the man who could not tolerate cunnilingus finds that he becomes gradually desensitized to oral sex, and the woman's responsiveness becomes a turn-on for him. Cunnilingus becomes an integral part of their lovemaking. Most inhibitions can be significantly reduced, even if not totally resolved. The goal is to lessen the negative impact so that desire is not blocked. An example is a woman who did not like deep (French) kissing, which her husband found erotic. She enjoyed lip and neck kissing, which became a regular part of their lovemaking. She became comfortable putting her tongue in his mouth, but did not enjoy reciprocal deep kissing. There are some sexual techniques that are not comfortable for an individual or couple. This needs to be accepted and worked around. For example, use of lotions is commonly recommended as a way to enhance touching. Couples are encouraged to experiment with different fragrances to discover those they find sensuous. However, some people dislike the feel of lotion on their bodies. This inhibition is accepted and worked around. Enjoy other aspects of touching, such as varying pleasuring positions, combining manual and oral stimulation, alternating one-way and mutual touching, standing rather than lying down, and enjoying erotic touch in the shower or bath.

In deciding whether to overcome, modify, or cope with an inhibition, assess its severity and how much it interferes with sexual desire. How strong is your motivation for change? How much energy and persistence will it take? Ideally, you view confronting the inhibition as a challenge, enlist your partner's support, put in the time and energy needed to succeed, and persevere until the inhibition is overcome. Unfortunately, some inhibitions are chronic and severe, the partner colludes in maintaining the inhibition, motivation for change is low, there is a significant secondary gain for maintaining the status quo, or the couple has a history of unsuccessful change attempts. In this situation, reducing the harm caused by the inhibition is a more realistic strategy. Contrary to the overpromises of "pop psych," not everything is curable.

Next, choose a change strategy. Good intentions are not enough; you need a plan. The most successful strategy is gradual step-by-step change, reducing the inhibition by engaging in a pleasurable alternative. Implementing a change plan requires thought, time, energy, and communication. For example, in confronting an inhibition about requesting that your husband stimulate you genitally, begin by seeing him as your intimate sexual friend. Talk outside the bedroom, tell him what you want and how he can be supportive, put your hand over his and guide him, say what feels good, acknowledge what he does that you like, make verbal requests, reinforce what is working, and make further requests. When something is awkward or is not working, do not avoid or give up. Overcoming inhibitions takes practice, feedback, and creative problem solving.

The last step, which is usually ignored, is maintaining and generalizing gains. Couples make initial changes only to regress to the old inhibition. Going back to "square one" is not only frustrating but makes it harder to regain motivation to confront the inhibition again. A major impediment with a longstanding problem is the weight of the chronicity. Failed attempts at change are more demoralizing than the initial problem. To avoid that trap, implement a relapse-prevention program. It is normal to have lapses and setbacks, especially when stress interferes.

Benign neglect and avoidance result in the inhibition regaining control. If you have overcome an inhibition about touching yourself during partner sex, continue doing this on a regular basis. Otherwise, self-consciousness and thoughts that self-stimulation is wrong regain strength. The most important relapse-prevention strategy is to acknowledge and reinforce healthy sexual attitudes, feelings, and behavior. A second strategy is to anticipate occasional anxieties, inhibitions, or lapses; be prepared to emotionally problem solve and get back on track. Do not allow a lapse to become a relapse.

individual and couple responsibility for changing inhibitions

The best way to change inhibitions is by assuming responsibility for your sexuality and becoming part of an intimate sexual team. Take personal responsibility; change for yourself and for the good of the marriage. Your spouse cannot coerce you to change or make changes for you, but you can influence and support each other in the change process.

It is unusual for partners to have the same inhibitions. Even when both partners have inhibitions, they are different. Empathize with and support your partner in challenging his or her inhibitions. The most destructive role is being your partner's worst critic, blaming, and making her or him feel guilty. That is not in your best interest, the best interest of your partner, or the best interest of your relationship. The person responsible for change is more invested in the process, but partner encouragement and support are vital. Sex is a team sport; you win or you lose as a team.

Often, inhibitions involve your spouse. This is particularly true of emotional inhibitions. Rather than the inhibited partner feeling like the "bad guy" and becoming defensive or counterattacking, the team approach allows both partners to be on the side of growth, challenging inhibitions, and building an intimate couple sexual style.

emotional inhibitions

The chief guideline is to deal with emotional inhibitions outside of the bedroom. Sexuality is the wrong context in which to play out emotional disappointments and conflicts. For example, when anger inhibits sexual desire, identify the source of the anger and address it. Anger, rather than anxiety, is the most common emotional cause of ISD. The traditional argument is that you cannot feel sexual in the bedroom if you are angry outside of the bedroom. Although sometimes a feeling is so powerful that this is true, it is not the case for the majority of couples. Our suggestion is to recognize that there is both an anger problem and a sexual problem. Ideally, you address the problems concurrently (a "both–and" approach). You can deal with anger issues over the kitchen table while rebuilding trust, intimacy, and touching in the bedroom. Unfortunately, the traditional belief that sex will take care of itself when you resolve emotional conflicts is not the reality for most couples.

Once sex has gotten off track, you need to focus directly on sexual issues for change to occur. The question is whether one or both partners are open to touching and sexuality even when they are still angry. If you had to wait for everything to be in sync emotionally before being sexual, there would be a dramatic increase in no-sex marriages. Couples can deal with anger issues while concurrently revitalizing their sexual relationship. A prime function of sexuality is to energize the bond. This increases motivation to address difficult issues, including conflict and anger.

Sex is more than genitals, intercourse, and orgasm. Sexuality includes self-esteem, body image, intimacy, touch, and openness to erotic scenarios. The mind is your main sexual organ. Feeling comfortable, open, and sensual provides the basis for erotic feelings. Emotional inhibitions cause sexual roadblocks that especially affect desire. Inhibitions interfere with sexual anticipation. Although this is more common for females, it can be just as inhibiting for males.

The key to overcoming inhibitions is feeling that you deserve sexual pleasure. Identify the value of sexuality for you and your relationship. Is it in your best interest to allow emotional inhibitions to dominate your sexuality? Emotions that had a positive function (to maintain autonomy, express hurt or anger, maintain perspective, or allow space to regroup) can keep you stuck in a self-defeating emotional and sexual pattern.

The relationship between thoughts and emotions is complex. The cognitive therapy approach involves challenging self-defeating thoughts, perceptions, and assumptions. Reinforce thoughts and perceptions that are rational, productive, and congruent with your sexual values and goals. Challenging self-defeating thoughts and assumptions facilitates intimacy and sexuality (Epstein & Baucom, 2002). For example, if the emotional inhibition involves fear of vulnerability or rejection, identify habitual thoughts such as "If I'm open, I'll be hurt"; "The more I care, the more painful the rejection"; "I won't let my spouse own me"; and "I won't beg for intimacy." Are these cognitions in your best interest? Do they serve a positive function for you or couple sexuality?

The best way to deal with negative attitudes is to replace them with positive, realistic cognitions. Use these each time you are tempted to fall into the inhibited pattern. Self-esteem is strengthened by a healthy, intimate relationship. There is a positive, reciprocal relationship between self-esteem and marriage. The healthy cognition is "I can be me in an intimate sexual marriage." Marriage should not contribute more than one third to one's self-esteem, but a satisfying, stable marriage fulfills needs for intimacy and security better than any other human relationship (Doherty, 2013).

Traditionally, married couples stayed together regardless of the quality of the relationship. Stigma against divorce, family pressure, religious sanctions, and community norms supported marginal marriages. Couples remained married unless there was a major disruption such as physical abuse of the spouse or children or if one of the spouses abandoned the family. In our current culture, low-quality or marginal marriages do not survive. If you value the marriage, you have to commit to satisfaction, security, and healthy sexuality.

Emotional inhibitions can be challenged. Take the risks necessary to reconnect with your spouse. If the inhibition involves overcommitment to one's family of origin or stress due to an unsatisfactory job, it is the person's responsibility to address this. One element of a change plan is to enlist the support of your spouse. For example, if a woman wants to switch jobs, her husband increases his contribution to housework and child care so that she has the time and energy to write inquiry letters and network. If the decision is to limit extended family contact, the partners convey to their respective relatives the parameters of the time available. It is easier to say no to social demands if both partners do it together.

There is great value in confronting emotional inhibitions. Successfully challenging inhibitions improves psychological well-being and increases the feeling that you deserve sexual pleasure. A powerful cognition is pride in seeing yourself as a survivor, not a victim. Another helpful cognition is that "living well is the best revenge."

challenging sexual inhibitions

How does one help her or his partner to overcome sexual inhibitions? Is the key to be sexually free, with no inhibitions? Is the sexual liberation philosophy correct? No! Focus on developing a comfortable, pleasure-oriented couple sexual style. It's not a matter of "anything goes." You do not have to prove anything to yourself, your partner, or anyone else. Focus on the present; you do not have to compensate for the past.

Some sexual inhibitions can be totally overcome or significantly changed, whereas others must be coped with and worked around. Seldom do people have the same sexual inhibitions, so it is hard for the partner to understand and empathize. For example, consider the husband who makes fun of his wife's preoccupation with breast shape or her sensitivity about heavy thighs. Or the wife who cannot understand why her partner is so concerned about the size of his penis or why he gets anxious when she plays with his buttocks. Accept your partner's sensitivity. Do not put your partner down or try to talk her or him out of it. Listen in a respectful, caring manner to your partner's feelings and perceptions. Be an intimate friend and supporter, not critical or demanding.

People do not magically overcome sexual inhibitions. Change is a gradual process that occurs over weeks, months, and, yes, even years. Barry recalls a man who had a strong aversion to looking at, much less touching, his wife's vulva. After 6 months of therapy, taking very small steps, he was able to successfully engage in manual clitoral stimulation, but he needed to do so with his eyes closed. Both he and his wife were pleased with the progress; this inhibition no longer controlled desire and pleasure. Two years later, the man wrote on his follow-up form that he now enjoyed giving manual stimulation and especially seeing the pleasure in his wife's eyes.

It is easiest to change sexual attitudes after changing sexual behavior. Feelings do not change until there have been a number of successful experiences. Orgasm is important and a natural culmination of arousal and erotic flow. However, orgasm is not the best measure of success. The best measure is desire and satisfaction. Women find this easier to accept than men. Women can recall highly satisfying experiences that did not include orgasm. Men rigidly measure sex by intercourse and orgasm. If pressed, the man discloses that on occasion he has ejaculated but felt little satisfaction. Experiences with pleasuring help identify emotional, sensual, and erotic sources of satisfaction in addition to intercourse and orgasm.

Throughout this book, we take a pro-sexual attitude. Confronting past abusive or traumatic sexual experiences is a challenge facing many people. Clients tell Barry that they have trouble maintaining pro-sexual attitudes and feelings because of experiences with childhood sexual abuse, incest, rape, or sexually transmitted infections (STIs); have been peeped at or exposed to; or have been made to feel guilty or shamed. In addition, they mention current negative experiences that include being sexually harassed at work, receiving obscene phone calls, coping with infertility caused by an untreated STI, or feeling psychological stress because of a sexual dysfunction. This is in addition to the frustration and stigma of a no-sex marriage. With these past and present negative experiences, it is possible to adopt a pro-sex attitude?

Negative motivation does not promote change; it serves to keep the individual and couple "stuck." Do not feel blamed or blame yourself for negative sexual attitudes and feelings; this just piles on the negativity, which makes the problem worse. Positive motivation, attitudes, and actions promote change. Can any healthy function for you or your relationship be derived from maintaining negative sexual attitudes? Very unlikely. What would be the result of adopting a pro-sexual attitude? It would mean seeing sexuality as a good thing, an integral part of you as a person, and feeling that you deserve to express sexuality in a manner that promotes your intimate sexual relationship.

What can you do and what can your spouse do to facilitate this change? One way to promote pro-sexual attitudes is through encouragement from an authority figure. For example, almost all religions are pro-sex in marriage. Barry suggests that Catholic clients consult with a priest. The husband and wife are amazed when the priest tells them that having intercourse is spiritually a good deed, equivalent to saying a prayer. Although you might think, "That's not what the nuns told me in grade school," you are a married adult and deserve sexuality to be a positive part of your life and relationship. Another source of permission giving is parents. When you were an adolescent, parents' admonitions were controlled by fear, especially fear of you getting pregnant, contracting a sexually transmitted disease, or falling in love with the wrong person and derailing your life. Talking to parents as a married adult is very different. Parents who had disappointing (and even disastrous) marriages and sexual problems are supportive and encourage you to enjoy marital sexuality.

Your spouse is the most important person in helping to change your attitudes. The role of both partners is to be genuinely empathic and supportive, not patronizing or coercive. The one–two combination of personal responsibility and acting as an intimate sexual team promotes change.

What to do about specific sexual inhibitions? For example, consider the man who is unable to talk during a sexual experience or to touch after orgasm, or the woman who is not comfortable giving genital stimulation or can only be sexual in the dark. The couple's task is to build a comfortable, pleasure-oriented sexual style that promotes intimacy and satisfaction. There is no "one right way" to be sexual. You do not have to perform to a rigid sexual criterion. The strategy is a gradual step-by-step plan to build comfort, acquire psychosexual skills, and encourage free sexual expression.

A common sexual inhibition is fear of not maintaining an erection. Rather than panicking when this happens, the couple is encouraged to use a "trust position" to reinforce physical connection. Partners can lie side by side and hold hands. Some couples find it more comfortable for the woman to lie in the man's arms, with minimal movement or verbal communication. Develop a trust position and way of being together that reestablishes comfort and intimacy when there are erection issues.

Sometimes you end the sexual encounter with the trust position. At other times you return to pleasure-oriented touching or engage in erotic touch to orgasm, thus expanding your sensual and erotic repertoire. Manual, oral, or rubbing stimulation to facilitate arousal is of great value in overcoming erectile dysfunction. Realizing you can achieve arousal and orgasm with erotic sex rebuilds confidence. Couples who have a flexible sexual repertoire that allows for normal variation in male and female pleasure and eroticism do not remain stuck in self-defeating inhibitions (McCarthy & Breetz, 2010).

The woman who wants to feel comfortable giving genital stimulation begins by rubbing her partner's penis against her thigh, moves to rubbing her body against his (including his genitals), and holding his penis while they are kissing. They might stop at that point or progress to her stimulating his penis with a vibrator, beads, or her hand. As she feels sexually responsive, she is open to his rubbing his penis between or against her breasts, engaging in mutual manual stimulation, or manually stimulating him while he stimulates her orally.

A major change in sexual technique during the past generation is increased enjoyment of oral sexuality. The "chic" erotic scenario is for the woman to be multiorgasmic with cunnilingus and then fellate the man to orgasm, with the woman swallowing the semen. If you are not comfortable with this, does it mean you are inhibited? It does not. We urge you as a couple to develop a comfortable, pleasure-oriented approach to oral sex. You do not have to prove anything to yourself or to your partner.

Some women enjoy cunnilingus naturally flowing to orgasm. Some women are not receptive to cunnilingus unless they are highly aroused before beginning oral stimulation. Some people find mutual oral sex (simultaneous cunnilingus and fellatio) extremely arousing, whereas others find it distracting or a turnoff. Many women prefer manual, rubbing, or intercourse stimulation and choose not to engage in oral sex. Some men enjoy fellatio to orgasm; others do not because it means they cannot engage in intercourse. Many men enjoy movement during oral sex; others prefer to lie passively and take in pleasure. Some people genuinely enjoy giving oral sex; others engage in it because it is arousing for the partner. Like other aspects of sexuality, the couple's focus is to develop a comfortable, pleasurable style of oral sexuality.

Exercise: Challenging Inhibitions

Each partner lists emotional and sexual inhibitions that subvert sexual desire. Next to each item, write whether your goal is to overcome, reduce, or work around the inhibition. Your spouse provides insights, perceptions, and feelings, but does not talk you out of or into anything. It is your inhibition and your responsibility to develop a change strategy. Discuss with your partner how he or she can be helpful. For example, a woman's inhibition might involve not enjoying sexual touching while semiclothed. The goal is to lower the inhibition so that she can receive and give stimulation while semiclothed. Her partner should not try to talk her into mutual stimulation but should be supportive of her goals. Her focus is to develop comfort with receiving kissing and hugging semiclothed, not feel pushed to do more.

Once you have established mutually acceptable goals, begin the change process. Clearly spell out steps to take and the ways in which your partner can be supportive. A crucial guideline is to move at the change pace that is comfortable for the person with the inhibition. Equally important, the person can veto or stop uncomfortable stimulation but not stop or avoid touching (which reinforces anxiety). If you feel anxious, switch to a trust position. Examples include putting your head on your partner's heart, lying in your partner's arms, or sitting facing each other while keeping eye contact and placing your hand on your partner's cheek.

Do not try to change more than two inhibitions at a time. Avoid the trap of being overly ambitious. For instance, if each person targets two emotional and two sexual inhibitions, both partners lose focus and become discouraged. A common pattern is to make significant progress then regress. It is crucial to generalize gains and prevent relapse. It is better to significantly change two inhibitions rather than to experience mixed progress and frustration in six areas. Remember the adage, "Two steps forward, one step back," and persevere.

Be clear and specific about change steps, communicating as an intimate sexual team. One advantage of working with a therapist, as opposed to doing this on your own, is that the therapist helps you process what you have learned, deal with frustrations, and design and alter psychosexual skill exercises and encourages you to maintain focus and motivation. Change is seldom quick or easy. If change is easy for you, consider this a cause for celebration.

The more specific the inhibition, the easier it is to change. Sexual inhibitions tend to be easier to change than emotional inhibitions. It is simpler to break the cycle of avoidance than to build a comfortable, pleasurable couple sexual style. Talk about and acknowledge improvements and plan your next steps. Set aside time to talk at least once a month and preferably weekly. If the inhibition has not been resolved within 6 months, we strongly urge you to seek professional help.

BETH AND CRAIG

Beth and Craig had argued about inhibitions during the entire 8 years they had been in a relationship, the last 4 as a married couple. They met through an "in search of" ad Craig had placed. Beth was intrigued that rather than writing an upbeat, overpromising ad, Craig admitted to shyness and being a critical person. He was looking for a woman who would tolerate initial hassles and discover the gem of a person underneath.

Beth felt comfortable with the giving–helping role. She realized that Craig was more than shy; he suffered from social anxiety. Sex was a particularly sensitive area. Craig had an uncommon sexual dysfunction—ejaculatory inhibition. He became easily erect and moved quickly into hard-thrusting intercourse. Even after an hour of intercourse, he would ejaculate less than one third of the time. Beth found Craig's approach to sex both intriguing and off-putting. She was used to men who had premature ejaculation and brought her to orgasm manually. Craig's sexual intensity and intercourse pattern presented a different dimension. Beth did not believe she could reach orgasm with intercourse and was pleasantly surprised when she was orgasmic during intercourse with Craig. On the other hand, she tired of Craig's incessant thrusting. After 12 minutes, she stopped lubricating and found sex boring and tedious. If intercourse extended beyond 20 minutes, it became physically irritating.

Craig and Beth felt that their relationship was emotionally validating and satisfying. Craig enjoyed Beth's warmth and giving. Beth was able to disarm his criticalness through humor. She realized that Craig longed for acceptance and a trusting relationship.

Craig was more successful professionally than personally. His background was in accounting and computers, and he was a consultant specializing in streamlining financial systems. This was a good professional match with his personality; he enjoyed detail work and analytical problem solving. The couple took advantage of the perks of Craig's job. Beth had the professional flexibility (she was a successful freelance editor) to accompany him on trips, taking advantage of frequent flyer miles and free accommodations. They admired each other's professional expertise.

Beth had one sexual inhibition. She was not comfortable lying in bed nude after sex and put on her granny gown, which Craig found anti-erotic. In addition, Beth had two emotional inhibitions. She was wary of the institution of marriage and did not trust men, including Craig, to be sexually faithful. This resulted in a paradox. Beth was loving, giving, and humorous, which enhanced the quality of their relationship. However, she was tentative and unwilling to commit. Craig offered stability and security, but Beth was not buying. This worked on his insecurity—fear that Beth would leave because of his ejaculatory inhibition. Beth assured Craig that the problem was not whether he ejaculated but his frustration and emotional distance when he did not.

Craig wanted to marry a year after their meeting, but it took 2 years of his lobbying, her parents' and friends' urging, and Beth's desire for children to convince her. Craig believed that a marital commitment would eliminate Beth's emotional inhibitions. He was upset when that did not occur and blamed her, which infuriated Beth. She had hoped that marriage would help Craig's ejaculatory inhibition. She never said it to Craig, but she worried that it would impinge on their ability to get pregnant. Beth had ambivalence about a lifelong marriage commitment but no ambivalence about children. She was thrilled that after 19 months of marriage and only 3 months of trying, they became pregnant. Craig was just as pleased. He, too, had silently feared that they would not be able to conceive. They did not share these fears with each other until after becoming pregnant.

Beth and Craig enjoyed parenting, but with less time and energy, conflicts over sexual and emotional inhibitions increased. Beth resented prolonged intercourse and had neither the time nor the patience to lie in bed afterward. As Beth became less sexually desirous, her fear that Craig would have an affair increased. Craig felt defensive and blamed for something he had not done and had no intention of doing. Craig kept it secret that he masturbated daily and was orgasmic 100 percent of the time. Craig found masturbation easier and more satisfying than intercourse.

The stimulus for entering couple therapy was an emotionally charged incident. Beth was holding the baby and needed to tell Craig something, so she interrupted him while he was showering. Beth realized that he was masturbating. Craig was mortified; Beth was apologetic but later became angry. She felt betrayed by his masturbating, that it was his way of having an affair. Beth did not oppose masturbation; she had masturbated since age 19 and felt free to masturbate when Craig was out of town. However, Craig's masturbation felt like a compulsive activity that took place when she was available. She was devastated to learn that he was easily orgasmic by himself. During couple sex, he was only orgasmic once a month. Beth was not sure whether to blame herself or Craig. Interestingly, it was Craig who made the call to the therapist. It was sad that it took this crisis to initiate their seeking help because Beth and Craig were excellent candidates for couple sex therapy.

Although Craig and Beth argued and blamed each other for inhibitions, they had not honestly and objectively assessed what the inhibitions were and disclosed them to their spouse. Craig became easily erect, but his level of subjective arousal was low. Because he had an erection he felt silly asking for erotic stimulation. Craig did not find intercourse alone stimulating but thought he was supposed to. The concept of subjective arousal (i.e., feeling turned on) was new to Craig but not to Beth. Beth was aware that her subjective arousal was usually greater than her objective arousal (i.e., vaginal lubrication) and just assumed this was true for Craig. Realizing that he became erect at a low level of subjective arousal was a revelation. Beth was eager to give manual and oral stimulation to build his subjective arousal. This increased involvement and eroticism for both. It was Beth's idea to continue erotic (multiple) stimulation during intercourse. Craig was especially responsive to testicle stimulation while thrusting. Giving breast stimulation increased his erotic involvement. As subjective arousal increased, so did his pleasure at being orgasmic. Craig learned to value couple sex and agreed to masturbate only when Beth was not available.

The therapist took a different tack with Beth's inhibitions. These were conceptualized as an inability to accept intimacy and security. Beth's parents divorced when she was 3. Her mother chose not to remarry; her father was divorced an additional two times. Two of Beth's siblings were divorced (one successfully remarried), and another sibling was in an unhappy first marriage. Beth's best friend had been abandoned when her husband left her for his business partner. Furthermore, Beth was an avid fiction reader and moviegoer, and affairs are a major theme in the media. Her favorite movie was *An Unmarried Woman,* which deals with the strength a woman needs to cope with her husband leaving for a younger woman. Beth loved being emotionally giving but hated feeling emotionally vulnerable.

Traditionally, religious, family, and community pressure ensured that marriages remained intact. A man having affairs or a mistress was frowned upon but accepted as long as he did not disgrace the family or abandon his wife. This double standard is less culturally accepted now and was totally unacceptable to Beth. Yet she felt vulnerable and helpless in dealing with her fear of Craig having an affair. The therapist suggested five things: (1) an upfront commitment on both Beth's and Craig's part to remain monogamous; (2) an agreement to disclose any potential risk situation and talk about it before acting on it—an excellent technique to confront the secrecy affairs thrive on; (3) an agreement that if there was a sexual incident, the spouse would be told within 72 hours; (4) that both partners would put time and energy into enhancing sexual intimacy; and (5) that after a sexual experience, Beth would put on underpants, lie in bed, and talk about intimate feelings. Beth was pleased that Craig would have a positive role rather than just complaining about her inhibitions. As inhibitions decreased, what had been a good marriage turned into an excellent marriage. Intimacy and sexuality thrived in a secure milieu.

the importance of freely flowing emotional and sexual intimacy

Inhibitions block the flow of intimacy and sexuality. This drains the marital bond of energy and good feelings. Decreasing inhibitions frees emotional and sexual energy, and couples report a surge of energy and sexual desire. The couple is operating on all six cylinders instead of limping along on four. It is difficult to gauge the negative impact of inhibitions until you are free of them.

Inhibitions—whether personal or relational, emotional or sexual—subvert sexual desire. Some inhibitions can be totally overcome, others significantly reduced, and still others need to be coped with so they do not control the person or relationship. Inhibitions function as a means of withholding, although this is seldom intentional. Guilt–blame struggles concerning inhibitions result in marital alienation. Taking personal responsibility and working as an intimate sexual team help free you and your relationship from the tyranny of inhibitions.

summary

Couples become trapped in the pursuer–distancer dynamic as well as the blame–counterblame pattern. This is self-defeating. The positive alternative is to understand personal, partner, and couple inhibitions, both emotional and sexual. Inhibitions drain sexual desire, intimacy, and sexual energy. Each person needs to take responsibility for her or his own inhibitions. Your partner's role is to be a supportive, intimate team member in the change process.

Key Points

- In confronting emotional and sexual inhibitions, the person and couple need to choose a strategy: (1) resolution, (2) modification, or (3) cope with and work around the problem.
- Reducing inhibitions increases energy and sexual desire.
- Dealing with inhibitions is a combination of personal responsibility and being an intimate sexual team.

CHAPTER 11

Creating Erotic Scenarios: Vital Sexuality

Intimacy and nondemand pleasuring are necessary, but not sufficient, for sexual function. For arousal and orgasm, you need erotic scenarios and techniques. When people think of erotic sex, they recall movies featuring passion and romance in new couples or extramarital affairs. Have you ever seen erotic marital sex in the movies? Is there eroticism after marriage?

You can create eroticism in your relationship and revitalize sexual desire and vitality. Eroticism, intercourse, and orgasm are not the core of a sexual relationship, but they are integral components. The prescription for a healthy sexual relationship is integrating intimacy, nondemand pleasuring, and erotic scenarios and techniques.

Couples plagued by inhibited sexual desire (ISD) and a no-sex marriage do not affirm erotic scenarios. Premarital sex was exciting because of newness, romantic love, passion, and wanting to please your partner. Yet the couple had not developed the comfort, communication, and freedom to share special turn-ons and erotic scenarios. Young partners, especially males, find that sexual function is easy and predictable. However, sexual quality is often mediocre or worse. If poor-quality sex becomes the norm, then anticipation declines and frustration increases. Do not treat your sexual relationship with benign neglect. This leads to resentment, alienation, and avoidance. Eventually, one or both spouses develop ISD. Unless the partners push to maintain contact, they fall into a no-sex relationship.

Couples with primary sexual dysfunction are particularly open to a new approach. Building a healthy couple sexuality is easier because the concept of developing bridges to desire and erotic scenarios is new and inviting. Optimism is high that awareness, comfort, being an intimate team, nondemand pleasuring, and erotic scenarios to facilitate desire are novel and empowering concepts.

A significant number of couples had good-quality sex and then lost desire and eroticism. For some, satisfying couple sex ended with the birth of their first child. For others, sexual intimacy was destroyed by a sexual conflict (an affair, a dysfunction, or an unplanned pregnancy), a practical conflict involving jobs or living conditions, or an emotional conflict involving not feeling valued. These are examples of secondary ISD, which is much more common than primary ISD, especially among men. When the couple avoids touching, sexual comfort and sexual skills atrophy. What had been easy and flowing becomes awkward, self-conscious, and difficult. It is reassuring to know you have experienced eroticism so you can experience it again in the future. It is hard to accept that you cannot magically turn back the clock. However, you can build bridges to desire and create erotic scenarios. Knowing that you have the potential for eroticism is helpful, but you have to be open to experiment, communicate, and play.

sexual desire and eroticism

Is it possible to maintain a sexual relationship with minimal eroticism? Some couples have a pattern in which one spouse (usually the male) initiates sex once a week. Sex is functional, even though not vital. For other couples, sex is tied to becoming pregnant, is viewed as a duty, or is part of the marital commitment.

Anticipating erotic, fun sex is a major motivator in revitalizing sexual desire. Sharing erotic flow and being orgasmic is energizing. The essence of eroticism is scenarios and techniques that increase involvement, arousal, and erotic flow. This includes, but is not limited to, intercourse. Ideally, the arousal of each spouse plays off the other's arousal. The "give to get" pleasure guideline is generalized to giving and getting erotic stimulation. The main aphrodisiac is an involved, aroused partner. Couples find that giving and receiving multiple stimulation before and during intercourse enhances eroticism. The more you turn your partner on, the more turned on you feel. Mutual arousal and multiple stimulation (partner interaction arousal) is the most common way to build high levels of eroticism.

Feeling open, receptive, and sexually playful is the underpinning of eroticism. Think of arousal as a 10-point scale, where 0 is feeling neutral and 10 is being orgasmic; you cannot jump from 0 to 8 with erotic scenarios. Sexual response assumes your openness and receptivity to touching and pleasuring—and being at least 4 and preferably 5 or 6 on the arousal scale before transitioning to erotic scenarios and techniques.

Erotic techniques during the pleasuring phase include mutual manual stimulation; his doing oral breast stimulation and manual vulva stimulation while she caresses his penis; her giving fellatio while he does breast stimulation and utilizes fantasy; kneeling, kissing, and engaging in mutual genital stimulation; watching a sexy movie, undressing each other, and erotically touching; verbalizing or playing out a sexual fantasy; standing in front of a mirror so that you have visual feedback while doing manual and oral stimulation. There are a variety of pleasuring positions; variations in stimulation; and use of external stimulation such as fantasy, lotions, music, sex toys, movement, online videos, and playful erotic scenarios.

Multiple stimulation can be integrated during intercourse. Why cease multiple stimulation because your penis is in her vagina? Many couples find that multiple stimulation is most erotic during intercourse. This includes switching intercourse positions two or three times; enjoying kissing or breast stimulation; using the man's hand, woman's hand, or vibrator for additional clitoral stimulation; the woman giving testicle stimulation; fantasizing during intercourse; enjoying buttock or anal stimulation; using intercourse positions (like side-by-side) that facilitate body contact; and taking a break for manual or oral stimulation, then resuming intercourse.

Eroticism and orgasm are important, but they are not the core of sexuality. Desire and satisfaction are the critical elements of a healthy sexual relationship. Unless you experience anticipation, receptivity, and involvement, even the most erotic scenarios and techniques will not elicit desire on a regular basis.

creative and erotic sex

When people think passion, excitement, and eroticism, they focus on premarital sex or extramarital affairs. Why are people willing to take sexual risks with a new person but not with their spouse? Erotic sex connotes new, illicit, swept away, "fun but dirty." Can couples with chronic desire problems learn to enjoy sex that is intimate, unpredictable, playful, erotic, and satisfying? Yes!

It is not technique alone, or even primarily, that serves to eroticize sex. Sexuality is enhanced by anticipation; playfulness; experimentation; and, above all, awareness of feelings and openness to creative expression. Sexual creativity emanates from three sources: awareness of feelings, thoughts, and fantasies; a dynamic process between you and your partner that includes touching, teasing, and nonverbal cues; and openness to experimenting with erotic scenarios and techniques. Eroticism need not reach a Hollywood-level lustful performance. Critical components are playfulness, unpredictability, multiple stimulation, creativity, and letting go. Erotic sex can and does exist in the context of a marital bond. Intimacy and eroticism complement each other. Erotic sex energizes the couple bond and adds a special dimension to your relationship.

guidelines for erotic experiences

Creative sexuality is a voluntary, pleasure-oriented, mutual experience. A major poison for desire is intimate coercion. This involves sexual demands in which the stated or implied threat is that if one person does not give the other what he or she wants there will be a negative consequence. This type of sex is neither intimate nor voluntary; it is a command performance under threat of punishment. Intimate coercion includes the threat of an affair if the spouse does not have sex, withholding love or money if a specific sex act does not occur, being distant or angry if there is no sex, or using sex as a bribe.

What is erotic for one partner might feel "kinky" or distasteful to the other. Experimentation should not be a means to prove anything to anyone or involve performance demands, manipulation, or coercion. Focus on eroticism, not performance; on requests, not demands; on honesty, not manipulation. Remember, you are trying to revitalize sex with your intimate sexual friend, not coerce the person to have sex your way.

Exercise: Creating Erotic Couple Scenarios

One of the most fascinating aspects of sexuality is the differences in what people find erotic. When exploring turn-ons, you do not have to prove anything to yourself, your spouse, or anyone else. Request and share scenarios and techniques that heighten your desire and eroticism.

The man makes the first initiation. From a smorgasbord of erotic turn-ons, choose what you would like to try or design something of your own. Erotic couple scenarios include slow, mutual kissing and touching followed by rapid, intense intercourse; making love while watching a favorite R- or X-rated video; being sexual in the shower or right after so that both of you are fresh for oral sex; reading a sexual fantasy aloud or playing out the fantasy; using a favorite lotion to heighten erotic sensations as you and your partner stimulate each other to orgasm; quick, intense intercourse followed by afterplay where you give her as many orgasms as she wants; having intercourse standing up or with her sitting on the bed and you kneeling; mixing manual and oral sex until both of you are highly aroused, then having intercourse in the woman-on-top position while you engage in manual clitoral stimulation and your partner strokes her breasts. Create scenarios that are personally inviting and an erotic turn-on. Your partner is open to your requests and desires. You both share turn-ons that heighten subjective and objective arousal.

The woman designs her creative erotic scenario(s). This is a sharing, not a competition. You can explore external turn-ons and use milieu and special techniques to heighten eroticism. Your partner can veto anything he finds negative, but he is encouraged to be open and experimental. Examples include being sexual in front of a mirror and enjoying visual feedback; watching an erotic or X-rated video; being sexual in the guest room, living room, or family room; using vibrator stimulation; being sexual on a deserted beach; having sex in a shower or Jacuzzi; using play aids (a feather, silk sheets, mittens); being sexual in the back seat of the car like carefree adolescents; using "toys," like loosely tied ropes or a paddle for spanking; being sexual at a bed-and-breakfast, upscale hotel, or funky inn; lighting a scented candle and putting on his favorite music; and being sexual under the stars during a camping trip.

When creating scenarios, individually or mutually, partners are open to each other's feelings and requests. Do not set artificial barriers between sex play and intercourse. You can experiment with positions, multiple stimulation, and expressing feelings. Bask in creative, flowing, erotic sexuality. Creative sexuality does not end with orgasm. You can be playful and creative so you really enjoy afterplay.

Intimacy and eroticism can be successfully integrated. Eroticism builds anticipation, desire, and vitality.

realistic sexual expectations

Couples envy friends in a new relationship who are in love and lustful and who brag about fantastic sex. Instead of going for ice cream after a movie, they rush home to have sex. It is hard not to be envious. The romantic love, passionate sex phase is great, but it is precarious and time limited. Unfortunately, "hot sex" couples have high rates of dysfunction later, especially no-sex relationships. Part of the problem is the natural transition of time and experience, but the prime cause is unrealistic expectations. Passionate, driven sex does not last. It needs to be replaced by mature, intimate sexuality that integrates eroticism to energize the marital bond. That is a positive, realistic expectation. Striving to return to the lustful, passionate, super-charged sex of the first few months is unrealistic and crazy making.

Empirical studies of sexually well-functioning, happily married couples present a very different view than the media hype. The average married couple has sex one to three times a week. The normal range of sexual frequency is between four times a week and once every 2 weeks. In 35 percent to 45 percent of sexual experiences, both partners feel desirous, aroused, orgasmic, and satisfied. So the ideal mutual, synchronous sexual scenario occurs less than half the time, even among well-functioning couples (Frank, Anderson, & Rubinstein, 1978). Other patterns include one partner being highly satisfied while the other feels good; one person being satisfied while the other finds it okay; and one feeling satisfied, whereas the other just goes along for the ride. These are acceptable and realistic, but quite different from the "hot," perfect sex portrayed in movies and novels. Of particular interest is that 5 percent to 15 percent of sexual experiences are mediocre, disappointing, or dysfunctional. That, too, is a realistic part of couple sexuality. You know that the couple is cured when they are able to laugh or shrug off a negative experience. They look forward to getting together in the next few days when they are feeling desirous, receptive, and responsive.

What is a realistic expectation regarding "hot" erotic scenarios? If you have one or two extraordinary sexual experiences a month, count yourselves lucky. You cannot expect each encounter to be special, nor can you expect each erotic scenario to be fabulous. Erotic scenarios sometimes turn out to be duds. This is not to discourage you but to emphasize realistic expectations. If 85 percent of erotic scenarios are successful, you can feel very good about yourselves as a sexual couple.

DANIELLE AND JACOB

Danielle was 34 and in her first marriage to 47-year-old Jacob, for whom this was a second marriage. Jacob had two adolescent children from his first marriage. Danielle met Jacob through work. They were friends for 2 years before becoming sexually involved. Danielle's premarital pattern was that she always had a boyfriend and sex went fine, although as the relationship progressed, sex became less important. She was 30 when she became involved with Jacob; they had been married 4 years.

Jacob was 26 when he entered his first marriage. He was disappointed when sex slipped into a once-a-week Saturday night routine—functional but unexciting. Divorce had been difficult. His wife left, saying that he was more interested in his job and hobbies than in being a husband. The years between marriages were stressful. Jacob did not enjoy the dating scene, although there was an erotic charge at the start of a new relationship.

Jacob had been a professional mentor for Danielle. He was attracted to her intelligence and enthusiasm, which combated Jacob's dour life outlook. Jacob felt attracted, but it was a safe attraction. He enjoyed hearing stories of the ups and downs of Danielle's relationships. They attended a convention in Boca Raton, Florida—a romantic milieu. After the inaugural speech, they went with a group for dinner, which evolved into drinking and dancing. Jacob was acutely aware of how attractive Danielle looked and what a sexy dancer she was. Jacob felt awkward and resisted dancing but impulsively suggested that they have a drink at the bar on the beach. After two drinks, Danielle suggested dancing on the sand where no one could see them. They still argue about who seduced whom.

The first 6 months were a very exciting time. They kept the fact they were a couple from work colleagues, which added to the sense of intrigue. Jacob felt sexually revitalized, as if he were 26 again. Danielle felt totally in love and amazed at having a relationship with a man of Jacob's maturity and professional status. Their weekends away were especially exciting. They forgot about work and really cut loose. Danielle had never been involved with an older man and was pleased to find that the stories and jokes her girlfriends told were not true. Jacob was sexually desirous and sophisticated with excellent ejaculatory control (this had been a problem in Danielle's prior relationships).

Romantic love and passionate sex are great at the beginning of a relationship but set a couple up for frustration and resentment later. Unfortunately, this was the outcome for Danielle and Jacob. Nonsexual factors interfered first. Danielle expected to win over his children (which she did 2 years later), but the initial meetings were tension-filled competitions for Jacob's attention. When the relationship became a source of office gossip, management urged Danielle to find another job as soon as possible. Jacob tried to facilitate placing her with a prestigious organization but was unsuccessful. Danielle felt increasingly uncomfortable and took a less than satisfactory job offer.

The romantic bubble had burst. However, they vowed to maintain the relationship. The decision to marry was with the hope that marriage would revitalize their relationship. Sex was strained but functional. Frequency had decreased to once or twice a month. Both were tentative in initiating and wished the other would take the lead—a common pattern. Marriage seldom revitalizes sexuality, nor does the honeymoon. They were sexual three times during the 2-week honeymoon, but it was not free-flowing sex. The constant comparison to their 6-month romantic, passionate sex phase depressed and devitalized them. They could not live up to that magical comparison. Three years later, when they consulted a sex therapist, he advised them to remember those 6 months fondly as a symbol of attraction and desire but to stop using this as a comparison and not try to replicate it. They needed to build an intimate, erotic couple sexual style in the present.

Danielle and Jacob were a demoralized couple in a low-sex marriage. To make matters worse, Jacob was experiencing performance anxiety and erection problems. Danielle was turned off by Jacob's tentativeness and apologizing—qualities that were not sexually appealing. Danielle wanted a baby. Her hope was that trying to get pregnant would revitalize sex. Although sex with the intention of becoming pregnant can be an aphrodisiac, that is not how it worked for Jacob. He worried about the pressure of intercourse based on a fertility timetable. He was ambivalent about starting a second family in his late 40s, although he felt guilty about cheating Danielle of the opportunity to have a child. It was a depressing impasse. Danielle's gynecologist was not helpful; instead he was judgmental. After 3 stressful months, Danielle's friend suggested they consult a couple sex therapist.

The therapist was respectful and empathic. Danielle and Jacob felt relieved to hear that pregnancy was not a quick fix for sexual problems. The concept of working as an intimate sexual team was particularly attractive for Jacob, who felt overwhelmed by guilt, self-blame, performance anxiety, and ambivalence. Each spouse had an individual psychological–relational–sexual history session.

Danielle felt bewildered, betrayed, and cheated by Jacob and the marriage. Although she did not voice it, she was angry that her career plans had been derailed. She resented that she, rather than Jacob, had been forced to leave the organization. Danielle blamed herself for Jacob's erection problem, feeling that her attractiveness and seductiveness had failed. She feared a marriage where both sex and children were missing. Danielle felt that she had lost sexual creativity and eroticism.

Jacob felt defeated by sex, marriage, and life. He was more depressed than ever. He felt shame over letting down Danielle personally, maritally, sexually, in her career, and in keeping her from having a child. These emotions negated Jacob's desire for couple sex. He masturbated one or two times a week and was able to get an erection and ejaculate, so he knew "it still worked."

In the couple feedback session, the therapist confronted these negative emotions. He proposed a plan to revitalize intimacy, introduce nondemand pleasuring, and develop a new couple eroticism. The feedback session provided a mirror through which Danielle and Jacob could identify the "poisons" of guilt, anger, shame, and withdrawal, which drained sexual desire and marital vitality. Performance orientation, inhibitions, and avoidance dominated sexuality, while depression and demoralization characterized their relationship. This feedback put the pieces of the puzzle together for Danielle and Jacob. No wonder they had a low-sex marriage. Confronting inhibitions and focusing on building bridges to desire had a strong appeal.

It was not until the 10th week of therapy that they began discussing erotic scenarios. The therapy process and nondemand pleasuring exercises resulted in gradual but sure improvement. There were frustrations and setbacks, but they stayed on the same team and felt that touching was on track, serving as a way to connect and build intimacy. Danielle's anger was acknowledged and dealt with, which freed sexual energy. Danielle realized that Jacob was still attracted to her. Once Jacob stopped apologizing, his attractiveness quadrupled. Danielle enjoyed pleasuring, and her arousal was arousing for Jacob. Performance anxiety was greatly reduced when Danielle agreed to initiate sexual encounters. However, Jacob's desire and arousal lagged behind that of Danielle, who was enthusiastic about manual and oral stimulation. Jacob's obsession about whether intercourse would succeed or fail dampened his sexual desire.

The therapist suggested that Jacob take the lead in designing and playing out erotic scenarios. He provided Jacob with a smorgasbord of choices—discussing them in the session and referring him to the chapter on special turn-ons in the book *Sexual Awareness* (McCarthy & McCarthy, 2012; listed in Appendix B). Jacob was hesitant, but Danielle assured him that she was open to his erotic requests. The following week included pleasurable experiences, but Jacob did not make an erotic initiation. He came to the session depressed and expecting to be censured. Jacob easily fell into the trap of feeling guilty and defensive, which was sexually paralyzing. This was in no one's interest. Jacob needed encouragement and a positive impetus, not punishment.

The therapist loaned Jacob a psychoeducational erotic video, suggesting that he and Danielle watch it and discuss scenarios and techniques that they would be open to trying. Jacob found the tape freeing and a turn-on. It gave him permission to be sexually selfish. Realizing that Danielle became aroused by arousing him was a powerful impetus. Jacob requested that Danielle be totally passive while he teasingly turned her on. When she was highly aroused, he requested oral stimulation while he lay on his back and she knelt (which allowed him to continue stimulating her). She put him inside her from the female-on-top position and stroked her breasts as they engaged in rapid in–out thrusting. This scenario was almost as arousing for Danielle as it was for Jacob.

Danielle's erotic scenario was quite different. Just like bridges to desire, having "his," "hers," and "our" erotic scenarios is of great value. Erotic scenarios are not a competition. Danielle found milieu and accoutrements key for her sexual desire and eroticism. She took the opportunity to experiment with creative lighting. She loved different colors and fragrances of candles. In her scenario Danielle put five candles in the bathroom where they took a sensual bath and five others in the guest bedroom for later. Danielle luxuriated in the bath, enjoying the smells and colors of the candles reflecting off the walls. She stood while Jacob orally stimulated her. She allowed herself to let go and have a series of orgasms. As a side effect of sex therapy, Danielle developed a multiorgasmic response pattern.

Danielle returned to the bath and had a glass of wine. Jacob told wonderful fantasy stories. It was one of her favorite things about him. They went into the guest room, and Danielle tied Jacob's hands over his head. This allowed him to be passive—something she liked but Jacob found hard to do because he was always trying to stimulate her. Danielle found it arousing to pleasure Jacob when he was passive, especially playing with his penis around her breasts. She was orgasmic rubbing against him. They then had intercourse with her on top, moving her hips in a circular rhythm. Danielle designed a creative afterplay.

They lay on their backs watching the candles play off the ceiling and talked about their dream vacation. This was a symbolic affirmation of their intention to remain a vital intimate couple.

At therapy termination, Danielle and Jacob knew that their marital bond and couple sexuality were solid. Sex was less frequent than in their first 6 months, but it was based on genuine attraction and openness to each other's sexual needs. They trusted that desire and eroticism would remain vital. Their decision to enjoy sex with the intention to get pregnant was a further sexual incentive.

Danielle and Jacob were committed to maintaining a vital sexual bond; they would not allow themselves to regress. They adopted three relapse-prevention strategies: (1) setting monthly intimacy dates that focused on sharing feelings and nondemand pleasuring, (2) setting an erotic date with a prohibition on intercourse if there had been a negative experience or they had not been sexual for 2 weeks, and (3) introducing an erotic technique into their sexual repertoire every 6 months to keep sexuality vital.

creative sex and desire

You look forward to watching movies, each of which is different. Some will be Academy Award quality, others okay or disappointing. A few movies are so good you watch them two or three times. Creative sex is like anticipating a really good movie; you hope it turns out to be special, but nothing is guaranteed. Even so, anticipation enhances desire. This holds true for sexual encounters.

The essence of creative sexuality is not technique; it is awareness of sexual feelings and willingness to take a risk and play out a scenario. Creative sex can be planned or spontaneous. A healthy sexual relationship mixes spontaneous and intentional erotic experiences. Creative sex can be experimental, using external turn-ons (role-enactment arousal). Creative sex can also involve tuning into internal feelings (self-entrancement arousal) and sharing them in an open, erotic manner. The most powerful aphrodisiac is not an esoteric technique; it is an involved, aroused spouse (partner interaction arousal).

The most popular erotic technique is oral sex. There are a variety of positions, techniques, and sequences and variations such as one-way or mutual stimulation and use of fruit or flavored lotions. People differ in their preferences and turn-ons. Some prefer oral sex as a pleasuring technique, others as a means of reaching orgasm. Some prefer whole body and visual contact; others want a sole focus on receiving oral stimulation and keep their eyes closed. For some, multiple stimulation is the key to arousal; others prefer one erotic focus at a time. Some prefer slow, seductive stimulation, while others desire fast and lustful stimulation. It is not a right–wrong question but a matter of personal preference and sequencing. Creative sex means awareness of feelings and desires and freedom to express these in the context of an intimate, erotic relationship.

individual and couple scenarios

Individual scenarios are easier to design and introduce. It is a matter of taking a risk and making requests. The partner is open to playing out your erotic scenario, knowing that he or she can veto or alter a technique that is unacceptable. Although people worry about being coerced into doing something they find aversive, the typical situation is that shyness or inhibition blocks the person from requesting erotic scenarios and playing erotically.

Creative couple scenarios require communication and mutuality. Instead of taking turns, let sex play be mutual. When feelings, touch, and sexual expression flow, your experiences of eroticism enhance those of your partner. Couple scenarios are an erotic extension of the "give to get" pleasure guideline. Choose your favorite place to play sexually (the den, dining room, guest room, outside on a secluded porch). You need not plan a detailed scenario. Be open to feelings and requests; let sexuality flow. Have favorite external turn-ons readily available if you decide to introduce them—a lotion, a mirror, a sexy story, beads or feathers, a vibrator, an erotic video, scented candles. Be free and playful. Be open to positions: standing, lying, kneeling, and sitting. Have your favorite music on. Dance, touch, be seductive. Do not place an artificial barrier between erotic play and intercourse. Communicate what you feel and want through touch, words, and movement. Allow eroticism to flow into intercourse. Experiment with positions and multiple stimulation during intercourse. Express feelings and allow sexuality to flow. Creative sexuality does not end with orgasm. Stay together and enjoy afterplay. Express affectionate, sensual, romantic, pleasurable, and playful feelings verbally as well as through touch.

enhancing your erotic relationship

If companies put as little time and energy into their businesses as couples put into their marriages, we would have a bankrupt country. A chief guideline in maintaining an erotic relationship is to place a priority on couple time. Valuing your relationship is the foundation for eroticism.

You can spot people who are in a new relationship or having an affair. They are attentive, aware of each other, playful, and seductive. When people think of eroticism, they think of youthful couples, extramarital affairs, or the jet set, not of themselves. Can a married couple fan the flames of eroticism?

An important sexual enhancer is a couple weekend without the kids. This gives you the time and freedom to be an expressive couple and do things you enjoy—hiking, antiquing, shopping, sleeping late. Enjoy a bed and breakfast, luxury resort, rustic inn, or camping. Choose what fits you. Sexuality is an integral part of the weekend instead of sex being the last thing you do at night when you are both exhausted. You can be sexual when you awake; take a shower and go back to bed; have sex after a walk; indulge in a "nooner"; have sex before or after a golf game or hike, before or after a nap, before dinner, or as dessert; or have an early evening sex date and then sit on the porch and have a drink as afterplay.

Another way to enhance your erotic relationship is by enjoying fantasies. Sexual fantasies are the most common form of multiple stimulation. People associate fantasies with masturbation, but 75 percent of married men and 50 percent of married women utilize fantasies during partner sex. Fantasy is a natural, healthy bridge to desire and eroticism (Morin, 1995). What makes sharing difficult is that fantasies are the most private part of you, which increases personal vulnerability. Most sexual fantasies are about unusual or unacceptable people, behaviors, or situations, and many are bizarre. Common fantasy themes include sex with an unattainable or inappropriate partner, forced sex, group sex, watching people being sexual, gay sex, and illegal sexual activities. What gives fantasies their erotic charge is that they are different from what you usually do and who you really are.

It is hard enough to accept your own fantasies much less share them with your spouse. Although many sex books encourage acting out fantasies, we believe that it is unwise to act out fantasies unless both partners are genuinely comfortable with this. Fantasy and behavior are separate realms. What is exciting and erotic as a fantasy can become destructive and self-defeating when acted out. Being turned on by a fantasy is not the same as desiring to experience that sexual behavior. Most fantasies are best kept as fantasies. For most couples, verbally sharing a fantasy is better than acting it out, but even then it can rob this fantasy of its erotic charge.

If you decide to play out fantasies, we suggest these guidelines: Only involve the two of you, do not be physically or psychologically coercive, and do not humiliate or intimidate your spouse. Either person can call a time-out or veto a technique. Remember, there is no place for intimate coercion in your sexual relationship.

summary

Breaking the pattern of a no-sex marriage requires communication, effort, and courage. Erotic scenarios elicit and maintain sexual desire and vitality. Creative scenarios enliven your relationship and prevent relapse. Erotic scenarios and techniques enhance intimate sexuality.

Key Points

- Eroticism is an integral component of healthy individual and couple sexuality.
- Intimacy and eroticism are different dimensions. The challenge is to integrate intimacy and eroticism into your couple sexual style.
- Although erotic scenarios and techniques are important, the essence of creative couple sexuality is awareness of sexual feelings and willingness to take a risk and play these out.

PART 3

Relapse Prevention

CHAPTER 12

Maintaining Gains: Keeping
Sexuality Healthy

You have broken the pattern of inhibited sexual desire (ISD) and a no-sex marriage. Congratulations! However, you cannot rest on your laurels or take sexuality for granted. Generalizing and reinforcing healthy couple sexuality is crucial. You have come a long way. You owe it to yourself, your partner, and your bond to maintain gains and not allow a relapse.

It is unrealistic and self-defeating to believe that each sexual encounter will involve equal desire, pleasure, eroticism, and satisfaction. It is equally unrealistic to believe that touching and eroticism will always flow easily. Establishing positive, realistic, nonperfectionistic goals is crucial for relapse prevention. A positive, realistic expectation is that sexuality will energize your intimate bond. Sexuality is a positive, integral part of your lives and relationship. By reinforcing healthy sexual attitudes, behaviors, and feelings, you are inoculated against future problems. Whether the sexual experience is joyful, satisfying, okay, mediocre, or dysfunctional, you remain an intimate sexual team. Both people are committed to maintaining intimacy and to not falling into the avoidance trap. Giving and receiving pleasure-oriented touching is the essence of couple sexuality.

The core of relapse prevention is awareness that intimacy and sexuality need continual time and energy. Sexuality cannot be treated with benign neglect. Consider a mediocre, negative, or dysfunctional experience as a lapse and ensure that it does not cause a relapse into ISD and a no-sex relationship. Relapse prevention is an active process, behaviorally and emotionally.

specific strategies and techniques

When couple sex therapy is about to end, Barry suggests 10 guidelines to ensure that gains are maintained. The partners agree to utilize three or four personally relevant guidelines to ensure that their hard-won gains are generalized and reinforced (McCarthy, Ginsberg, & Fucito, 2006).

1. Continue to dialogue as a couple on a regular basis. One advantage of therapy is that on a weekly or biweekly basis you engage in serious communication about your relationship. When therapy ends, keep the schedules you cleared for regular meetings at the therapist's office for yourselves. Use this time to go for a walk, have a sexual date, go to dinner, problem-solve a difficult issue, or have an intimate experience. Devote time and energy to maintaining your intimate sexual bond.
2. Schedule a 6-month follow-up therapy session. This ensures that you remain accountable to each other and to the therapist. Intimacy and sexuality cannot be taken for granted. Commitment and accountability prevent relapse.
3. Schedule a nondemand pleasuring session at least once every 4 months, preferably monthly or bimonthly. Setting aside time for a pleasuring session (with a prohibition on intercourse and orgasm) reinforces communication, sensuality, and playfulness. This allows you to experiment with new pleasuring scenarios and techniques—an alternative pleasuring position, body lotion, a new setting or milieu. Maintaining pleasuring and sensuality is a solid foundation for couple intimacy, which serves to combat relapse.
4. When a problem occurs, treat it as a lapse, a mistake to learn from. Do not permit it to become a relapse. Even among happily married couples with no history of sexual dysfunction,

5 percent to 15 percent of sexual encounters are mediocre, unsatisfying, or dysfunctional. People are not perfectly functioning sex machines. There is an inherent variability and flexibility to couple sexuality. Do not panic or overreact to a mediocre or negative experience. Rather than hoping it will never happen again (an unrealistic expectation), learn coping techniques so that you do not relapse into old habits. Whether it occurs once every 10 times, once a month, or once a year, more likely than not there will be occasions when the man loses his erection, the woman experiences pain during intercourse, or one or both partners do not feel sexual desire. This need not be a cause for panic or blame. Accept this as disappointing but not as a tragedy or being back at square one. You can laugh or shrug off the experience and make a sexual date within a few days when you are feeling desirous, receptive, and sexually open. Better yet, you can enjoy a sensual massage or an erotic scenario. A negative experience can turn into a pleasurable one.

5. Maintain positive, realistic expectations about marital sex. In movies (where healthy marital sexuality is almost never portrayed), sex is spontaneous, intense, nonverbal, passionate, and perfect. The reality for married or partnered couples is that fewer than half the encounters include equal desire, pleasure, eroticism, and satisfaction. If you experience movie-quality sex once or twice a month, you are a very lucky couple. If sexuality is to remain positive and nurture your intimate bond, you need to accept flexibility and variability. Adopt the Good Enough Sex (GES) broad-based approach to touching and eroticism. Sexuality meets a variety of individual and couple needs. Sometimes sex is a tension reducer, sometimes a way to share closeness; at other times sex is a passionate experience, a way to heal an argument or to share pleasure, or a bridge to reduce emotional distance. Often, it is better for one partner than the other. That, too, is a realistic expectation.

6. Plan intimacy dates or weekends without children. Sex therapy confronts the rigidity of the male always initiating sex with the expectation that all touching should end in

intercourse. Both people are free to initiate intimacy, pleasuring, and sexuality. Especially valuable is a weekend away (without children) at least once a year. Couples report better sex on vacation.

7. Generalize and expand your sexual repertoire. There is no "one right way" to be sexual. Each couple develops a unique style of initiation, pleasuring, eroticism, intercourse, and afterplay. The more flexible the couple sexual style and acceptance of the multiple roles and meanings of touching and sexuality, the greater the resistance to relapse. Develop a comfortable, functional, and satisfying couple sexual style that meets your needs and energizes your bond.

8. You can cope with mediocre or negative sexual experiences. The single most important technique in relapse prevention is the ability to accept and not overreact to experiences that are mediocre, unsatisfying, or dysfunctional. Any couple can get along if everything goes well. The challenge is to accept disappointing or dysfunctional experiences without panicking or blaming. Miscommunication about a sexual date, a minimally arousing sexual interaction, or an erectile or orgasmic dysfunction—these happen to all couples. Intimate sexual couples accept occasional mediocre or dysfunctional experiences and take pride in having a resilient couple sexual style.

9. Develop intimate and erotic ways to connect and reconnect. Intimacy includes sexuality, but it is much more than sexuality. You need a variety of ways to connect, reconnect, and maintain connection. These include five gears (dimensions) of touch—affectionate touch, sensual touch, playful touch, erotic touch, and intercourse touch. In traditional sex-role socialization, men emphasize sexual connection and women affectionate connection. Ideally, both partners are comfortable initiating intimacy and sexuality. This promotes a variety of ways to remain intimately attached and build bridges to sexual desire. The more ways you have to maintain intimate and sexual connection, the easier it is to avoid relapse.

10. Each of you makes sexual requests, and as a couple you develop special erotic scenarios. The importance of having a variety of sexual alternatives and scenarios cannot be overemphasized. Couples who express intimacy through massage, taking walks, bathing together, and engaging in semiclothed or nude sensual touch have a flexible, satisfying repertoire. Couples who are open to "quickies," prolonged and varied erotic scenarios, various intercourse positions, multiple stimulation during intercourse, and both planned and spontaneous sexual encounters have a strong, resilient sexual relationship. A flexible, variable sexual repertoire is a major antidote to relapse. Sexuality that meets a range of needs, feelings, and situations will serve you well in maintaining gains and preventing relapse.

assumptions behind relapse prevention

The best strategy for relapse prevention is a broad-based couple sexual style that is comfortable, intimate, pleasurable, erotic, and satisfying. Intimacy, nondemand pleasuring, and erotic scenarios and techniques, combined with realistic expectations, ensure healthy sexuality. This guards against sexual problems, especially with the aging of the partners and the relationship.

People who trust each other to deal with problems are in a much better position than those who magically hope that nothing goes wrong. Resilient couples are confident in their ability to deal with difficulties and lapses. Relapse prevention is more than luck; it is confidence in yourself, your spouse, and your relationship. You can deal with stress and disappointment while remaining an intimate sexual couple. Affectionate, sensual, playful, erotic, and intercourse experiences are flexible and can withstand occasional problems, dysfunction, or disappointments. The most important component is motivation. You are an intimate team that is committed to maintaining a vital sexual relationship.

TRACY AND SEAN

When they started treatment, Tracy and Sean had been married 3 years, had a 1-year-old daughter, and had not been sexual since she was born. Unbeknownst to Tracy, Sean began an affair with a divorced woman from his office when Tracy was 4 months pregnant. Sean used the pregnancy as a justification for the affair, rationalizing that Tracy did not enjoy sex when pregnant. Sean was an example of the adage that affairs are easier to get into than out of. The stress of a double life caused by the affair, plus adapting to a new baby, resulted in marital alienation.

Tracy suggested marital therapy. Sean was resistant, afraid that the affair would be revealed. When Tracy found a therapist who specialized in sex therapy, Sean relented and agreed to go. Consulting a professional confronted the couple with the seriousness of the problem. Tracy was sad and angry over the lack of intimacy and sexuality. She alternated between blaming herself and blaming Sean.

Sean minimized the impact of the affair, although he realized the precarious state of their marriage and the problem of sexual avoidance. In his individual session, Sean told the therapist about the affair, feeling relieved to disclose this secret. After the first few months, the affair was no longer exciting or satisfying, but he could not extricate himself. The affair was becoming increasingly destructive. Sean could not devote the time and energy needed to revitalize the marriage while distracted by the drama of the affair.

In their conjoint session, the therapist asked Tracy whether she was willing to help Sean terminate the affair. This was a novel strategy, but the more they discussed it, Sean felt that this was what he needed. Tracy would not tell the other woman the affair was over, but she agreed to actively support Sean in confronting this secret sexual life.

Tracy was hurt to learn that Sean was having an affair but felt validated that her intuition had been right—that there was a specific cause for feelings of alienation. Tracy and Sean invited the woman to their home for lunch. To be sure that emotions remained in check, no alcohol was served. Sean showed her the baby and said that he and Tracy were recommitted to the marriage and that they needed to devote time and energy to rebuilding their marital and family bond. He hoped this would not interfere with their professional work relationship, but there could be no personal relationship. The woman was upset. It was an awkward, uncomfortable lunch, but the message was clear and unequivocally communicated. Tracy and Sean agreed to a 5-minute check-in weekly to ensure that there would be no secrets between them. Sean agreed that if a high-risk situation arose, he would tell Tracy within 72 hours. This agreement freed Sean and Tracy to focus on revitalizing their trust and sexual bond.

Realizing how much work it takes to rebuild trust and intimacy increased their motivation not to allow an affair or any another crisis destabilize their marriage. Six months after they resumed being a sexual couple, Tracy unexpectedly broke into tears. This occurred after she had been orgasmic and was feeling close to Sean. At first, Sean was defensive and wondered if Tracy was doing this as a guilt-inducing manipulation. Tracy was clear that it was neither manipulative nor to punish Sean; it was a genuine flashback, causing a feeling of unexpected sadness. You cannot change the past, nor does guilt help rebuild intimacy. What is helpful is turning toward each other as intimate allies.

Renewing intimacy is a joint challenge. Trust is not a simple process. It requires talking and emotionally supporting each other through stresses and disappointments. When Tracy cried or Sean was frustrated, rather than go their separate ways they used their trust position: Tracy put her head on Sean's heart, and he stroked her hair. They found that being quiet, yet together, was better than trying to talk the problem to death.

Two years after the completion of couple sex therapy, Tracy and Sean felt secure in their marriage. Intimacy was a forte. Sexuality was pleasurable, erotic, and satisfying. They felt proud that the marriage had survived a stressful crisis and no-sex period.

The strategy that was most helpful was thinking of themselves as an intimate sexual team fighting against the common enemy of ISD. The most helpful technique was building bridges to desire. Before a sexual date, Tracy took time for herself while Sean watched their child. Tracy became comfortable using a vibrator during partner sex, and Sean integrated loving and erotic feelings. Sean's favorite bridge was taking a shower while Tracy was putting their child to sleep and then getting together. Tracy's favorite bridge was being sexual when their child was out of the house and being watched by someone else.

The therapist encouraged them to develop a specific relapse prevention plan. Tracy worried that this was overkill because they were doing well, but Sean was in agreement about how important it was to maintain their gains. He felt responsible for the intimacy and trust problems and was committed to doing everything he could to ensure that the marriage remained satisfying, secure, and sexual. Sean suggested that they get together for coffee and a serious conversation at least once a month to make sure that there would be no relapse. The quality of their sex was much improved. Sean enjoyed showering before sex (which facilitates oral sex). Tracy committed to initiating sex at least once a week. She wanted marital sexuality to remain vital, integrating intimacy and eroticism.

Sex with the intention of becoming pregnant enhances desire. Sean and Tracy remained emotionally and sexually connected throughout their second pregnancy. By the 5th month, Tracy preferred erotic sex to intercourse. Sometimes it was mutual and sometimes asynchronous. Although he preferred intercourse, Sean was open to whatever was comfortable for Tracy. Neither Tracy nor Sean was hypervigilant about an affair. They were confident that they would discuss a high-risk situation rather than be secretive or act out.

Tracy and Sean valued an intimate, erotic, secure marriage. They did not take each other for granted. Sexuality was a positive, integral part of the marriage, and they were committed to keeping it that way.

relapse prevention versus crisis intervention

In movies and novels, once a problem is resolved people expect to live happily ever after. It doesn't quite work that way in real life, where relapse is a distinct possibility. Prevention is superior to a crisis and the need for crisis intervention. Sadly, a significant number of couples fall into the trap of a second sexual crisis caused in part by "magical thinking." The partners hope that if they do not worry or talk about sex, it will not be a problem. We do not promote fear or obsessing. However, we do advocate an active relapse prevention approach—and a problem-solving approach if sexuality gets off track.

The best example of relapse prevention involves guarding against ISD as an overreaction to erectile dysfunction. The goal of sex therapy when erectile difficulty occurs is to regain comfort and confidence with erections, resulting in renewed sexual anticipation and desire. A man's inability to maintain an erection that is sufficient for intercourse might occur once a month or once a year. This is a normal part of male sexuality, especially after age 40. When an erectile difficulty causes the man (or woman) to overreact and avoid sex, sexual desire is vulnerable.

**Exercise: Your Personal and Couple Plan for
Preventing Relapse**

Take the theory and good intentions of relapse prevention and make them personal and concrete. Each person needs to be aware of vulnerabilities and traps. What can you do to ensure that you will not fall into these traps? How can your partner be helpful and supportive? Individually and as a couple, commit to doing what is necessary to ensure that your intimate sexual bond remains vital and resilient.

This exercise involves two phases. First, write down personal and couple traps. Writing facilitates clarity and specificity. Then, discuss how to prevent falling into these traps.

An example of a trap for the husband is becoming discouraged or obsessed with career disappointments, which depresses sexual desire. The coping mechanism is to share career perceptions, feelings, and alternatives with your wife, professional colleagues, or both. Your career is only one factor contributing (at most one third) to your self-esteem. If career problems are not changeable, it is crucial to find other sources of self-esteem and satisfaction. One source is emotional and sexual intimacy. Your partner can initiate both supportive hugs and satisfying sexual encounters.

An example of a trap for the woman is that orgasms are not as easy as in the past, but you are reticent about requesting additional erotic stimulation. As sex becomes lower quality and less satisfying, your anticipation and desire decrease. You are more irritated by than receptive to your partner's sexual initiations. To counter this, you introduce personal and external turn-ons to enhance sexual involvement and pleasure. You request additional erotic stimulation, realizing that your satisfaction is as important as his. His role is to be a giving partner, not to pressure you or make your orgasm his responsibility. Both of you are open to erotic scenarios and techniques that enhance quality and facilitate desire and satisfaction.

The most common trap is self-consciousness about sexual initiation. Psychosexual skill exercises can increase awareness and comfort without the side effects of self-consciousness. Sexual initiation becomes easier. Each of you identifies what you can do to make initiations personal and inviting.

The second phase of this exercise is to explore strategies and techniques to keep couple sexuality vital. Discuss intimacy and sexuality in a clear, positive, realistic manner. The answer is not to quit your job so that you are stress free or to send the children to their grandparents for a month. Examples of realistic plans are that each of you initiates an intimate experience once a week and a couple weekend without children every 6 months; if there has been no sexual contact for 2 weeks, you agree that he will initiate a nondemand pleasuring experience on Sunday afternoon; on Friday night after the kids are asleep you rent an R- or X-rated video; you plan an erotic date at least every 2 months, with the understanding that you will not proceed to intercourse; every 6 months you shop for a new sensual lotion or a sexy outfit; each of you initiates a favorite erotic scenario once a month. Commit to developing at least one individual scenario and one couple scenario each year that reenergizes couple sexuality.

Repeat this exercise yearly.

ensure that a lapse does not become a relapse

For some behaviors, a lapse (returning to a self-defeating or destructive behavior) is serious and unacceptable—partner abuse, using heroin, driving while intoxicated, exhibiting yourself, or setting fires. For the majority of behaviors, although you try to avoid lapses, they do occur and you must deal with them. Examples include fear and avoidance, obsessive–compulsive behavior, and depressive thinking. Behaviors that are a continuous part of the person's life (mood, anxiety, eating) are more likely to involve lapses than are behaviors that are dichotomous and can be abstained from (cigarettes, stealing, drug use). With sexual functioning—specifically, desire—occasional or intermittent lapses are likely.

Lapses in martial and sexual behavior are normal. The most important issue is how you ensure that a lapse does not turn into a relapse. A lapse involves a temporary situation, a specific regression. Examples include pushing sex when your partner is not receptive; reacting to a mediocre or negative experience with blame; miscommunicating when one partner wants intercourse and the other wants a sensual experience; overreacting when the man loses his erection or the woman is not orgasmic; going along with a sexual initiation even though you are not really interested; having sex in the middle of the night, which you had agreed was not acceptable; trying to have sex after an argument when your partner is still alienated. These are normal occurrences. Among couples with no sexual problems, 5 percent to 15 percent of sexual experiences are mediocre, disappointing, or dysfunctional. The key is to ensure that occasional lapses do not become a full-blown relapse.

What is a relapse? A relapse is a regression to dysfunctional ways of thinking, behaving, and feeling. It is a return to infrequent sex (less than once every 2 weeks), ISD, and avoidance. Anticipatory anxiety replaces positive anticipation; the partners no longer feel they deserve sexual pleasure and resort to guilt and blaming. They stop acting and feeling like an intimate sexual team. Do not allow yourselves to regress to the cycle of anticipatory anxiety, tension-filled sex, and avoidance.

A relapse is more distressing than the original sexual problem because it is more difficult to regain motivation. The first time you confront ISD and the no-sex marriage, you learn new concepts, skills, and exercises that challenge this problem. Sharing intimacy, nondemand pleasuring, and erotic scenarios are powerful reinforcers. Dealing with a relapse (whether for the first or eighth time) is more difficult. There is no new dramatic strategy; rather, you must implement and reinforce techniques that you know are helpful in rebuilding sexual intimacy and desire. The challenge is to remain motivated and focused on maintaining a healthy couple sexual style.

It is crucial to address and recover from a lapse. Feelings of intimacy, pleasure, eroticism, and being an intimate sexual team become stronger and more resilient. It is easier to deal with issues and problems early on and not allow the avoidance that results in a full-blown relapse.

How to prevent relapse? When a lapse or negative experience occurs, you need to acknowledge this rather than deny that it happened or magically wish it will never happen again. Recognize the lapse and actively deal with it rather than avoid, pretend, or overreact. Learn from mistakes. Sexual self-esteem and couple intimacy need not be controlled by problems. A healthy strategy is to set an intimacy date for the next day or two. Some couples choose a pleasuring experience, with an explicit ban on intercourse; others prefer to go with the flow. It is crucial to challenge avoidance. Some couples choose a nongenital pleasuring date to reintroduce touching, confronting avoidance in a sensual, as opposed to erotic, manner. Continuing to share intimacy and pleasure is a powerful strategy to prevent relapse.

Couples do not decide to regress to a no-sex marriage. It is a result of benign neglect. It is easy to procrastinate, be diverted by other things, and fall into old habits. Sexuality often takes a back seat. While sexuality should not be the top priority in marriage, it should be a positive, integral component. Treating sexuality with benign neglect does not work. Sexual desire is like any other activity; if you ignore or avoid it, sexuality becomes self-conscious and uncomfortable. The positive feedback loop of anticipation, pleasurable experiences, and a regular sexual rhythm gives way to the negative feedback loop of anticipatory anxiety, tense and failed intercourse, and sexual avoidance. Anxiety and avoidance feed on themselves. Inhibition and avoidance need to be confronted and replaced by a regular rhythm of anticipation; intimacy; pleasuring; and erotic scenarios, including intercourse.

summary

You have come too far to relapse into a no-sex marriage. Confronting the sexual problem was a team effort. Maintaining and reinforcing intimacy and sexual pleasure likewise are team processes. Value intimacy and eroticism, recognize and avoid personal and couple traps, and ensure that a lapse does not become a relapse. Value GES and your couple sexual style.

Key Points

- You need to invest time, energy, and creativity to maintain an intimate, sexual, and satisfying relationship. You cannot take intimacy and sexuality for granted.

- Relapse prevention is an active individual and couple process. You need a specific, personally relevant plan to generalize gains and prevent relapse.
- By its nature, couple sexuality is variable and flexible. The most important issue is to accept disappointing or dysfunctional sexual experiences as normal but not allow this to lead to relapse. Value GES and take pride in being an intimate sexual couple.

CHAPTER 13

Intimate Attachment: Enhancing Your Bond

INTIMACY DATES ARE the single most important technique in maintaining a satisfying sexual bond. We have emphasized the importance of intimacy in overcoming sexual avoidance and the no-sex marriage. Intimacy dates are a powerful resource in preventing relapse and reinforcing marital satisfaction.

Both planned and spontaneous experiences are valuable. Most intimacy dates are planned and anticipated. Couples with children and jobs find that if they do not set aside couple time it does not happen. Enjoy spontaneous intimate times; they are special. However, do not put your marriage in jeopardy by being the romantic who devalues intentional and planned dates because you idealize spontaneity and natural feelings.

Sexual intimacy is like a garden: It requires consistent attention, planning, tending, and weeding. Similarly, intimacy requires the couple to deal with negative emotions and difficult issues. Intimacy is so much more than a "feel good" concept. Intimate couples share hurt and angry feelings as well as close and loving feelings. They deal with disappointments and problems as well as hopes and successes. Intimacy involves sharing a range of feelings and experiences, sexual and emotional. If sexual intimacy were dependent on each person always feeling positive, most couples would have a no-sex marriage. Emotional and sexual intimacy is anchored in knowing and accepting your partner, with her or his strengths and vulnerabilities and loving and disappointing characteristics (McCarthy & McCarthy, 2004). An advantage of an intimate sexual marriage is that you feel loved and accepted for who you really are, for both your positives and your vulnerabilities.

Intimacy dates range from a half-hour talk on the porch over a beer to a night out dancing or at a movie, a weekend at home without the children, or a couple trip to a resort for a week. Each couple has preferences for types of activities and places to stay. The core of quality intimate time is feeling close and involved, not the activities or places.

What is the relationship between intimacy dates and sexual dates? Intimacy dates can lead to intercourse, but that is not their chief reason. Intimate dates always involve emotional connection, usually involve affection, could include sensual activity, might transition to erotic feelings, and might involve intercourse and orgasm. Intimacy dates must not fall into a predictable, mechanical routine that always leads to sex.

Intimacy dates are inviting and facilitate anticipation. There is a range of ways to express feelings and a variety of potential outcomes. Closeness builds desire as long as there is not a spoken or unspoken expectation that it must lead to sex. Traditionally, this appeals to women, but increasingly men (especially over 40) appreciate the benefits of a nondemand approach to touching. It is possible (and desirable) to share intimacy without intercourse. It is also possible (and sometimes particularly exciting) to share sexuality without feeling emotionally intimate. Passionate, lustful sex adds spice to the marriage.

Most couples prefer an intimate foundation for sexuality. The prescription for maintaining sexual desire is integrating intimacy, nondemand pleasuring, and erotic scenarios. Couple sexuality works best when each person values both intimacy and eroticism.

We encourage weekly intimacy dates. If a couple goes more than 2 weeks without an intimate experience, that is a cue to reconnect. Otherwise, the risk of self-consciousness and avoidance grows and eventually leads to inhibited sexual desire (ISD). You cannot make up for lack of intimacy by having an intimate weekend every 3 months any more than you can make up for not regularly watering the garden by soaking it on occasion. Maintaining a regular rhythm of emotional and physical connection promotes sexual desire.

valuing marital intimacy

Traditionally, very different gender learnings and values were placed on intimacy. In the 1980s, "pop psych" books and talk shows focused on differences between women and men, treating them as if they were totally different species. Scientific studies found just the opposite; there are many more similarities than differences between women and men, including the desire for intimacy and sexual satisfaction (Hyde, 2005).

What distinguishes women and men is not their needs but their fears. Women and men share a need for both intimacy and sexuality. Men fear intimacy for two reasons. The first is that they will have to sacrifice autonomy, especially in regard to time and career. Their second fear is that intimacy is a ruse to criticize and coerce them to change. The fear women have about intimacy is giving up their sense of self to serve and protect the man. Too much of female self-esteem is tied to the nurturer–protector role. You are a healthier person and a better nurturer if you balance personal needs with the needs of others. Intimacy does not mean giving up yourself. Autonomy, including valuing your "sexual voice," facilitates genuine intimacy.

Intimacy involves openness in sharing positives and negatives without a hidden agenda to manipulate your spouse. Genuine intimacy allows both the man and the woman to value individuality and maintain self-esteem as an autonomous person. Change is based on a positive influence model, not on coercion or threats of abandonment.

Intimacy is key in maintaining emotional connection and serving as a bridge to sexual desire. Partners who care about each other will not allow sexuality to fade. Caring and trust set the stage for sexual risks—whether initiating sex in a new way, trying a different pleasuring scenario, experimenting with an intercourse variation, or integrating fantasies into an erotic scenario. Intimacy facilitates desire and satisfaction, which are more important than arousal and orgasm in maintaining a vital sexual bond (McCarthy & Wald, 2012).

intimacy dates at home

When couples think of dates, they think of going to dinner, a sporting event, a concert, or taking a weekend jaunt. These are fine, but the core of intimacy is expressing emotion and sexuality in everyday life where you live—at home. It costs less money but does not require less time, thought, or planning. It means having privacy—ensuring that children are asleep or at someone's house, the answering machine is on, the phone is off the hook, and you agree not to answer the door. It is crucial to be aware and receptive. Too often, couples relegate intimacy to bedtime, when they are tired and emotionally drained. Minimal contact cannot pass for quality couple time. Sleeping next to your spouse 7 nights a week does not mean that you share intimacy. Minimal contact deadens sexual desire. You are only half there; you may be emotionally present, but marginally involved. Boredom and routine subvert intimacy and anticipation, decreasing desire.

Intimacy dates can occur in the morning, afternoon, or early evening. They might involve a walk, sitting on the porch, having a drink and an appetizer, luxuriating in a sensuous bath, sitting at the kitchen table planning a couple or family vacation, or putting on your favorite music and dancing in the living room (with or without clothes). The intimacy date might focus on plans and hopes, sharing feelings, a sensual massage with a new lotion, disclosing a sensitive topic from the past, discussing an important family issue, problem solving a financial difficulty that is interfering with intimate feelings, or having fun playing a board or card game. It might be a time to be emotionally and physically close, or it can be a playful scenario you hope will evolve into a sexual encounter. Intimacy dates are different from the nitty-gritty interactions that involve kids, chores, money, house, and work. This is a special time for a quality emotional and/or physical connection.

intimacy dates outside the home

Emily enjoys being at home. Barry loves to go for day trips, to a play and dinner, and especially on a couple weekend trip. Intimacy dates outside the home are worthwhile to plan and anticipate. Emily jokes that half the fun of a weekend trip for Barry is anticipating, which he begins a month before. Although it is important to have activities with children, other couples, and families, intimacy dates are a one-on-one activity.

Intimacy dates can be elaborate, like a couple vacation that lasts a week or two. But more commonly they entail an evening date or a half-day outing. Although spontaneous dates are a special treat, most intimacy dates are planned. The key is not to fall into a predictable routine of doing the same thing, going to the same place, or talking about the same stuff. We both love movies, but if every date involved a movie, it would become stale. What about bowling or exploring a small town? Eating at an ethnic restaurant or attending community theater? Trying canoeing or horseback riding? Taking a hike in the mountains or having a picnic along the river? Sharing a story from childhood that you never told your spouse? Re-reading love letters you have not looked at in 10 years? If you usually stay at hotels, what about going to a rustic inn or a romantic bed and breakfast? What about the children staying overnight with friends while you go dancing and then come home for a sexual evening in the living room (a combination of an inside and outside date)?

One factor that makes marriage special is that you trust your spouse will not make fun of you when you take a risk that does not turn out well. We urge you to take psychological and sexual risks and try new things—a new restaurant, a new activity, disclosing a hope or dream, a new sexual scenario. If the food is a disaster, the activity is boring, the new idea terrible, the sexual scenario a dud, accept this. Your spouse will not blame or make fun of you. Intimacy is not just sharing close and good feelings; it is sharing disappointing and frustrating experiences.

RITA AND TONY

Sex was a problem throughout Rita and Tony's relationship. The best sex had been in the 8-month period prior to marriage, even though premarital sex had never been more frequent than twice a week and always took place at Tony's initiation. Rita suffered with ISD and was minimally involved, only occasionally aroused, and almost never orgasmic. Tony was angry and punishing when Rita said no to sexual overtures. The cycle of his anger and her avoidance was strongly ingrained. The only time they had frequent sex was when they were trying to get pregnant.

Rita and Tony were professionally and financially successful and enjoyed their two children. However, 9 years into the marriage, sexual frequency was four to six times per year. Sex was functional for Tony and not unpleasant for Rita. However, Tony's anger over lack of sexual frequency was a source of great marital stress. Rita's resentment of Tony's blaming escalated, as did her emotional alienation.

Couple sex therapy was not an easy process, but it was successful. Talking about the problem as a couple issue was the core strategy. Tony's backing off from sexual demands and anger allowed them the space to develop a comfortable couple sexual style. Tony established himself as Rita's intimate sexual friend, not her punishing critic. Rita developed an arousal–orgasm pattern that was different from those described in female sexuality books. Her response to sexual stimulation was rapid; slow pleasuring was counterproductive for her. Rita used a vibrator to enhance arousal, which quickly resulted in orgasm. Tony was supportive rather than feeling threatened or being judgmental.

A major breakthrough for Rita was making initiations and sharing her emotional and sexual conditions for a satisfying experience. Rita enjoyed being orgasmic, but orgasm was not her top factor for a fulfilling sexual life. What mattered was the emotional dimension. She needed to feel close to and open with Tony, without the hovering demand that all touching culminate in intercourse. Rita needed to feel desirable and turned on before stimulating Tony. She preferred to be orgasmic with Tony's manual stimulation or vibrator stimulation before beginning intercourse. Tony enjoyed afterplay (most males tune out sexually after reaching orgasm). Although Rita appreciated this, afterplay with a focus on orgasm did not fit her sexual style. For Rita, afterplay was for closeness, not sexual response. They developed afterplay scenarios that were playful and intimate, a crucial element in Rita's sense of sexual satisfaction.

Rita and Tony had established a vital, satisfying sexual bond and were committed to maintaining it. They had come too far and wanted to ensure there would not be a relapse. A prime component of their relapse prevention program was intimacy dates. The agreement was that one week Tony would initiate, the next week Rita would. This ping-pong system of initiation worked well.

Rita and Tony initiated very different intimacy dates. Almost all of Rita's initiations involved dates at home. Rita did not value pleasuring but did value emotional and affectionate attachment. Rita loved sitting on the screened-in porch with a glass of wine while Tony gave her a foot massage. They shared feelings about their lives and relationship with an understanding that they would not talk about children or finances during an intimacy date. Rita could spend up to 2 hours on the porch. She cared as much about listening to Tony's feelings and perceptions as about sharing her own. She enjoyed affectionate contact while talking, which facilitated closeness and attachment. Usually, the intimacy date ended with a kiss and getting on with their tasks. Sometimes, Rita would suggest they go upstairs and make love. Tony was intrigued by how quickly Rita would get aroused, a very different pattern than before sex therapy. Talking and affection on the porch were Rita's "foreplay." Once Rita was aroused she enjoyed stimulating Tony.

Tony's initiations were more varied. Most of his intimacy dates occurred out of the house. Tony loved going to clubs to listen to jazz. Other activities included canoeing and having a champagne picnic on the banks of the river or hiking up a hill and watching the sunset. Tony preferred a different style of touching. He was big on holding hands, playful touching, and kisses on the neck and ears. Tony loved to tell stories and construct fantasies (both about an ideal life and sexual fantasies). Rita found this entertaining and would weave her fantasies with his. Tony liked to play sexually in the car, which Rita found a turn-on as long as he remained attentive to driving. Tony initiated sex approximately 75 percent to 80 percent of the time, and usually Rita was open to it. If she was not, Tony accepted this and did not pout or punish, a dramatic improvement over the prior pattern.

Tony and Rita placed high value on spontaneous intimacy dates. Between two careers and two children, the opportunity seldom arose, but when possible it was special. On one spontaneous date, Tony came home early from work to take care of their ill son. An hour later, after the child had fallen asleep, Rita called, saying that her meeting was cancelled. Tony suggested that she come home. He would fix a salad, and they could have a glass of wine. It was fun playing hooky from work and responsibility. It was a relaxed, engaging hour—talking, being silly, and having sex before their boy awoke. He enjoyed seeing his parents together in the middle of the afternoon.

Rita emphasized the importance of intimacy for her sexual desire, and Tony accepted that emotional intimacy was valuable for their marriage. Closeness was key for Rita; playful touching was key for Tony. For some couples, intimate time is a good opportunity to discuss tough issues and sad situations and to resolve conflicts. This was not how Rita and Tony used intimacy dates. They focused on positive feelings, touching, and feeling attachment. Difficult issues and conflict resolution were dealt with in a different milieu, outside of their intimate time.

Tony did not need intimacy for sexual desire but accepted this need in Rita. An important component of a viable marriage is awareness of individual preferences for intimacy, touching, and eroticism. Accept this, rather than engaging in a "right–wrong" power struggle. Accepting and appreciating differences reinforces intimacy. Conflicts over differences no longer interfered with the couple's sexual intimacy. Trust that Tony was her intimate partner provided a powerful underpinning for Rita's sexual desire.

blocks to intimacy

A major block to intimate communication is based on gender socialization and misunderstanding. A significant fear in a man is that his wife will use intimacy as a cover to criticize and coerce him to change. A major female fear is that her husband will withhold intimacy as a way to punish her for sexual difficulties or for saying no to sex. This reflects the traditional gender socialization that males value sex and devalue feelings and that women value feelings and devalue sex. This simplistic dichotomy is reinforced by the media, pop psych books, and same-gender friends. Gender wars interfere with all kinds of male–female relationships, especially marriage. The more meaningful the relationship, the more destructive the rigid gender stereotypes.

Be aware of differences and vulnerabilities, but do not turn these into stereotypes and prejudices. Respect your partner's individuality. How can you work as an intimate sexual team to confront and reduce blocks, inhibitions, and anxieties?

Pop psych books advocate greater communication and intimacy—the more the better. This is a new psychological myth. Empirical research has identified four viable couple styles:

1. Best friend (soul mate)—the most intimate style
2. Emotionally expressive style
3. Complementary style
4. Traditional (conflict-minimizing) style—the least intimate

Which do you think is the most common couple style? It is the complementary couple style that balances individual autonomy with moderate amounts of intimacy. Who are the most stable (least likely to divorce) partners? Conflict-minimizing, traditional couples.

The relational couple style and the couple sexual style are not the same. The relational couple style refers to how the couple organizes their marriage, especially dealing with differences and conflicts. The couple sexual style refers to balancing each partner's sexual voice with being an intimate sexual team that integrates intimacy and eroticism. The concepts are not adversarial, but it is crucial that your couple sexual style promote sexual desire and satisfaction to energize the marital bond.

Our marriage is based on the complementary couple relational style and the best friend couple sexual style. However, the best friend sexual style is not the right fit for the majority of couples. The key to a satisfying, secure marriage is to establish a level of intimacy and a mutually acceptable way to deal with differences and conflicts. Sexual intimacy problems include extremes of too much intimacy (stifling individuality and causing enmeshment) or too little intimacy (causing a lack of connection that results in alienation). Each couple must find a level of sexual intimacy that promotes desire.

As intimacy increases, so does vulnerability. How vulnerable is each spouse comfortable being? For some people, intimacy means giving up emotional control. How does each person feel about control? Can you share control with your partner? What level of sexual intimacy fits best for you? How can intimacy facilitate sexual anticipation and desire? Some couples feel so emotionally close that they lose erotic feelings. Too much intimacy can smother desire. One of the most important balances in marriage is maintaining individual autonomy while sharing couple intimacy. Eroticism and intimacy are not adversarial dimensions; they are complementary and enhance satisfying couple sexuality.

Intimacy is only one bridge to desire. Playfulness, fantasy, erotic movies, tension release, teasing touching, and lust are other bridges. Most (but not all) couples find that intimacy dates are a vital link in enhancing sexual desire. Intimacy dates are most important for complementary and best friend couples.

Exercise: Intimacy Dates

Theory is one thing; implementation and practice are another. In this exercise, use the ping-pong system of initiation to establish a pattern of intimacy dates that facilitates sexual desire.

For a 2-month period (enough time to experiment and form an intimate pattern), the man initiates an intimacy date during his week and the woman initiates during her week. Each person explores his or her preferred style of expressing intimacy. Experiment with in-house and going-out dates; formal, planned dates and informal, spontaneous dates; dates that involve sexuality and dates that focus on feelings and affection; half hour dates and day dates; activity dates and talking dates. Develop a comfortable, inviting pattern. Be aware that there are three somewhat different styles: his, hers, and our intimacy styles. It is unusual for both people to have the exact same intimacy preferences. Yet, by definition, intimacy is a shared experience. Intimate couples accept and enjoy differences in styles and preferences. They do not insist that their style is superior.

After 2 months, share with your partner aspects of these intimacy dates that you appreciate and want to continue. If there is something about intimacy dates you find off-putting or counterproductive, disclose that along with a specific suggestion of how to make the date comfortable and inviting. How do you integrate intimacy so that sexual desire is enhanced? Being an intimate couple promotes desire, sexual satisfaction, and marital happiness.

for better or worse

The United States has the highest divorce rate among developed countries. Traditionally, stability was taken for granted, no matter what the quality of the marriage. People tolerated physically abusive, alcoholic, emotionally alienated, and dysfunctional marriages because of family, cultural, economic, and religious pressures to stay together. Destructive marriages continued "for the sake of the children" or the vow "for better or worse." No-sex marriages, low-sex marriages, sexually dysfunctional marriages, or marriages where intimacy needs were negated were tolerated. We are advocates for revitalizing marriage and reducing the divorce rate, but the pendulum should not swing back to the self-defeating ideology of staying in a destructive or fatally flawed marriage.

A healthy marriage involves satisfaction, stability, and sexuality. Successful marriages that survive a no-sex phase—whether this has been the case for 8 months or the marriage has not been consummated for 8 years—possess healthy sources of motivation. These include supporting each other through difficult times, being good parents, sharing a dream of a house or a business, dealing with a chronic problem in a supportive manner, overcoming poverty or alcoholism, receiving care and support from extended family, and having a religious or spiritual commitment to the marriage. You have a sense of pride in having survived and thrived.

Often, the couple maintains a genuinely intimate, if not sexual, bond. Enjoying affection and physical closeness while maintaining respect and trust form a solid base from which to revitalize sexual intimacy. Religious or spiritual beliefs anchor the marital bond for many couples. These are positive prognostic signs for overcoming a no-sex marriage. You have persevered through better and worse.

How can intimacy reinforce good experiences and feelings while buffering the couple when problems recur? A prime function of intimacy is to nurture the marital bond and generate special feelings. This is very different from "romantic love" feelings that are celebrated in songs, movies, and novels. The promise of romantic love is that there will be only better, not worse. Romantic-love couples do not survive a no-sex period.

Intimate couples have a special feeling about surviving a painful time. A sign of a viable marriage is the ability to cope with crisis and loss without destroying the bond of respect, trust, and intimacy. Intimate feelings are badly stressed by ISD. But as long as a sense of intimacy remains, sexual desire can be revitalized. You do not want to again stress your marital bond, and intimacy dates are a powerful strategy to prevent relapse. When you value your spouse and marriage, it is hard to deny and avoid sexual issues. The function of sexual intimacy is to energize the marital bond. Intimacy has the protective function of not allowing the couple to ignore or avoid core issues, including sexuality.

Intimacy dates are not sufficient to promote sexual desire, but they do establish a base for attachment. For many couples, intimacy dates are the easiest bridge to sexual desire. For example, the couple talks over a cup of coffee or while gardening. After sharing a special time together, it is easier to initiate sex later that day. You can have a drink on the deck or put on music and dance—an intimate way of being together that flows into a sexual encounter.

Couples who are separated by business travel find intimacy dates a more successful way to reconnect than having intercourse. It is harder to turn on sexually when you feel emotionally unconnected. A passionate coming together works better for unmarried than for married couples (or maybe that is just in the movies). Intimacy dates provide a means to feel emotionally connected and enjoy affectionate touch. This can lead to a sexual encounter that day or the next. Both emotionally and physically, intimacy serves a bridging function. When Barry returns from a work trip, it is rare for us to be sexual that night. Typically, the next morning we have an intimacy date—go for a walk or bike ride and then out to breakfast. This serves as a bridge to being sexual later that day or the next.

summary

Overcoming a no-sex marriage and revitalizing sexual desire almost invariably include increased intimacy. One of the best ways to ensure that you will maintain and generalize sexual gains is to recognize and reinforce the vital role of emotional and sexual intimacy. A key is to recognize that not all intimacy can or should result in intercourse. Intimacy is a prime bridge for sexual desire, but that is not its major function. Time to emotionally share, touch, enjoy, and experience sensuality is crucial in maintaining a satisfying marriage. Intimacy is not the sole bridge to sexual desire, but it is an important bridge. Intimacy dates can be planned or spontaneous, at home or away, initiated by one spouse or mutually, and involve half an hour or a whole weekend. Some intimacy dates are nonphysical, some affectionate, some sensual, some playful, some erotic, and some include intercourse. Intimacy dates are a prime means to generalize gains and prevent relapse.

Key Points

- Intimacy provides the solid foundation for a sexual marriage.
- Having an intimate attachment in good times and bad is a prime component of a satisfying, secure marriage.
- Intimacy dates have value in themselves as well as serving as a bridge to sexual desire.

CHAPTER 14

The Erotic Marriage: Lusting for Life

CAN MARRIED SEX be erotic? We hope we successfully answered that question in Chapter 11, "Creating Erotic Scenarios." Can marriage remain erotic? Not only can it, but maintaining an erotic marriage is in your best interest so that sexuality energizes and makes your marital bond special. Much of this book has focused on intimacy, nondemand pleasuring, and bridges to sexual desire. Intimacy, anticipation, touch, and pleasure are the bedrock for generalizing and reinforcing sexual gains. However, they are not enough. Eroticism is integral to sexual satisfaction and relapse prevention.

People associate "hot" or "passionate" sex with a new, intense, illicit relationship—a premarital or extramarital affair. These are powerful but unstable, transitory sexual experiences. "Hot" sex connotes the "fun but dirty" approach of X-rated movies, sex shops, and non-socially acceptable exploits. Eroticism is associated with premarital sex, extramarital sex, and kinky sex. Is it naive to believe that married sex can remain erotic? We are convinced—theoretically, empirically, and in our lives—that sex in an intimate marriage can be creative, erotic, and satisfying. Keeping marital sex erotic is a powerful strategy for preventing relapse. Ideally, the foundation is an emotionally intimate, secure marital bond, including a solid involvement with nondemand pleasuring

(Metz & McCarthy, 2012). Erotic scenarios and techniques are the crucial additional ingredients that promote desire, arousal, orgasm, and vitality.

It is not technique alone—or even primarily—that eroticizes sexuality. Eroticism is enhanced by spontaneity, playfulness, experimentation, and above all awareness of feelings and openness to creative expression.

An erotic marriage is based on three sources: awareness of feelings, thoughts, and fantasies; a dynamic process between you and your partner that includes touching, teasing, and seductiveness; and openness to experimenting with erotic scenarios and techniques. Be aware of sexual feelings and desires, and take the risk to play them out. Do not worry about performing to the standard of a Hollywood movie or porn video. Share and value the special turn-ons of eroticism.

For marital sex to remain vital, you need to challenge routine and mechanical sex, which is the death knell for desire. Eroticism calls for creativity, energy, and expression. Eroticism cannot be taken for granted. It must be actively cultivated. Be aware of erotic feelings, thoughts, fantasies, and scenarios. Eroticism elicits sexual desire and builds anticipation. Touching, teasing, unpredictability, and seductiveness are enticing, adding spice and adventure to couple sexuality. Romantic, seductive, and playful touch is not reserved for premarital or extramarital affairs; it is an integral component of marital sex. The core of erotic marriage is openness to a variety of sexual scenarios and techniques, which builds anticipation. Whether this occurs once a month or seven times a year, sharing creative, erotic scenarios allows you to be a vital sexual couple. This is a powerful antidote against regressing to a no-sex relationship.

the myth behind extramarital affairs

Cultural attitudes toward extramarital affairs are schizophrenic, On one hand, affairs are viewed as immoral and a reason to terminate the marriage; on the other hand, they are perceived as seductive, erotic, and a way to break out of the doldrums of marriage. On daytime soap operas, marriage is a kiss of death. The couple is either written off the show or has an affair to generate excitement and drama. Affairs add tension, conflict, and suspense to novels and movies. Without the torment of affairs, country music would lose its best-selling theme.

Sometimes the crisis leading to a no-sex marriage is the discovery of an extramarital affair. The most effective therapeutic strategy is to deal with the meaning of the affair; rebuild the trust bond; and develop a new couple sexual style featuring strong, resilient sexual desire. Most couples make a firm commitment not to have another affair. If a potential high-risk situation arises, the partner agrees to discuss it beforehand with his or her spouse. This is a powerful technique for confronting a potential affair. People talk about an affair in terms of being "swept away" by romantic or lustful feelings. With the technique we advocate, you and your partner make a planned decision in choosing to have or not have an affair. This means assuming responsibility for your sexual behavior. Discussing the meaning of a potential affair with your spouse raises consequences for you and the marriage. You do not just fall into a secretive affair.

Couples who value intimacy, security, and sexual desire are advised against extramarital affairs. Affairs have a high potential to subvert your marital bond, especially for traditional and soul mate couple styles. Affairs are most easily accepted by emotionally expressive couples who value making their own rules.

Why are affairs erotic? Can you expect the same type of eroticism from marital sex? Extramarital affairs are erotic in the same way that premarital affairs are. Newness, illicitness, adventure, quest for acceptance, and excitement of the unknown drive an affair. By their nature, affairs are sexually powerful but unstable. When the partners move in together or marry, the sexual charge dissipates. Stability and security disrupt the eroticism. Erotic affairs have a high risk of turning into no-sex marriages.

Affairs and marriage are different experiences. There are three erotic strategies that married couples can learn from affairs—although you do not have to have an affair to gain these insights: (1) the value of anticipation; (2) the importance of fantasy and of planning a sexual encounter; and (3) the sexuality-enhancing effects of playfulness, creativity, and unpredictability. An example is people who meet at a hotel for an afternoon sexual tryst. Both partners set aside the time, have someone cover for them at work or for child emergencies, are assertive enough to ask for the day rate, and fantasize about and anticipate the sexual encounter. This is not the "natural, spontaneous sex" of movies and soap operas. Yet it is very erotic.

Why should this be the domain of unmarried people? If you are married, you do not have to pay for a hotel room; you can meet for an afternoon delight at home. On the other hand, why not meet your spouse at a hotel? A new setting can be erotic. Couples can go to a rustic inn, a bed and breakfast, or an X-rated motel. One reason that sex is better on vacations or weekends away is that this allows you to be sexual in a new environment. Anticipating this getaway builds sexual desire. Some people (Barry is a good example) very much enjoy fantasizing and looking forward to an intimate sexual weekend. The setting and milieu facilitate special, erotic feelings. You can feel playful, creative, and free to let go. Creative, erotic sex can be maintained in a marriage. You do not need an affair.

Exercise: Maintaining an Erotic Marriage

A good way to revitalize eroticism in your relationship is to review the exercise from Chapter 11. What did each person identify as special turn-ons? What were favorite erotic scenarios and techniques? Do these continue to elicit anticipation and desire? Be clear with your partner about how to integrate eroticism into lovemaking so that it remains special. Are there erotic scenarios and techniques that previously elicited sexual desire but no longer do so? Don't be embarrassed; this is normal. Sexual techniques that felt erotic 5 years ago may now feel "worn out," even boring or mechanical. Not only can you drop these scenarios, we urge you to. Boring, routine, minimally involved sex subverts and eventually can destroy desire. Even if the sex is functional, it does not enhance vitality or satisfaction.

To maintain a creative, erotic marriage, put time and energy into sexuality. Each partner suggests at least one and preferably two special turn-ons to experiment with during the next 6 months. Be clear and specific (writing it first makes it easier to discuss). Do not just say, "I want to try oral sex in the morning"; say, "I want us to shower the night before, and I want you to wake me by orally stimulating me." Do not say, "Be passive"; say, "Let me control this sexual scenario; put your hands behind your head, or I can tie your hands with a silk scarf." Do not say, "Be natural"; say, "I want to try a sexual experience where we don't talk. Let's share eroticism through eye contact, movement, and touch."

Each partner initiates at least one and up to three erotic scenarios. This could include a major external stimulus like planning a couple weekend, buying a DVD for the bedroom so that you can watch erotic videos, getting a hot tub, or going on a camping trip and being sexual under the stars. More commonly, it is a nitty-gritty addition such as having a pillow with a message of "tonight" on one side and "sorry" on the other; a special light or scented candle in the bedroom; being sexual in the shower or bathtub; or using a vibrator, beads, or feathers for erotic play.

A common form of creative sexuality is a bimonthly sexual date, with freedom to play sensually and erotically, but with a prohibition on intercourse. Many couples find that this is their most sexually fun time. You can experiment with alternative pleasuring positions, a new lotion, music, a different time of day, varying amounts of light, different types of clothing, one partner giving pleasuring or mutual pleasuring to orgasm, or being turned on but not going to orgasm. Sexual dates (whether planned or spontaneous) allow you to experiment with personal and external turn-ons to facilitate eroticism.

The essence of creative sexuality is creating a special intimacy, sharing yourself emotionally and sexually—sometimes being warm, sometimes erotic, sometimes fun, sometimes lustful. Sexuality is more than genitals, intercourse, and orgasm. Creative sexuality is usually mutual, with each partner contributing to the erotic scenario. Mutuality requires both verbal and nonverbal communication. When thoughts, feelings, and sexual expression flow, each partner's arousal enhances the other's. This is an extension of the "give to get" pleasuring guideline—giving and sharing eroticism.

Couples have a favorite room (or rooms) for creative sexuality. For some, it is the bedroom; for others, it is the den, the living room, in front of the fireplace, or the guest room. Unlike in other exercises, we advise against designing a specific scenario.

Be open to your creative feelings. Let the sexual scenario be as free and playful as possible. Experiment with a multitude of positions—standing, lying, kneeling, or sitting. In creative sexuality, there are no artificial barriers between sex play and intercourse. Allow creative eroticism to flow into creative intercourse. Experiment with positions, multiple stimulation during intercourse, expressing feelings, and making erotic requests. Intermix intercourse and erotic sexuality. Creative sexuality does not end with orgasm. Enjoy afterplay. You can express affectionate, sensual, romantic, and playful feelings verbally and nonverbally.

JOHN AND JENNY

The fact that John and Jenny were married with a 2-year-old daughter and that Jenny was 5 months pregnant was a tribute to their love, commitment, and persistence. They had met 15 years previously as sophomores at a state university, a romantic college couple. There was plenty of playfulness, romanticism, and eroticism. The quality of sex might not have been great, but it was frequent and exciting.

In the 5 years after college, John and Jenny were an on-again, off-again couple. The emotional turmoil of breaking up and getting back together provided drama and intrigue that allowed them to ignore intimacy issues. Jealousy and comparisons inherent in dating others provided an emotional and sexual charge. At 27 they began living together, and 3 years later, they married. This dating and relationship pattern was common for their peer group. Another unfortunate commonality was that the best sex they experienced was while dating. Living together did not improve couple sexuality.

They married despite a poor sexual relationship. In the first 4 years of marriage, they had intercourse less than 25 times. Throughout living together and being married, they had been a no-sex couple. Jenny had an affair in the 2nd year of the marriage. Contrary to popular mythology, affairs are most likely to occur early, not late, in marriage (Allen et al., 2005). It was a brief affair with a married man from work. When John heard rumors of the affair, he was agitated but not surprised. There was anger but more angst, with feelings of guilt and blaming. A side effect of the affair was that John and Jenny totally stopped marital sex, which had been marginal anyway. For some couples, an affair is a wake-up call, an opportunity to revitalize intimacy and sexuality. For John and Jenny, it added to marital alienation, serving as another reason to avoid sex.

They had tried individual, marital, and couples group therapy. Individual therapy had been particularly valuable to John, challenging his depressive view of life and encouraging him to take career risks and switch to an organization that rewarded his innovative ideas. Marriage therapy and couples group therapy served to normalize their struggles and reinforce that they were a viable couple. Unfortunately, it reinforced the mistaken view that sex would improve only when all the other emotional and marital issues had been dealt with. For the majority of couples, the optimal strategy is to address sexual issues concurrently with emotional and relational issues (McCarthy & Thestrup, 2008b).

It is easier to conduct sex therapy with a committed couple than with a tenuous couple. John and Jenny entered sex therapy with a great deal of marital commitment but with self-defeating sexual attitudes and feelings. They were an affectionate couple but not an erotic couple.

The structure of nondemand pleasuring exercises, followed by erotic psychosexual skill exercises, was of great value. Jenny was responsive to the permission-giving aspects of sex therapy, especially experimenting with erotic scenarios and techniques. She was turned on by playing out scenarios in which she was the dominant partner. John was responsive and aroused by Jenny's arousal; her sexuality was an aphrodisiac for him. Jenny was afraid that to maintain erotic feelings, she would have to exaggerate the dominance scenarios, something she was not interested in. The therapist suggested that they continue to use erotic scenarios with a dominance theme but broaden them rather than make them extreme. Each spouse had a right to veto anything that was psychologically or sexually uncomfortable. The core theme was not to do anything sexually at the expense of their partner or the relationship.

For John, the best way to maintain eroticism was by setting aside time for sexual dates. John enjoyed varied sexual experiences: sex in a hotel, sex at the in-laws' house (especially in the living room during the middle of the night), sex under the stars on a camping trip, sex in the middle of the day. Jenny could appreciate this, but for her eroticism was closer to home. Jenny felt that for sex to be an integral, vital part of the marriage, they had to be erotic at home with the reality of her pregnancy. Jenny would awaken early because of pressure on her bladder. If she could not go back to sleep, she would awaken John by sucking on his penis; she enjoyed seeing him in the combination state of arousal and drowsiness. She liked the quickie intercourse of woman on top, where she did the thrusting. John was orgasmic and went back to sleep. Jenny cuddled against him, which allowed her to fall asleep.

People do not think of pregnancy as erotic, but maintaining emotional, affectionate, and sexual contact during pregnancy is important. The birth of a second child is a major transition for the marriage and family. Maintaining sexual vitality was a priority for Jenny and John. Jenny found the sitting–kneeling intercourse position particularly erotic and fulfilling. She looked forward to the third trimester to use this again. Jenny sat on a low-slung chair with a pillow for back support and scooted to the end. There was no pressure on her stomach or on the fetus. John knelt in front of her with pillows under his knees for support, his penis at the same height as her vulva. This position allowed eye contact, kept both hands free for touching, and offered the ability to kiss and caress and engage in multiple erotic stimulation. John gave clitoral and breast stimulation, and Jenny did testicle and buttock stimulation. They planned to continue to use this position after the baby was born.

If Jenny did not feel like being sexual herself, she pleasured John to orgasm. Jenny enjoyed one-way (asynchronous) sex. Feeling control over John's arousal and watching him just before orgasm was gratifying. John preferred mutual sex but found asynchronous sex erotic. John and Jenny felt more intimately connected than during the first pregnancy.

With two young children and two careers, they realize it will be a challenge to maintain a quality sexual relationship, but it is a challenge they are prepared to meet. Erotic scenarios and techniques are not the core of their intimate relationship but an important component in keeping sexual desire vibrant. John and Jenny value intimacy, nondemand pleasuring, and eroticism.

special sexual experiences

Should every sexual experience be special? That is a self-defeating expectation. Even for well-functioning couples, less than half of encounters involve equal desire, pleasure, and eroticism. Positive, realistic expectations promote sexual satisfaction. In truth, 40 percent to 50 percent of sexual experiences are very good for both partners; of these, 5 percent to 10 percent are special. If you have one or two special sexual experiences a month, you can count yourselves lucky. This is quite a different way of thinking from the way sex is portrayed in movies or soap operas, where it is always perfect and special. These concepts will not sell songs or movies, but they fit the reality for married and partnered couples and enhance sexual satisfaction.

What makes a sexual experience special? It is the feelings, not the technique or the orgasm. Sometimes feelings are intensely sexual—a hot and lustful erotic flow, letting go, experiencing sexual abandon, feeling free. Sometimes feelings are intensely intimate—loving, close, full of pride in overcoming inhibitions, self-validating, reflecting deep satisfaction with your partner and relationship. Special sexual experiences energize your bond like a shot of adrenaline. If each encounter were highly erotic, it would not feel special.

Creative sexuality is sometimes a special experience, sometimes very good, sometimes satisfactory, and sometimes a bust. We encourage couples to take sexual risks, but there are no guarantees the risk will result in a special erotic experience or even a successful one. This is not to discourage creative sexuality. You will not have special erotic experiences unless you are willing to take sexual risks.

An advantage of an intimate relationship is that you can risk failure without being embarrassed or frightened of your partner's reaction. Trust in your partner allows you to share feelings, your body, and eroticism. This results in intense, creative experiences and special sexual encounters. At other times it results in failure—we hope with the ability to laugh at or shrug off stupid or silly experiences.

Intimacy and erotic feelings are more important than the sex itself. Couples feel closer and more open during pleasuring and afterplay than during intercourse. An insight from one of Barry's clients was that "intercourse and orgasm are great, but they're only a small part of making love. For us, a special part of sex is taking a walk and talking afterward." Afterplay is an integral component of lovemaking. Integration of erotic and intimate feelings facilitates encounters that you remember for months and even years.

making requests for special turn-ons

How can you make clear, erotic requests without these becoming self-conscious demands? One technique is to separate verbal requests from sexual encounters. One of the worst times to talk sex is in bed right after a sexual experience. You do not need an instant replay with a detailed critique. Some of the best places to talk sex are on walks, in the car during a long drive, sitting on the porch, or over coffee at the kitchen table. Some of the best times are the day before a sexual encounter, an hour before a sexual date, the next morning, and the day before going away for a couple weekend. Make requests for special turn-ons in a comfortable, anticipatory manner that invites your partner to be open, experimental, and playful.

The main miscommunication regarding sexual turn-ons is that your partner feels pressure to perform and give you exactly what you want. Rather than a sexual sharing, it feels like a command performance. To stay away from that trap, be clear that your request is to engage with your spouse so that pleasure and eroticism are enhanced. Experience this together; be open to your partner's feelings and desires. Direct or indirect coercion has no place in couple sexuality.

Special turn-ons keep your sexual relationship vital and exciting. Marital sexuality is different from premarital sex or extramarital affairs. Special turn-ons involve experimentation and playfulness and promote integration of intimacy, pleasuring, and eroticism. Some turn-ons remain vital for 20 years or longer. More commonly, the couple adds or revises sexual scenarios and turn-ons so that they retain their erotic capacity. It is like cooking a special meal; over time you can spice up the ingredients.

Creative sexuality and special turn-ons are not the same but are complementary. Both require openness to your own and your partner's feelings. Both require taking risks and making requests. Because special turn-ons are specific and planned, there is potential for awkwardness, self-consciousness, and performance pressure. If you value an erotic marriage, experimenting with special turn-ons and encouraging your partner to be an involved sexual friend are crucial. This is the best way to combat self-consciousness.

Creative sexuality is a team effort. Although it is common for some experiences to be more erotic for one partner than for the other, your arousal and involvement act as an aphrodisiac for your spouse. This is another example of the "give to get" pleasuring guideline. Your arousal will increase your partner's arousal. When a man was 20, his arousal was autonomous, needing nothing from his partner. Beginning in his mid-30s and increasing with age, male arousal is enhanced by the woman's arousal. For many couples in their 50s and beyond, female arousal is easier and more predictable than male arousal. The woman's special turn-ons are good not only for her but for him and their sexual relationship.

The prescription for healthy sexuality—integrating intimacy, non-demand pleasuring, and erotic scenarios and techniques—reaches fruition as the couple matures. The importance of creative sexuality and special turn-ons increases with both the age of the couple and the age of the marriage.

summary

Bridges to sexual desire, intimacy dates, and nondemand pleasuring are major strategies to maintain healthy couple sexuality. The importance of erotic scenarios and techniques cannot be underestimated. Seeing yourselves as an erotic couple and enjoying erotic flow and orgasm play integral roles in maintaining a sexually vital relationship. Erotic dates keep sex special and energize your intimate bond. Creative sexuality and special turn-ons ignite your sexual relationship. Eroticism is not the core of sexual desire, but it is an integral component. You, your spouse, and your relationship benefit greatly when you make the effort to maintain an erotic marriage.

Key Points

- Contrary to media and cultural myths, you can maintain a creative, unpredictable, playful, and vital erotic marriage.
- Lustful and erotic scenarios complement intimacy and pleasuring.
- You owe it to yourself, your partner, and your relationship to continue to experiment with erotic scenarios and techniques.

CHAPTER 15

Valuing Couple Sexuality

INHIBITED SEXUAL DESIRE (ISD) and a no-sex marriage pose a major threat to relational satisfaction and viability. When sexuality is pleasurable and functional, it is a positive, integral part of marriage but not a dominant factor—contributing 15 percent to 20 percent to relational vitality and satisfaction. The main functions of couple sexuality are to create shared pleasure, deepen and reinforce intimacy, and act as a tension reducer to cope with the stresses of life and marriage. Sexuality energizes and makes your bond special. Sex that is dysfunctional, inhibited, or nonexistent plays an inordinately powerful negative role, becoming 50 percent to 70 percent of the relationship, draining intimacy and threatening stability. Paradoxically, bad sex has a more powerful negative role in a relationship than good sex has a positive role.

This book has presented concepts, strategies, techniques, guidelines, psychosexual skill exercises, and case studies to help you understand and confront ISD. Knowledge and awareness are necessary but not sufficient to address the complex problem of the no-sex relationship. Intimacy and sexuality are best understood as a couple issue. It is crucial to maintain motivation so that the problem is resolved and sexual desire revitalized.

221

Once the self-defeating pattern of the no-sex marriage is broken, do not be passive and expect sexuality to take care of itself. Your sexual relationship needs continual thought, communication, energy, and time. We have been married for 47 years and still need to devote time and energy to maintaining sexuality as a positive, integral part of our lives and relationship. A desirous, pleasurable, erotic, and satisfying sexuality energizes your bond. Intimacy and sexuality keep your relationship vital and special.

Couples with a satisfying sexual relationship and no dysfunction still have to put time and energy into sexuality. The movie, media, love song, and fiction approach to sexuality sells products but leads to self-defeating, unrealistic expectations. Acceptance of sexual variability and flexibility helps you maintain positive, realistic expectations. Your comfort with and anticipation of sexuality and the belief that you deserve sexual pleasure are the bedrock of couple sexual desire.

You cannot wait for everything to be perfect before you become open to being sexual. Do not expect every experience to be earth-shaking. Mutual desire, arousal, orgasm, and satisfaction are ideal, but in truth, sex is not always equal or mutual. The quality of your intimate sexual experience is more important than frequency of intercourse. Do not allow sex to fade away. Keep your intimate connection intact with touching that occurs both inside and outside the bedroom. Sometimes it is affectionate touch, sometimes sensual touch, sometimes playful touch, sometimes erotic touch, sometimes intercourse touch. Both partners must be committed to maintaining a vital sexual bond. Try to go no longer than 2 weeks without some kind of sexual contact. Sex cannot be taken for granted or treated with benign neglect. Sexuality requires time, mindful awareness, communication, and energy.

If this is true for couples who have no sexual problems, it is crucial for couples with a history of ISD. Maintaining a vital sexual bond and preventing relapse are individual and couple commitments. When sexuality functions as a shared pleasure, a means to reinforce intimacy, and a tension reducer to deal with the stresses of life and marriage, you have a powerful relationship resource. When you maintain an intimate sexual connection through good and bad times, you can be confident (although do not become overconfident) that sexuality will continue to enhance and energize your bond.

how much intimacy? how much sexuality?

In Chapter 6, we discussed couple sexual styles (complementary, traditional, soul mate, and emotionally expressive). Each partner helps develop and individualize the chosen sexual style. A crucial dimension is finding a mutually comfortable level of intimacy. Lack of intimacy and not valuing the marriage are self-defeating. However, the opposite is not true. People who say the only thing that matters in life is marriage and give up individuality for coupleness, strive for intimacy at the cost of personal well-being, or believe that sex six times a week is more important than anything else are setting themselves up for failure. The key is to find a healthy balance between autonomy and intimacy. More intimacy is not necessarily better. This also holds true for sexuality. Being sexual six times a week is not better than being sexual twice a week. For some couples frequent sex is an impulsive, compulsive, destructive pattern that subverts their relationship.

How does a couple reach a comfortable understanding about intimacy? It is easier to say what not to do. Do not elevate intimacy to becoming a test of marriage. Do not sacrifice individuality. Do not confuse intimacy and intercourse. Do not treat intimacy solely as a "feel good" concept. What promotes intimate sexuality? Each partner must honestly ask herself or himself what the healthiest balance is between autonomy and coupleness. This is not a matter of being "politically correct" or giving the "socially desirable" response but determining what best fits each individual and the relationship so that sexuality energizes their bond.

In our marriage we share almost all thoughts and feelings about psychological, relational, and sexual issues. We have a female friend whose parents had a bitter divorce in which emotional secrets were exposed during a hostile divorce litigation. Although she trusts her husband and is committed to the marriage, she does not share emotionally sensitive issues with him (she does discuss these with female friends). We also have a couple of friends who share a great deal emotionally, relationally, sexually, and parentally. However, their financial lives, especially investments and retirement funds, are handled separately. Theirs is a strongly held philosophical position. They do not respect partners who are dependent on one another financially (which includes us). A last example is a couple in which the man travels extensively on business and is out of town at least half the time. Their agreement is that when they are together, their relationship is a priority. When apart, they have separate lives, which includes not asking questions about what they do or how they spend their time. Many married couples (including us) would find this unacceptable, but it has worked well for this couple.

Each person needs to ascertain whether there are prerogatives and feelings he or she will keep separate from the marital bond. We advocate telling your spouse about this parameter, but many people prefer that it remain implicit. We suggest two guidelines. First, be sure that maintaining autonomy in this area is in your best interest, not a defensive or avoidant response. Second, be sure that this parameter does not undermine your spouse or couple sexuality. Your challenge is to integrate autonomy and intimacy in a manner that facilitates self-esteem and sexuality. Psychological well-being is enhanced by valuing both self-esteem and an intimate sexual marriage. These are complementary, not antagonistic.

Autonomy involves individual needs, preferences, and desires. Intimacy involves couple emotions, understandings, and agreements, thus establishing a comfortable, nurturing level of attachment. Do you want a "soul mate" level of sexual intimacy? This is the cultural ideal and the model we have adopted in our marriage, with our variation of being intimate and sexual friends. However, it is not the right model for the majority of couples. This is especially true for couples with a history of ISD. Often the sexual problem is compounded by unrealistically high expectations about intimacy, which results in hurt, anger, blaming, and devaluing the relationship and sexuality.

Striving for the maximum amount of intimacy is the wrong strategy for most couples. A healthier strategy is to develop a comfortable level of intimacy that balances autonomy and coupleness. Be sure that this level of intimacy enhances sexual desire. For many couples, intimacy is the main bridge to desire; for others, intimacy is a lesser factor. What is comfortable and healthy for you, emotionally and sexually?

accepting and valuing

A common cultural myth is that women value marriage and men value sex. Marriages are healthier when the man and woman value both emotional and sexual intimacy. The culture and media emphasize gender differences, even gender wars. This is not scientifically true, nor does it promote marital or sexual satisfaction (Hyde, De Lamater, & Hewitt, 1998). Relationships in which both partners value intimacy and both value sexuality do not regress to a no-sex state.

Divorce is hard on both men and women, but contrary to popular mythology it is more difficult for men. Physical and mental health for never-married or divorced men is poorer than for married men. Men are more likely to remarry than are women. The data are clear. Men need marriage. If that is so, why is it that men do not put a high value on marriage? Valuing one's wife and marital sexuality is not part of the masculine image. Men in second marriages are more likely to value their current marriage than are men in first marriages (McCarthy & McCarthy, 2006). Valuing a marriage is not contingent on your spouse or your marriage being perfect. Valuing means that you accept, respect, and care about your spouse and your marriage, with its strengths and vulnerabilities, special characteristics, and weaknesses.

Contrary to cultural myths, women value sexuality as much as men do (Heiman et al., 2011). One reason that sex therapy is more accepted by women is its emphasis on broad-based sensual and sexual expression, integrating intimacy and eroticism. Valuing touch—affectionate, sensual, playful, erotic, and intercourse—goes a long way toward building and maintaining sexual desire. A major barrier to valuing sexuality was the woman's belief that sex had to be on the man's terms—that "real sex is intercourse and orgasm." We are strong advocates of intercourse and orgasm, but there is more to "real sex" than that. The core of sexuality is giving and receiving pleasure-oriented touching. Desire, pleasure, eroticism, and satisfaction are more important than intercourse and orgasm.

Sexuality is not like money. There is no competition in which there is one objective measure, and one wins or loses. Sexuality is not a zero-sum game. Sexuality involves an integration of attitudes, behaviors, and feelings. At its core, sexuality is a couple concept rather than an individual concept. Sexual satisfaction is based on subjective feelings—not on frequency of intercourse or number of orgasms. The more you accept the importance of broad-based sexuality—the Good Enough Sex (GES) model—the stronger your bond will be. This inoculates you against sexual dysfunction and ISD as you and your relationship age.

the importance of being an intimate sexual team

Valuing intimate sexuality and accepting broad-based sexuality—especially having a variable, flexible sexual repertoire that includes affectionate, sensual, playful, erotic, and intercourse touch—are crucial. The intimate team concept is the core factor in maintaining a healthy sexual bond. A major roadblock is the traditional male–female double standard. The male is afraid that accepting the team approach is giving in to his partner, that it makes him less of a man, and that the result will be less intercourse and fewer orgasms. He resentfully holds on to the narrow definition of sex as intercourse. Barry heard a male client say, "We haven't had sex in 3 years, so she owes me 156 orgasms." What a self-defeating approach!

Sexuality is integral to who you are as a man, a woman, and a couple. The issue is how to express affection, sensuality, playfulness, eroticism, and intercourse so that these promote desire and satisfaction. When you value touching and being an intimate sexual team, you will have a vital, satisfying, secure marriage.

These concepts are of particular value for individuals with a history of negative or traumatic sexual experiences. These include childhood sexual abuse, incest, rape, sexual humiliation or rejection, a painful divorce, sexual harassment, an unwanted pregnancy, sexually transmitted infection, and guilt over masturbation or fantasies. Feeling responsible for sexuality in the context of an intimate relationship is validating. You no longer feel victimized and controlled by past trauma. You are a proud survivor who deserves sexual pleasure. Sexuality enhances your life and intimate relationship. One of the most healing and healthy cognitions is "living well is the best revenge."

Negative sexual experiences or traumatic incidents can occur in childhood, adolescence, young adulthood, or adulthood. It happens to men as well as women. ISD and a no-sex marriage compound past negative sexual experiences. Take responsibility for your sexuality, take pride in being a survivor, trust that your spouse is your intimate sexual friend, enjoy touching and pleasure, and see sexuality as something that enhances your life and relationship. Intimate sexuality is a personal victory and source of pride for the survivor and the relationship (Maltz, 2012).

Negative experiences affect couples, not just individuals. Couples with a history of alienation, drug or alcohol abuse, affairs and distrust, separation and threats, physical or emotional abuse, or sexual coercion take pride in overcoming these problems and becoming an intimate, secure sexual couple. These painful experiences would have destroyed less caring, committed partners. Surviving the bad times and developing a satisfying sexual marriage is a source of personal and couple pride.

On the other hand, abusive or destructive marriages are not worth maintaining. A marriage that negates one or both partners' psychological and sexual well-being should be ended, not saved.

You have worked as an intimate sexual team to address, understand, and change destructive emotional and sexual patterns. You could not do this alone; you needed the support and involvement of your partner. Together, you have revitalized your relationship. Reestablishing intimacy and sexuality is a couple task. This is even truer in maintaining an intimate, sexually satisfying marriage. When both partners value intimacy and eroticism, sexual desire and satisfaction are reinforced.

accepting nonperfect sexuality

Barry's clinical work has convinced him that no couple has a perfect marriage or a perfect sex life. One of Emily's pet peeves with self-help books is that they overpromise a perfect solution for everyone. This is intimidating and makes partners less accepting of their relationship and couple sexuality. Our joke is that because we do not have a perfect marriage or perfect sex, why should anyone else?

All relationships have strengths and vulnerabilities, as do all individuals. There are no couples that report equal desire, arousal, orgasm, and satisfaction every time. Human sexuality is inherently flexible and variable—the chief argument for the GES approach for male, female, and couple sexuality. The key to maintaining sexual desire is anticipating sexual pleasure and having positive, realistic expectations. Perfectionism is poison for sexual desire. Sexual competition or comparing yourselves with an ideal couple subverts desire. The myth that sex should compensate for past problems robs your relationship of intimacy and pleasure. Acknowledge changes, enjoy pleasure and eroticism, commit time and energy to reinforce your intimate bond, and enhance your couple sexual style. Do not strive to be perfect, do not make comparisons with other couples, and do not try to compensate for the past.

A common anxiety is that if you are not hypervigilant, you will regress to a dysfunctional, or at least boring, sexual relationship. How much is enough? How do you know when you are "accepting," as opposed to "settling"? What are positive, realistic expectations for intimacy and sexuality?

As a couple you need to establish a comfortable, satisfying sexual style for yourself—not in comparison with a perfect ideal, a romantic love fantasy, or even the guidelines we propose. Broad-based sexuality facilitates enjoyment of affectionate, sensual, playful, erotic, and intercourse touching. Intimacy and sexuality help you accept and value your spouse and marriage rather than sex being a drain or source of stress. Sexuality energizes and makes your bond unique.

We hope the following is true for you:

- Sexuality now contributes 15 percent to 20 percent to relational satisfaction.
- Sexuality is a shared pleasure; it reinforces intimacy and serves as a tension reducer rather than a source of tension.
- No longer do ISD and sexual conflict play a dominant role in your lives and relationship. Intimacy and sexuality reinforce marital vitality and satisfaction.

If this is not the case, we strongly suggest couple sex therapy. Reading the material in this book gives you a better understanding of the problems and the challenges surrounding ISD as well as resources for change. Therapy provides the motivation to address complex problems and frustrations, deal with setbacks, and individualize the change process. Appendix A provides information about choosing a sex, couple, or individual therapist.

ISD has been shadowed by embarrassment, shame, guilt, and stigma. What a paradox that a problem that affects 40 million to 60 million Americans has been shrouded in secrecy and denial. However, sexuality can become a positive and integral part of your bond. Intimacy and sexuality have many dimensions—with individual, couple, cultural, and value differences. You are an individual, and your relationship with your partner is unique. Choose what fits the two of you, and do not indulge in comparisons with anyone else, including our models and guidelines. You owe it to yourselves and your relationship to use the resources necessary to feel good (not perfect) about intimacy and sexuality in your lives.

valuing couple sexuality, not just sexuality

In revitalizing couple sexuality, being an intimate sexual team is crucial. A 43-year-old man who developed erectile dysfunction (ED) and ISD after he stopped drinking said that if it were just about having orgasms, he would not have cared about revitalizing marital sexuality. Since age 14, he had always associated sex with alcohol abuse. He did not know how to be sexual in a sober state, and at 43 he had little desire to learn. He was afraid that frustrations about ED and feelings of humiliation would lead him back to alcoholism. This viewpoint was reinforced by his Alcoholics Anonymous (AA) sponsor and many group members. Sex is not a major topic at AA meetings because so many recovering alcoholics associate sex with drinking. They fear that sexual problems will destabilize their lives and recovery.

With the help of his wife and a couple therapist, this man realized there was a whole world of intimacy and sexuality to be explored. He learned that sexuality is more than penis, intercourse, and orgasm. He felt better about himself, his spouse, and their marriage as he became more comfortable with the variable, flexible GES model.

Because he could no longer depend on alcohol to lower inhibitions, he was afraid he would be stuck at the opposite extreme—inhibited, self-conscious, obsessed with his penis, and failing at intercourse. With his wife's active involvement, he learned a new style of pleasure-oriented touching. He became comfortable with sensual, playful, and erotic touch. They enjoyed a broad, flexible couple sexual style that included intercourse and orgasm but not as the sole means of being sexual. Intimacy and sharing pleasure were more important than intercourse. This also involved major changes in his partner's view of sexuality. Although she enjoyed the intimate, erotic, and flexible aspects of their sexuality, she missed (as did he) easy, predictable intercourse.

If it were just about spontaneous desire, easy arousal, intercourse, and predictable orgasms, most couples would give up on sex after a few years of marriage. If it were just about orgasm, people would masturbate rather than have couple sex. Masturbation is easier and more controllable, predictable, and reliable than partner sex. Intimacy and sexuality have multiple roles, dimensions, and meanings. Sexuality is more about desire and satisfaction than intercourse and orgasm. Quality is more important than frequency. Sexuality can reinforce, energize, and make your bond special. At its core, marriage is a respectful, trusting commitment that requires emotional and sexual intimacy to thrive. A marriage can survive without orgasm; it cannot survive without touching and emotional attachment.

What does this mean in terms of your valuing couple sexuality? Establishing an intimate connection that includes affectionate, sensual, playful, erotic, and intercourse touch is crucial. A no-sex relationship is especially draining when emotional and touching attachment is absent. Ideally, you would have a vibrant sexual relationship, with easy arousal and orgasm almost all the time. However, that is the exception, not the norm. Couples develop their unique style of intimacy and eroticism. It is crucial to affirm that you are an intimate sexual team. Pleasure-oriented touching is integral to your bond. Broad-based, flexible sexuality is valued by both partners. Try to maintain erotic contact at least three times a month. Not all touching has to or should culminate in intercourse; touching is valued for itself—as affection, a way to connect, an erotic stimulus, a bridge to sexual desire.

A major characteristic of couples who overcome a no-sex relationship is increased self-acceptance. You no longer need to prove something to yourself or your partner. You are committed to maintaining an intimate sexual relationship. The focus is on sexual quality and attachment more than on intercourse frequency. You do not compare yourselves with a romantic movie ideal or with the sexual high of a new couple. Value the quality of couple intimacy and sexuality that you have nurtured. Enjoy what is happening in the present; there is no need to compensate for the past.

summary

An intimate, satisfying relationship is highly valued. You should take pride in overcoming ISD and a no-sex marriage. Marriage and sexuality need continual time and psychological energy. Sexuality plays a vital, integral role in marital satisfaction as a shared pleasure, a means to reinforce intimacy, and a tension reducer when dealing with the stresses of life and marriage. Broad-based sexuality enhances special feelings and energizes your bond.

It takes courage to confront and change ISD and a no-sex marriage. You deserve credit for facing this secret, stigmatizing problem. Easy solutions, total cures, and "happily ever after" stories are for novels and movies, not real-life couples. Maintaining intimacy and sexuality is a couple task. Enjoy pleasure-oriented sexuality that is flexible and broad-based. You owe it to yourself, your partner, and your marital bond to maintain a vital sexual intimacy.

Key Points

- Valuing desire, pleasure, eroticism, and satisfaction is key to healthy couple sexuality.
- Devote thought, time, and energy to intimacy and sexuality so that it continues to have a 15 percent to 20 percent role in your relationship.
- Enjoy intimacy and sexuality into your 60s, 70s, and 80s.

Choosing a Sex, Couple, or Individual Therapist

 This is a self-help book, not a do-it-yourself therapy book. Individuals and couples are reluctant to consult a therapist, feeling that to do so is a sign of craziness, a confession of inadequacy, or an admission that their life and relationship are in dire straits. In reality, seeking professional help means that you realize there is a problem. You have made a commitment to address the issues and promote individual, couple, and sexual growth.

The mental health field can be confusing. Couple therapy and sex therapy are clinical subspecialties. They are offered by several groups of professionals—including psychologists, marital therapists, psychiatrists, social workers, pastoral counselors, and licensed professional counselors. The professional background of the practitioner is less important than his or her competence in dealing with your individual, couple, and sexual problems.

Many people have health insurance that provides coverage for mental health; thus, they can afford the services of a private practitioner. Those who do not have either the financial resources or insurance could consider a city or county mental health clinic, a university or medical school outpatient mental health clinic, or a family services center. Some clinics have a sliding fee scale based on your ability to pay.

When choosing a therapist, be direct in asking about credentials and areas of expertise. Ask the clinician what the focus of the therapy will be, how long therapy is expected to last, and whether the emphasis will be specifically on sexual problems or on individual, communication, or relationship issues. Be especially diligent in asking about credentials such as university degrees and licensing. Be aware of people who call themselves personal counselors, sex counselors, or personal coaches. There are poorly qualified persons—and some outright quacks—in any field.

One of the best ways to obtain a referral is to call or contact online a local professional organization such as a state psychological association, marriage and family therapy association, or mental health association. You can ask for a referral from a family physician, priest, minister, imam, rabbi, or trusted friend. If you live near a university or medical school, call to find out what specialized psychological and sexual health services may be available.

For a *sex therapy* referral, contact the American Association of Sex Educators, Counselors, and Therapists (AASECT; http://www.aasect. org). Another resource is the Society for Sex Therapy and Research (SSTAR; http://www.sstarnet.org).

For a *marital therapist,* check the Internet site of the American Association for Marriage and Family Therapy (AAMFT; http://www. therapistlocator.net) or the Association for Behavioral and Cognitive Therapies (ABCT; http://www.abct.org). Another good resource is the National Registry of Marriage Friendly Therapists, whose members are dedicated to helping relationships succeed (http://www. marriagefriendlytherapists.com).

If you are looking for a psychologist who can provide individual therapy for anxiety, depression, sexual compulsivity, behavioral health, and other issues, we suggest the National Registry of Health Service Providers in Psychology (http://www.findapsychologist.org).

Feel free to talk with two or three therapists before deciding with whom to work. Be aware of your level of comfort and degree of rapport with the therapist as well as whether the therapist's assessment of the problem and approach to treatment make sense to you. Once you begin, give therapy a chance to be helpful. There are few miracle cures. Change requires commitment; it is a gradual and often difficult process. Although some people benefit from short-term therapy (fewer than

10 sessions), most find the therapeutic process will require 4 months or longer. The role of the therapist is that of a consultant rather than a decision maker. Therapy requires effort on your part, both during the session and at home. Therapy helps to change attitudes, feelings, and behavior. Although it takes courage to seek professional assistance, therapy can be a tremendous help in assessing and ameliorating individual, relational, and sexual problems.

Resources: Books, Videos, and Trusted Websites

Suggested Reading on Couple Sexuality

McCarthy, B., & McCarthy, E. (2009). *Discovering your couple sexual style.* New York, NY: Routledge.

McCarthy, B., & McCarthy, E. (2012). *Sexual awareness: Your guide to healthy couple sexuality* (5th ed.). New York, NY: Routledge.

Metz, M., & McCarthy, B. (2010). *Enduring desire.* New York, NY: Routledge.

Perel, E. (2006). *Mating in captivity.* New York, NY: HarperCollins.

Suggested Reading on Male Sexuality

McCarthy, B., & Metz, M. (2008). *Men's sexual health.* New York, NY: Routledge.

Metz, M., & McCarthy, B. (2003). *Coping with premature ejaculation.* Oakland, CA: New Harbinger.

Metz, M., & McCarthy, B. (2004). *Coping with erectile dysfunction.* Oakland, CA: New Harbinger.

Zilbergeld, B. (1999). *The new male sexuality.* New York, NY: Bantam.

Suggested Reading on Female Sexuality

Foley, S., Kope, S., & Sugrue, D. (2012). *Sex matters for women* (2nd ed.). New York, NY: Guilford Press.

Heiman, J., & LoPiccolo, J. (1988). *Becoming orgasmic.* New York, NY: Prentice Hall.

Boston Women's Health Book Collective. (2011). *Our bodies, ourselves.* New York, NY: Touchstone.

Other Significant Sexuality Readings

Joannides, P. (2011). *The guide to getting it on: Other significant sexuality readings.* West Hollywood, CA.: Goofy Foot Press.

Maltz, W. (2012). *The sexual healing journey* (3rd ed.). New York, NY: William Morrow.

Michael, R., Gagnon, J., Laumann, E., & Kolata, G. (1994). *Sex in America.* Boston, MA: Little, Brown.

Snyder, D., Baucom, D., & Gordon, K. (2007). *Getting past the affair.* New York, NY: Guilford Press.

Suggested Reading on Relationship Satisfaction

Doherty, W. (2013). *Take back your marriage* (2nd ed.). New York, NY: Guilford Press.

Enright, R. D. (2007). *Forgiveness is a choice.* Washington, DC: American Psychological Association.

Gottman, J., & Silver, N. (1999). *The seven principles for making marriage work.* New York, NY: Crown.

Johnson, S. (2008). *Hold me tight.* Boston, MA: Little, Brown.

Love, P., & Stosny, S. (2008). *How to improve your marriage without talking about it.* New York, NY: Three Rivers Press.

Markman, H., Stanley, S., & Blumberg, S. (2010). *Fighting for your marriage* (3rd ed.). San Francisco, CA: Jossey-Bass.

McCarthy, B., & McCarthy, E. (2004). *Getting it right the first time.* New York, NY: Brunner/Routledge.

McCarthy, B., & McCarthy, E. (2006). *Getting it right this time.* New York, NY: Routledge.

Internet Sites: Mental Health

National Institute of Mental Health (NIMH), home page:
  http://www.nimh.nih.gov
NIMH, Anxiety: http://www.nimh.nih.gov/anxiety/anxietymenu.cfm
NIMH, Depression:
  http://www.nimh.nih.gov/publicat/depressionmenu.cfm
Obsessive Compulsive Foundation: http://www.ocfoundation.org

Internet Sites: Health

National Institutes of Health (NIH): http://www.nih.gov
National Institute on Alcohol Abuse and Alcoholism (NIAAA):
  http://www.niaaa.nih.gov
WebMD—information on many illnesses, including diabetes, cancer,
  and heart disease: http://www.webmd.com

Professional Associations

American Association for Marriage and Family Therapy (AAMFT): 112
  South Alfred Street, Alexandria, VA 22314-3061, (703) 838-9808,
  http://www.therapistlocator.net
American Association of Sex Educators, Counselors, and Therapists:
  1441 I Street, NW, Suite 700, Washington, DC 20005, (202) 449-
  1099, http://www.aasect.org
Association for Behavioral & Cognitive Therapies (ABCT): 305
  Seventh Avenue, New York, NY 10001-6008, (212) 647-1890,
  http://www.abct.org
Smart Marriages—The Coalition for Marriage, Family, and Couple
  Education, http://www.smartmarriages.com
Society for Sex Therapy and Research (SSTAR): 6311 W. Gross Point
  Road, Niles, IL 60714, (847) 647-8832, http://www.sstarnet.org

Sex Websites, Videos, and Toys

Go Ask Alice! web site: http://goaskalice.columbia.edu/
Kinsey Confidential web site: http://kinseyconfidential.org/

Good Vibrations: 938 Howard Street, Suite 101, San Francisco, CA
94110, (800) 289-8423, http://www.goodvibes.com

The Sinclair Institute: P.O. Box 8865, Chapel Hill, NC 27515, (800) 955-
0888, http://www.sinclairinstitute.com

Sex Smart Films: Promoting Sexual Literacy:
http://www.sex.smartfilms.com

REFERENCES

Allen, E., Atkins, P., Baucom, D. Snyder, D., Gordon, K., & Glass, S. (2005). Intrapersonal, interpersonal, and contextual factors in engaging in and responding to extramarital involvement. *Clinical Psychology: Science and Practice, 12,* 101–130.

Barbach, L. (1975). *For yourself.* New York, NY: New American Library.

Basson, R. (2007). Sexual desire/arousal disorder in women. In S. Leiblum (Ed.), *Principles and practice of sex therapy* (4th ed., pp. 25–53). New York, NY: Guilford Press.

Brotto, L., & Woo, J. (2010). Cognitive–behavioral and mindfulness-based therapy for low sexual desire. In S. Leiblum (Ed.), *Treating sexual desire disorders* (pp. 149–164). New York, NY: Guilford Press.

Cohn, R. (2011). *Coming home to passion.* Santa Barbara, CA: Praeger.

Diamond, L. (2003). What does sexual orientation orient? *Psychological Review, 110,* 173–192.

Doherty, W. (2013). *Take back your marriage* (2nd ed.). New York, NY: Guilford Press.

Epstein, N., & Baucom, D. (2002). *Enhanced cognitive–behavioral therapy for couples.* Washington, DC: American Psychological Association.

Fedoroff, J. (2010). Paraphiliac worlds. In S. Levine, C. Risen, & S. Althof (Eds.), *Handbook of clinical sexuality for mental health professionals.* (2nd ed., pp. 401–424). New York, NY: Routledge.

Foley, S., Kope, S., & Sugrue, D. (2012). *Sex matters for women* (2nd ed.). New York, NY: Guilford Press.

Frank, E., Anderson, A., & Rubinstein P. (1978). Frequency of sexual dysfunction in "normal" couples. *New England Journal of Medicine, 229,* 111–115.

Goldstein, I., Lue, T., Padma-Nathan, H., Rosen, R., Steers, W., & Wickler, P. (1998). Oral sildenafil in the treatment of erectile dysfunction. *New England Journal of Medicine, 338,* 1397–1404.

Gottman, J., & Silver, N. (1999). *The seven principles for making marriage work.* New York, NY: Crown.

Hall, K. (2004). *Reclaiming your sexual self.* New York, NY: Wiley.

Heiman, J. (2007). Orgasmic disorders in women. In S. Leiblum (Ed.), *Principles and practice of sex therapy* (4th ed., pp. 84–123). New York, NY: Guilford Press.

Heiman, J., Scott, J., Smith, S., Fisher, W., Sand, M., & Rosen, R. (2011). Sexual satisfaction and relationship happiness in midlife and older couples in five countries. *Archives of Sexual Behavior, 40,* 441–453.

Hyde, J. (2005). The gender similarities hypothesis. *American Psychologist, 60,* 581–592.

Hyde J., De Lamater, J., & Hewitt, E. (1998). Sexuality and the dual-earner couple. *Journal of Family Psychology, 12,* 354–368.

Johnson, S. (2004). *The practice of emotionally focused couple therapy* (2nd ed.). New York, NY: Routledge.

Laumann, E., Gagnon, J., Michael, R., & Michaels, S. (1994). *The social organization of sexuality.* Chicago, IL: University of Chicago Press.

Lobitz, W., & Lobitz, G. (1996). Resolving the sexual intimacy paradox. *Journal of Sex and Marital Therapy, 22,* 71–84.

Maltz, W. (2012). *The sexual healing journey* (3rd ed.). New York, NY: Morrow.

Masters, W., & Johnson, V. (1970). *Human sexual adequacy.* Boston, MA: Little, Brown.

McCarthy, B. (1997). Strategies and techniques for revitalizing a non-sexual marriage. *Journal of Sex and Marital Therapy, 23,* 231–240.

McCarthy, B. (2003). Marital sex as it ought to be. *Journal of Family Psychotherapy, 14*(2), 1–12.

McCarthy, B., & Bodnar, L. (2005). The equity model of sexuality. *Sexual and Relationship Therapy, 20,* 225–235.

McCarthy, B., & Breetz, A. (2010). Integrating sexual interventions and psychosexual skill exercises into cognitive–behavioral therapy. *The Behavior Therapist, 33*(3), 54–57.

McCarthy, B., & Farr, E. (2012). Strategies and techniques to maintain sexual desire. *Journal of Contemporary Psychotherapy, 42,* 227–233.

McCarthy, B., & Fucito, L. (2005). Integrating medication, realistic expectations, and therapeutic interventions in the treatment of male sexual dysfunction. *Journal of Sex and Marital Therapy, 31,* 319–328.

McCarthy, B., Ginsberg, R., & Fucito, L. (2006). Resilient sexual desire in heterosexual couples. *The Family Journal, 14*(1), 59–64.

McCarthy, B., & McCarthy, E. (2004). *Getting it right the first time.* New York, NY: Routledge.

McCarthy, B., & McCarthy, E. (2006). *Getting it right this time.* New York, NY: Routledge.

McCarthy, B., & McCarthy, E. (2009). *Discovering your couple sexual style.* New York, NY: Routledge.

McCarthy, B., & McCarthy, E. (2012). *Sexual awareness* (5th ed.). New York, NY: Routledge.

McCarthy, B., & Thestrup, M. (2008a). Couple therapy and the treatment of sexual dysfunction. In A. Gurman (Ed.), *Clinical handbook of couple therapy* (4th ed., pp. 591–617). New York, NY: Guilford Press.

McCarthy, B., & Thestrup, M. (2008b). Integrating sex therapy interventions with couple therapy. *Journal of Contemporary Psychotherapy, 38,* 139–149.

McCarthy, B., & Wald, L. (2012). Sexual desire and satisfaction. *Sexual and Relationship Therapy, 27,* 310–321.

McCarthy, B., & Wald, L. (2013). New strategies in assessing, treating, and relapse prevention of extramarital affairs. *Journal of Sex and Marital Therapy, 39,* 493–509.

McCarthy, B., & Wald, L. (in press). The psychobiosocial model of couple sex therapy. In Z. Peterson (Ed.), *Handbook of sex therapy.* New York, NY: Wiley-Blackwell.

Meana, M. (2010). When love and sex go wrong. In S. Levine, C. Risen, & S. Althof (Eds.), *Handbook of clinical sexuality for mental health professionals.* (2nd ed., pp. 103–120). New York, NY: Routledge.

Metz, M., & McCarthy, B. (2003). *Coping with premature ejaculation.* Oakland, CA: New Harbinger.

Metz, M., & McCarthy, B. (2004). *Coping with erectile dysfunction.* Oakland, CA.: New Harbinger.

Metz, M., & McCarthy, B. (2007). The "Good Enough Sex" model for couple sexual satisfaction. *Sexual and Relationship Therapy, 22,* 351–362.

Metz, M., & McCarthy, B. (2010). *Enduring desire.* New York, NY: Routledge.

Metz, M., & McCarthy, B. (2012). The Good Enough Sex (GES) model. In P. Kleinplatz (Ed.), *New directions in sex therapy.* (2nd ed., pp. 213–230). New York, NY: Routledge.

Morin, J. (1995). *The erotic mind.* New York, NY: Harper Collins.

Perel, E. (2006). *Mating in captivity.* New York, NY: Harper.

Rind, B., Tromovitch, P., & Bauserman, R. (1998). A meta-analytic examination of assumed properties of child sexual abuse using college samples. *Psychological Bulletin, 124,* 22–53.

Sims, K., & Meana, M. (2010). Why did passion wane? A qualitative study of married women's attributions for declines in sexual desire. *Journal of Sex and Marital Therapy, 36,* 360–380.

Snyder, D., Baucom, D., & Gordon, K. (2007). *Getting past the affair.* New York, NY: Guilford Press.

Stanley, S., Markman, H., & Whitton, S. (2002). Communication, conflict, and commitment. *Family Process, 41,* 659–675.